MW01639674

MANAGING PROBLEM LOANS

THE COMPLETE GUIDE FOR LOAN OFFICERS

MANAGING PROBLEM LOANS

THE COMPLETE GUIDE FOR LOAN OFFICERS

Peter S. Clarke

Dow Jones-Irwin
Homewood, Illinois 60430

Sponsoring editor: Jim Childs
Project editor: Suzanne Ivester
Production manager: Bette Ittersagen
Jacket design: Phil Kantz
Compositor: TCSystems, Inc.
Typeface: 11/13 Times Roman
Printer: R. R. Donnelley & Sons Company

Library of Congress Cataloging-in-Publication Data

Clarke, Peter S., 1941-
Managing problem loans: the complete guide for loan officers/ Peter S. Clarke.
p. cm.
Includes index.
ISBN 1-55623-206-3
1. Bank loans. 2. Collecting of accounts. 3. Loan officers. 4. Credit—Management. I. Title.
HG 1641 .C554 1989
332.1'753'068—dc20 89-32233
CIP

Printed in the United States of America
1 2 3 4 5 6 7 8 9 0 DO 6 5 4 3 2 1 0 9

CONTENTS

INTRODUCTION

Most bankers cannot unequivocally declare that they have been untouched by problem loans. Certainly it is a way of life in these tumultuous times of banking that virtually all of us are faced with problem or so-called workout loans.

In this connection, we would like to share some ideas on how to manage your loans and reclaim the collateral assets securing them. In addition, we aspire to provide the essential strategies that may be used for loan recovery once a debtor enters bankruptcy.

First of all, let us define a problem loan. Basically, it is one where repayment is in jeopardy, especially if the expected or anticipated source of repayment is no longer sufficiently available to repay the debt. Put another way, a problem loan can be defined as one where there has been a default in the repayment agreement resulting in undue delay in collection or in which there appears to be a potential loss.

Virtually all banks sustain problem loans; the key is to minimize the loss. Certainly reasons for nonpayment include business losses; declines in liquidity or working capital; overtrading (excess merchandise, purchased on credit, remaining unsold, burdening inventory turnover); failure on the part of the borrower to properly perform under contracts or other commitments; nonreceipt of payments or third-party client bankruptcy; death of a manager; and errors and omissions which may include fraud, casualty losses, and theft. Also, the borrower may be hurt by an economic downturn or a market decline which could play havoc in its business and also lower or deplete market asset values and the subsequent collateral values you rely on to recoup the loan. Many of us have faced this scenario in recent years as it relates to agriculture, steel, and the auto industries, and the severe economic impact lately in the Southwest on the real estate market and the oil-related segments of our economy. These are other good reasons why your bank should not concentrate in any one particular industry or business, even if it initially looks appealing.

The principal reasons banks have exposed themselves more to problem loans as a result of procedural breakdowns within their own system are as follows:

- Insufficient underwriting and lack of prior background checks and investigation of potential borrowers.
- Inadequate analysis of the real purpose and use of the loan proceeds, and the source of repayment.
- Lack of understanding of the borrowers' true financial needs and how the funds will benefit them. In this connection, the banker should fully comprehend the financial structure of the borrowing entity in order to better understand the company's financial condition and financing requirements. Also, banks have treated long-term problems with short-term solutions by extending quick-fix loans to many borrowers.
- Inadequate analysis of financial statements, perhaps because of apprehension about asking borrowers or their accountants pertinent questions.
- Ill-conceived loan terms extended by the bank.
- Poor review and audit of marginal loans.
- Overly aggressive loan officers who want to look good by attempting to book more loans for growth; this behavior allows officers to become more lax in lending criteria, thus, in effect, letting the competition set their lending standards as they seek to remain competitive.
- Poorly defined, excessively lenient, or poorly implemented and monitored credit policies and procedures.
- Inexperienced loan officers who incorrectly approve loans because they do not have the necessary expertise to evaluate and analyze credits and financial information, or because they may not have sought the proper counsel on making such loans, including neglecting to properly evaluate, document and collateralize loans.

- Easily persuaded loan officers who allow customers to intimidate, coerce, or overly sell them on making loans.
- Over-reliance on the analysis of a lead bank regarding credit decisions involving participations.

Factors that banks fail to follow up on once a loan becomes a problem range from neglecting the borrower to ignoring economic signals. Lack of follow-up details include:

- Lack of follow-up review, including the request and analysis of financial and other credit information; infrequent contact with the borrower and rare visits to the company's offices or plant.
- Poor monitoring of the impact of changing economic conditions on the company and its industry.
- Lack of control when granting too much credit for a company's overexpansion or for other uses such as acquisitions. Whenever you lend substantial funds to a borrower, as measured against the bank's legal lending limit, institute loan agreements with applicable covenants (often not adhered to by the company) in order to allow expansion in a judicious manner.
- Excess accommodations; that is, you place an albatross around the borrower's neck by allowing it to continue borrowing new money until the point of no return, whereby the debt is too great for the borrower to repay within a reasonable length of time.
- Reluctance to admit to a mistake or to even having a problem. As such, you avoid asking the difficult or tough questions once a problem is detected. This may lead to the "miracle syndrome" (the loan officer takes little or no action and hopes the problem will disappear or the situation will resolve itself).

Worse, bankers may cut off communication with borrowers once a problem has manifested itself, or they may resort to pressure tactics or threats to collect the debt. Such tactics could lead to a classic cause of action whereby the borrower files a lender-liability suit against the bank.

In the event of failure, the bank should always be able to look to a secondary source of repayment, which is usually its collateral. As many of you know, it is oftentimes very difficult to realize enough on your collateral, when push comes to shove, in order to pay off the borrower's debt.

Of course, the best time to recognize a problem loan is as early as possible. This is critical to future collection. In many instances, loan officers do not see trouble ahead, or do not move quickly enough once they realize there is a problem. Any delay in action often affects the kinds and numbers of ways to solve the problem. At times, a loan officer may lack the courage to address the situation. If the wrong officer is handling the credit or if he or she procrastinates, it frequently results in loan losses.

The very next step is a strong follow-up. This writer has personally seen many problem situations become worse because of inadequate follow-up. For instance, the inexperienced loan officer often allows the borrower to persuade him or her to make additional loans or to delay action on calling for payment on existing loans. The borrower is usually seeking a quick fix in order to hopefully delay the inevitable and temporarily continue operating. This is the hard part as the bank must come to a conscious decision on what action to take after analyzing and thinking through all the facts.

It takes courage for the loan officer to face up to the decision of cutting the borrower off and perhaps closing the doors of the business and attempting to repossess its collateral. This can be very difficult, especially since the typical banker will probably feel somewhat like a fish out of water when he or she has to liquidate the collateral—certainly a less friendly role than lending money. It becomes quite different for the banker who is generally market oriented and accustomed to accommodating customers to suddenly become a collector and perhaps even a liquidator of collateral.

Usually, the officer is the first one to detect a problem or realize if he or she in fact has a real loan problem. Officers should be encouraged to recognize their loan problems early and bring them to the attention of management.

In larger banks, problem credits are often transferred to a special workout unit, section, or department. Of course, valuable time may be lost in taking action by the time the special workout staff or department receives the responsibility of collecting on the credit. In many instances, this department will only assume loans over a certain limit and oftentimes the credit has been already identified as a serious problem based on a "substandard" classification or loan review grade. These departments commonly have different functional names, such as asset recovery, special asset, or loan reclamation department.

There are often many reasons why a loan should be transferred to the bank's special workout staff. Frequently, for example, loan officers do not have the expertise to continue handling the credit. Many times they lack objectivity or have lost it because they may be too close to the borrower and the situation; perhaps they had been persuaded to undertake something that was not too prudent or sensible in the first place. Becoming harsh or rigid now is simply too drastic a change for them to handle. Also, officers often do not have the additional time to handle a workout because it would consume the time they need to service their existing portfolios and to develop additional business.

Most loan officers often start off their careers in a conscientious manner as they seem willing to adhere to good lending principles; they make an earnest effort to comply with bank policies and procedures even though they have not gained the experience of a seasoned lender. With years of experience, though, they may become complacent and somewhat lax, expecially relative to documentation. Moreover, they begin taking more unwarranted credit risks.

At other times, the loan officer may start out very enthusiastic and make good progress in developing new business with high marks for marketing ability, but neglect or never receive sufficient or proper training in loan documentation and/or credit analysis. Eventually, in time, this lack of technical background or attention to detail will often catch up to this sales-oriented lender; loans granted may not only fail, but leave little recovery due to lack of credit standards, and improper documentation and collateral. Unfortunately, it is often easier to address the problem with a Band-Aid, rather than perform the surgery necessary to address the problem properly. Loan officers also find it difficult to give up the customer relationships they brought into the bank and have nurtured over time; or they may let their guard down with a long-term customer.

Obviously, these things lead to the need for better and more disciplined training for future lenders. It is not enough to have a formal training program or send future loan officer candidates off to banking schools, classes, and seminars, and then, after one to two years in training, more than likely spending most of this time in the credit department, to expect them to be fully equipped, astute veterans.

The training program must be well planned. Credit analysts and future officer trainees must be grounded in the fundamentals of credit and equipped with a broad background by having the opportunity to learn more about lending, especially the types applicable to the particular bank's portfolio and collateral. They must learn how to document different types of loans, write commitments, and prepare letter and loan agreements. Trainees also need to have exposure to loan review, asset recovery, including charge-off recovery, audit procedures, regulations, compliance laws, and special collateral monitoring functions. Further, they need an understanding of loan policy and procedures and some amount of grounding in the fundamentals of bank accounting, operations, and investments, including asset and liability management. All this is necessary in addition to becoming acquainted with the bank's various lending departments and learning how they operate. The novice should spend some time in each of these departments or areas. It would even be good if they could spend some time in the workout loan and the charge-off/recovery areas to attain a good understanding of what caused credits to become problems, how they are being worked, and how anything is being recovered or salvaged.

The young journeyman will gain invaluable experience, learning to understand both the positives and negatives of credits, the effects that incorrect or improper documentation has on the outcome of credit losses, and the importance of continuous monitoring of the credit and collateral. Indeed, the journeyman will become alert to signs of trouble and weaknesses in credits. He or she should gain training experience and knowledge by actual on-the-job training; better yet, the journeyman should not take up staff member time by being an unproductive observer. In this way, both the bank and trainee will gain from such an approach.

This may appear to be an ambitious goal, and it may take longer for the future lender to move onto the firing line this way, but certainly it should be worth it. Also, by broadening such training, these future lending officers should be better equipped to face the more difficult challenges in today's lending environment. Certainly, banks have had problems for one reason or another for not undertaking appropriate training. To work well, however, there needs to be good coordination. A training director and committee, with the support of bank management, would also certainly help improve the whole process. Trainees would also have to become more committed—to stick with the program—because it would take them longer to become loan officers.

Personally, I believe that even if a bank cuts back on an expensive training program involving numerous candidates, management can still hire permanent staff that may be trained by working them through each of these areas.

As such, there must be even better planning and coordination in utilizing quasi-permanent trainees productively, especially when budget constraints are firmly in place. An alternative would not only be to assign the permanent trainee or analyst to the credit department, but also arrange to have them work in each of these other areas as time permits, making sure they get the right exposure to work in the bank's various lending departments or areas. All in all, they will be better prepared for a future lending position.

Consider these points seriously as they will make for a better quality bank and staff in the long run. People are generally ambitious; this will give them some type of opportunity for training at all stages, and letting them aspire to greater achievements. In this day of constant job changing and lack of loyalty, you will also enhance their morale and you may find a more dedicated and loyal employee. Just estimate the cost of bringing in a new employee, plus the additional time and cost to replace them because they quit within a year or two, before ever becoming productive.

Throughout this text we will refer to the loan officer as the party managing the problem loan. Therefore, for our purposes, both the servicing loan officer and workout officer who is assigned to a special problem loan or workout department will be synonymously referred to as the loan officer.

Without doubt, problem loans have become a way of life for banks to live with today. In addition, lender liability lawsuits have more recently proliferated and have brought on a new wave of litigation for banks to deal with especially as it relates to problem loans. Indeed, many contemporary lenders have never before dealt with the problems many of us face in today's changing banking environment. Clearly, there is a need for the solutions spelled out in this book. What we want to address is how to deal with your existing and potential problem loans and how to best work out of them by obtaining the optimum return on each invested dollar. We also want to cover the special impacts and effects on loans in conjunction with potential lender liability and how to best deal within a bankruptcy or court controlled environment. All in all, the book offers bankers a practical tool to deal with problem loans.

CHAPTER 1

IDENTIFYING AND MONITORING PROBLEM LOANS

1.01 GENERAL

Generally, a problem loan is one in which the original terms or conditions have been violated or breached, often resulting in a default for nonpayment or default under the note, security, or loan agreements. A problem loan could also be one in which the original loan repayment terms have been altered because the borrower could not pay in accordance with the bank's requirements and needed extensions, renewals, or debt restructure. Also, a problem loan could be one in which the collateral margin was depleted, diminished, or dissipated to the point where the bank's risk increased substantially.

A problem may be manifested even before a note becomes due, while the borrower is still making payments. A declining financial condition is often reflected in such signs as slowness in receivable collections while bad debts increase, a slump in inventory sales, necessary writedowns in product values, or a rapid decline in gross and other profit margins. Problems may also appear in other more visible ways, for example, the recent death of a sole proprietor without sufficient life insurance, recent loss of some principal customers or market share, new competing or replacement product lines suddenly leaving the company in an obsolete position, or new styles replacing the one(s) produced by the borrower.

First, before attempting to solve or correct the problem, you should identify its causes. The factors outlined below may or may not have contributed to the problem.

1. Management:
   - Was incompetent.
   - Had limited experience in this field of business.
   - Was not active or had not spent much time in the business.
   - Had too many other business ventures.
   - Committed fraud.
   - Was Greedy.
2. Product:
   - Lacked demand.
   - Lacked quality.
   - Was provided by a marginal supplier.
   - Lost a key customer base or market.
3. Economy
   - Local or national economies or markets declined.

Factors such as those above could result in many problems, depending on the nature of the business. Some such problems and their warning signs are described as follows:

- Machinery becoming antiquated, equipment becoming idle or unusable, and overall excess plant capacity or space may be signs of a business depression or decline in customer base.
- Inventory obsolescence, run-off, or general decline in prices, value or demand are similar signs of trouble.
- Accounts receivable becoming slower or even uncollectible may be a sign of weakness in the quality of account debtors and their ability to meet their obligations. It may also be a sign of the borrower lowering its customers' credit quality standards or rating requirements.
- Weakness or softness in market values such as real estate often signals economic decline.

The following are some additional warning signals to be derived from financial statements and other credit information available to you:

• A general slowing in inventory turnover or "days supply on hand" may reflect a buildup of slow-moving, obsolete, or out-of-style inventory. Sometimes when the inventory turnover is not showing any improvement, even though sales are being realized, the company may be using up certain hidden reserves. This may not always be a negative sign.
• Declining quick ratios often reflect a concentration of inventory buildup resulting from an increase in accounts payable in conjunction with a decline in sales and concurrent receivables and a run-off of cash.
• Heavier debt/worth positions may result from losses and buildup of debt to support continued operations or from incorrect, improper, or unnecessary overexpansion.
• In order to assume the disguise of being a profitable operation, or to retain cash reserves, the company may have deferred routine expenses such as maintenance necessary for continued operations or may have postponed other expenses in order to continue business momentum.
• Significant or noticeable increases in merchandise returns evidencing poor product quality controls.
• A general increasing trend in allowances may evidence a guaranteed sales arrangement with buyers, consignment sales extended to others, or just a general let down in return policies in order to increase sales.
• An increasing trend in total trade debt outstanding may be the result of a buildup in inventory and slowdown in sales. It could also evidence other possible problems occurring with cash flow and working capital.
• Improper practices may be used to conserve cash or not reflect delinquencies. These include holding checks in the draw, thus not reflecting accurate payable agings or other accrual obligations.
• Other unusual activity may occur impacting cash flow. For example, owners or principals may be taking more out of the business in the way of salaries or draws, dividends, and loan repayments or advances to them from the company. Or, preferential treatment may be given to some creditors over or at the expense of others, irrespective of debt superiority or collateral held.
• A declining trend in the company's gross profit margin is the

leading barometer of the operating health of any business. It could be the result of price cutting to move the company's products or goods—at times a judicious move on the company's part in order to clear out old, stale, or overstocked inventory and obtain cash to reduce debt or purchase fresh, new merchandise. This should also help lower inventory levels and improve turnovers. At other times, a decline in the gross profit margin may be the result of a company incurring increasing cost burdens in the products it sells which cannot be passed on to customers. Obviously this is a more dangerous concern.

- A succession of new accounting firms auditing and examining a borrower's books and records could be the result of disputes with accountants over giving qualified or even disclaimer opinions because the company does not conform to generally accepted accounting principles (GAAP), or over the improper withholding of necessary financial information.
- Delinquencies in such accrual payments as taxes (e.g., personal and property, sales, use, and payroll) is a form of riding float and true unauthorized borrowing. Companies that do this are usually having serious financial difficulties. Such practices often result in vulnerability to IRS or other state or local taxing authority liens, which may jeopardize the continuation of the business and could tie up assets to the point of creating senior and superior liens in some instances.
- A rapid or steep decline in sales volume may result from poor quality control or decreases in product demand, market share, or product promotion, including not utilizing "good-enough" sales strategy.

1.02 EVALUATING THE RISK

If you have to assume that an economy must improve before the borrowing company may turn around, then you must make a calculated decision to carefully evaluate the risk of keeping the customer alive whether through debt restructure, extensions, moratoriums, or by essentially closing them down by making demand.

Other Risk Factors

You must determine many other factors about the borrower's business such as its market and financial controls.

Market

You must ask such questions as:

- Has the customer defined its own market?
- Does it have a niche in that market?
- How much has that market changed?
- Will the market recover?
- What new competition is there (products or companies)?

Financial Controls

You must determine what financial controls the borrower has in place such as:

- Does it have good financial and internal accounting controls?
- Does the borrower know its costs, and does it have an effective cost-control system in place?
- Does the borrower have receivables and inventory control systems in place (such as perpetual inventory controls, centralized purchasing)?
- Does the borrower have adequate controls over overhead and cost accounting control systems? Examples of such controls include carrying overhead into the inventory cycle and then costing it out as goods are sold, which is a new tax requirement for most businesses under the Tax Reform Act of 1986.

1.03 PROBLEM LOANS

The handling of problem loans often depends on the size of the loan in relation to the bank's legal lending limit (LLL) or house limit (amount set at some level below the bank's LLL), the complexity and type of loan involved (such as commercial, real estate, or energy), and any available collateral.

There are a number of reasons why a loan may become a problem. These may include an economic downturn in a particular industry—this is why banks should not allow their loan portfolios to become overly concentrated in any one particular industry. Some loans may just go bad and are not identified or monitored properly by the bank. There are other loans booked that, for various and sundry reasons, should never have been made in the first place.

General Reasons for Problem Loans

Lending syndromes have contributed heavily to the making of bad loans. Some of the more common syndromes include banks that enter a new or go-go type industry and banks that are compelled to react to what the competition is doing. Often a bank is not really aware of what the competition is doing but presumes what is going on and how they are doing it.

Bankers are human and sometimes make mistakes. They may not follow-up or may fail to act when something is recognized to be wrong. There are also those bankers who just cannot say no to a deal.

Banks certainly need comprehensive systems and personnel who understand how to identify and protect against problem loans. This means a good working loan and credit policy with all the necessary standards and procedures should be in place. In addition, procedures should be established regarding all support areas, such as loan operations, loan review, and compliance and regulations.

Four general early warning signals may foretell problem loans even before repayment schedules fail to be met. These are:

- *Financial*—as detected from financial statements and compliance with loan agreements.
- *Management*—as determined from meetings with principals.
- *Operations*—as evidenced from business or plant calls.
- *Collateral*—as evaluated from monitoring and inspecting collateral.

The loan officer should assume responsibility for any loans

that become problems especially if he or she originated the debt or has been servicing it for a reasonable length of time. This is because loan officers should be the first to recognize when a problem exists and know all the warning signals evidencing a potential problem.

Determining the Problem

Loan officers should immediately evaluate their files, including all collateral documentation, upon determining that they may have a problem loan on their hands. Certainly this is also a time when the loan officer may need to draw on the assistance of special support personnel within the bank or seek outside legal assistance.

As a loan officer, your first priority after special support personnel or legal counsel reviews the documentation, is to correct any deficiencies or collateral exceptions. Always first run lien searches to verify your collateral position. Be especially sensitive to other senior creditor liens and any recently recorded filings, whether they be first or second liens. Beware of properly filed purchase money security interests (PMSI) filed by other creditors who may come ahead of you on certain collateral items even though you filed a blanket lien prior to the other creditors' PMSI. Such items may have intrinsic value as they relate to the possible sale of the business. Are there any liens filed against the debtor, such as judgments or tax liens which could jeopardize future operations? You may need to request advice on possible remedies to correct the problem.

Some of the more common collateral errors include the following.

- Financing statements being filed in the wrong jurisdictions or not in all the appropriate jurisdictions.
- Lapse in filing a continuation statement on time after a financing statement has expired.
- Incorrect name of debtor; this occurs most often when using only a trade name instead of first showing an individual sole proprietor's name or corporate name.
- Use of inaccurate addresses.
- Change in the debtor's name or address; or perhaps the

debtor has moved the collateral to another jurisdiction more than four months ago without your knowledge.
- Wrong description of collateral; this often occurs in real property and mineral rights, i.e., reference to a working interest versus an overriding royalty interest.
- Collateral unknowingly transferred and sold to a buyer in good faith without the bank's knowledge.
- Collateral transferred to a directly or indirectly related entity without the bank's knowledge.
- Oversight on the bank's part by not taking a collateral interest in certain of the borrower's assets or those of a subsidiary or other related entity that may have been formed since you acquired your collateral interest.
- Collateral description not matching, i.e., when the description in security agreement(s) differs from what is in the financing statement, even taking into account that a more generic description is applicable to financing statements.

Make sure that staff completing or checking documents works from a pre-closing checklist which will describe what documents must be on hand and properly completed before funding and what documents may be carried as an exception until received. A post-funding review should also be undertaken to assure that documentation is in suitable order as specified by term sheets, commitments, and agreements. Consider the use of experienced loan closers or processors, documentation experts, and paralegals within your bank, or in-house attorneys depending upon the complexity of the documentation.

It is very important to determine your collateral position because this may affect your initial strategy which should include correcting any collateral mistakes or errors. Remember that if you do take any new or additional collateral, you need to wait out the 90-day voidable preference period before taking any further action.

In addition to a collateral review, you should undertake a financial review to determine the extent of the bank's credit exposure. This financial review should include the following steps:

- Overdraft history, letters of credit and other potential sources of direct and indirect liability with the bank must be reviewed.
- It may be appropriate to establish an internal level of debt the

bank might approve and the necessary collateral or guarantees before approving it.

• Financial statements should be reviewed. It may be appropriate to consider undertaking an exam or audit of the borrower's books and records, especially since the borrower may have unrecorded liabilities, (e.g., taxes, unfunded pensions, severance pay, vacation pay and sick-leave benefits); unknown contingent obligations such as guaranties, leases, buy-back agreements and warranties; pending litigation including securities litigation; and possible regulatory problems.

• Liabilities should also be checked for true maturity, and terms and conditions need to be determined when possible.

• Financial statements should also be reviewed for adequate reserves, for example liability, valuation, and capital allocations. Asset values should be judged as to whether they are accurate and prudent. Intangibles should be checked to verify the true value of tangible net worth and how much in intangibles or goodwill is being reflected in the balance sheet as well as whether it is being properly amortized. Also, statements should be reviewed for liquidity, true internal cash flow, and to determine how much in assets is not really current or is static and not representative of an operating asset or is not beneficial to productive use in the business.

Can the borrower realistically provide acceptable financial information for you at this time? Certainly, you should review and analyze any information received at this time from the borrower such as updated financial statements, schedules, and projections. You must compare actual results to proformas and projections.

There are also other critical financial matters you must consider. For example, if the borrowing base formula is being depleted, and the borrower is not paying you enough down to get the credit back into margin, your collateral is perhaps being liquidated to retire other creditors' debt, especially open (unsecured) trade credit. This also applies to a negative cash flow position as your collateral position is possibly being diminished in order to cover operating expenses. Furthermore, if the company is losing money and this is causing the equity deficit to increase, then your risk is being heightened based on the loss of a principle source of repayment and possible greater exposure to insolvency.

Loan officers should talk to their own in-house or outside

attorneys for advice. Discussion should include strategies for action relative to possible legal remedies while also considering legal pitfalls. Loan officers should discuss problems with the borrower's independent accountants, too, if possible. Statements should be scrutinized for evidence of misrepresentation and fraud. If you have access to the borrower's accountants, meet with them over financial details, and also discuss internal controls, as well as any weaknesses in this respect.

Financial Statement Spread Sheets and Analysis

Sometimes problem loans are evidenced in subtle ways, perhaps by the gradual deterioration in a borrower's financial condition, reflected in the financial statements the loan officer receives. For this reason, it is always good for the loan officer to review borrower statements upon receipt. Loan officers should seek assistance from their credit department in analyzing the trends evidenced in financial statements. These statements should first be transposed onto the bank's spread sheets for better ease of analysis. Spread sheets offer an easier method of comparing trends and making comparisons, because entries and totals are condensed side-by-side into a standard form which can more easily be analyzed. The spread sheet should also be presented in a format that will allow the loan officer to better analyze the numbers without requiring a written analysis by the credit department. Basically, the spread sheet will reflect comparative periods and should provide all the totals, percentages, and ratios necessary for the loan officer to analyze trends in the company's financial progress. The spread sheet should be completed by a credit analyst to reflect all totals in their appropriate categories and in a prudent fashion. This is generally accomplished by downgrading below the current asset line certain assets which were carried current and upgrading to the current section certain liabilities which had been reflected in the long-term or other liabilities section by the accountants.

One particularly interesting analysis of the borrower's business is the determination of what phase or cycle of business life they are in. Such phases include:

- *Experimental stage*. A start-up company incurring heavy R&D is a high risk. This may also be considered a time of formulation for a company.

- *Exploitation stage.* This stage is represented by companies making significant impacts in new markets such as high tech, communications, or computer systems. This is also a time when a company is taking action and concentrating on its efforts and objectives.
- *Stability stage.* This includes those companies that have momentum and have achieved a breakthrough resulting in structured systems and successful stabilization.
- *Decline/decay stage.* Companies at this stage have peaked at some prior period of their life cycle and are now declining or decaying due to such factors as economic changes or antiquated industries. This is happening today in the United States in certain fields involving the manufacture or marketing of outdated products.

Obviously, the best time to be lending to a company is at the least risky stage, which is the stability stage.

Follow-Up Approach

The bank should constantly follow up on monitoring credits. Follow-up procedures should include at least annual credit and analytical reviews including bank and trade investigations.

It is important to obtain financial statements on a regular basis, and to spread and analyze them at predetermined regular intervals. Make comparative statement analyses based on statement dates. Compare them to common-size statements. Robert Morris Associates maintains such comparisons based on its annual composite statement studies conducted with member banks around the country. You can do a better analysis by obtaining long-form reports including working capital and fund flow statements which contain informative footnotes.

The follow-up approach also requires making regular plant visitations which should include the inspection of collateral when possible. To monitor loans secured by intangible personal property (e.g., receivables) or tangible personal property (e.g., inventory and equipment), conduct on-site audits or exams of the borrower's books and records at intervals between fiscal periods. In this connection, you may need the assistance of special staff members within your bank, such as an asset-based lending, staff-support group. If your bank does not have this type of support, consider the use of internal accountants or auditors who may provide such assistance.

You should also follow up on negative feedback from the borrower's suppliers and customers and from other financial institutions indicating that the borrower is having financial difficulties or is unable to meet its obligations in a timely manner.

1.04 FORMAL COMMITMENTS

Consider the use of formal loan commitments involving larger or more complex loans. The loan officer can protect himself better if the credit is under a formal commitment, and the appropriate affirmative covenants are built into a letter or loan agreement with the borrower, whereby financial statements and any supporting schedules are to be received in a timely and frequent manner. The formal commitment differs from an informal one in that the former should be properly executed by both the borrower and bank and generally must be acknowledged. The formal commitment also creates a formal or contingently legal obligation on the bank to fund the debt versus the more informal agreement, which should be written, in advised letter form, without a legal obligation on the part of the bank to make future advances to the borrower.

Banks have frequently entrapped themselves into formal commitments by the way they have written letters of intent and informal letter commitments; therefore, even though the intent was not to offer a formal commitment, the bank did not write proper or sufficient qualifications into the letter to invalidate any potential possibility of the letter being construed as a formal commitment by the courts. This has become an issue today because of the rapid increase of lender liability lawsuits.

Letter/Loan Agreements

The difference between letter and loan agreements is that the letter agreement is usually a rather short document (often only a few pages), while the loan agreement is much more lengthy and can even be quite voluminous. Loan agreements are for large, complex loans. Typically, the longer document must not only be executed by both parties, but is generally required to be acknowledged. The letter agreement, on the other hand, may only be witnessed or attested by third parties for the borrower and bank. Most formal letter/loan agreements require borrowers to furnish financial statements on both an annual and an interim basis. The interim period may entail the requirement for monthly or quarterly statements. But loan agreements often require more frequent receipt of financial statements (i.e., monthly versus quarterly) than do letter agreements. Another difference obviously may be the sheer number of covenants, events of default, and rights and remedies found in a loan agreement. These agreements often require additional information and schedules that govern and control collateral if the debt is secured, particularly pertaining to tangible and intangible personal property assets of a company.

Covenants

Covenants cover both affirmative and negative requirements incumbent on the borrower. They are written to assist and guide most corporate borrowers to maintain an acceptable and solvent financial condition. This is often done by way of achieving various financial ratios and percentages, minimum dollar and (stair step) levels pertaining to working capital, equity, and borrowing base levels. In addition, the bank will often incorporate boilerplate covenants.

In this connection, banks place most of their financial covenant requirement emphasis on the borrowing company's balance sheet. Obviously, this is often less complicated to do because the bank can easily determine the company's overall health by its liquidity, working capital, debt, and equity levels. However, bankers should stress and apply more covenants to a company's profit and loss (P&L) and cash flow statements. In this connection, the bank should consider using some of the following ratio formulas to build in stability to earnings and cash flow. These formulas apply to business borrowers:

- **Internal Cash Flow minus (−) Retained Earnings Adjustments (net decreases) / Current Maturity Long-Term Debt (CMLTD).** Divide internal cash flow which is computed after adjusting internal operating accrual totals, minus any retained earnings adjustments on a net decrease basis, by CMLTD. This indicates a borrower's cash flow ability from operations to servicing its current portion term debt.

• **Internal Cash Flow minus (−) Retained Earnings Adjustments (net decreases) / CMLTD plus (+) Capital Expenditures.** This indicates a borrower's cash flow from operations to service its current portion term debt and to support any new capital expenditures (fixed assets).

• **Internal Cash Flow plus (+) Cash and Equivalents/Current Liabilities.** Divide internal cash flow plus cash and cash equivalents (e.g., marketable securities) by total current liabilities. This shows a borrower's ability to generate liquidity to meet current debt. The higher this ratio the better a company's ability to service current debt needs from cash flow, cash, and cash equivalents.

• **Break-Even Debt Service.** Calculate the borrower's break-even, after debt service, but eliminate noncash charges (e.g., depreciation, depletion, and amortization) that are not considered true cash expenses. Also, since the interest portion of debt is already included in the income statement, only the current portion of term debt should be added as a fixed cost in calculating the break-even point. This adjusted break-even formula will then reveal the amount of sales and/or revenues necessary to break even and service the current portion of term debt.

In addition, one of the more pertinent affirmative covenants is the receipt of financial statements in a timely manner. Usually with larger credits, annual audited statements must be received within 90 to 120 days of a company's fiscal year-end; the statement is normally accompanied by a no-default letter from the company's CPA. This letter reveals that the company is not in default of any covenants and if the company is in default, the CPA should indicate that in the letter and request a waiver. Required interim statements are another affirmative covenant; such statements whether monthly or quarterly should be received within 15 days of the statement date for monthly statements or up to 45 days from statement date for quarterly statements. Additional covenants may mandate receipt of collateral schedules on a monthly or more frequent basis. Types of schedules include borrowing base certificates, inventory reconciliations, and/or monthlv accounts receivable and payable or aging reports.

Liquidity and Working Capital Covenants

Most covenants involving the maintenance of dollar levels, percentages, and ratios are basically established to protect the solvency of the borrowing entity and to retain sufficient liquidity and working capital. Under the U.S. Bankruptcy Reform Act, solvency is established by a borrower's ability to meet scheduled debt payments in a timely manner and not solely on a positive net-worth test. Therefore, besides building in some of the more important cash flow covenants as indicated above, the bank should emphasize covenants that require adequate levels of liquidity or the attainment of sufficient levels of liquidity by building in stair-step (improvements) covenant requirements. Remember, liquidity level requirements vary greatly depending on the nature of the company's business, e.g., manufacturing, wholesaling, retailing, or service, and on its trading cycle (period of time it takes the company to convert its inventory to cash) and cash conversion cycle (trade cycle period including support it receives from the trade and accruals represented by the current liability side of the balance sheet). As an example, a manufacturer generally has a longer trading cycle than a wholesaler because it usually acquires inventory in its raw state and then processes it (work-in-process) to completion for sale, while a wholesaler would only need to buy the goods for resale. Obviously, the manufacturer would have a longer trading cycle which would also entail a heavier fixed cost or overhead burden because of the manufacturing cycle—thus the need for more working capital than the typical wholesale business.

Compliance Checks

The next key ingredient is for the bank's credit department to set up compliance checksheets to monitor the progress the borrowing company is making. These checksheets can be prepared manually or be computerized. Basically, all the covenants consisting of numbers, percentages, or ratios that can be calculated from the financial statements, received from the borrower within the required time period, or other collateral schedules or information should be displayed in appropriate columns on the compliance checksheet. Columns should be broken down by months, which is the normal cycle for these covenants to be checked by a credit analyst.

Each analyst should be assigned a certain number of credits to monitor each month. Junior analysts, who normally get many of these assignments because of their mundane nature, should realize it is very good for them to become experienced in the general convenant requirements of letter and loan agreements and to monitor the progress of a company's financial condition. The analyst should actually verify recent dates, and calculate amounts, percentages, and ratios, then insert them in the appropriate monthly columns. Any covenant that is not met should be clearly indicated by a violation marked in red or in some other way. The servicing loan officer should receive the results of the monthly checks pertaining to their credits. In particular, violations should be brought to the loan officer's attention in order that he or she might correct them.

As you can see, this is a good early warning system to inform officers of any pending problems. Usually, the officer will allow the borrower a waiver for not meeting the particular covenant; this does not mean that the particular covenant should not stay in force. If the violation is one that cannot be corrected within a reasonable period, the borrowing entity will often request an amendment to the particular covenant, which could either be a permanent waiver or change that the company could comply with; it will be up to the loan officer or higher level of authority (senior loan officers or committee), if above the loan officer's lending limit, whether to temporarily waive the covenant or permanently amend it.

This whole process, therefore, allows loan officers, even at higher levels of authority, to be involved in the monitoring and early detection of a problem credit.

1.05 MISCELLANEOUS PROBLEM LOAN IDENTIFICATION

The miscellaneous symptoms in recognizing a future problem loan include the following:

- Renewal of a loan several times instead of it being liquidated according to maturity schedule, in essence providing capital monies.

- Audited financial statements not being delivered to the bank on schedule.
- Evidence of drastic financial statement changes or losses from operations.
- Credit agency reports reflecting slowness in the trade, not previously shown.
- An increase in trade inquiries from vendors and suppliers.
- Notices of insurance cancellations.
- Notices and indications in public information records of legal action being taken against the borrower.
- Evidence of cash flow problems in checking accounts, e.g., overdrafts (ODs), numerous drawings on uncollected funds, and deposits rushed in frequently to cover checks being presented the same day.
- Detection of unusual activities of the borrower, or officers of the borrower (company), e.g., high living, gambling, excessive alcohol or drug problems.
- Major or drastic changes in management.
- Notice of tax liens, suits filed, or judgments being recorded.

If you do not have an in-house collection officer to step in after a loan becomes delinquent, the loan officer should move quickly especially when one of the above problems is observed. Having a third party in the bank review the credit proves beneficial because this provides a fresh look at the situation. In smaller banks an experienced collection officer or uninvolved third party can frequently turn up possible solutions that have been overlooked.

When you do not have an in-house collection officer, sometimes it is difficult to find that third party in a small bank who really has the skills to be of assistance. Indeed, you may have to look closely for that third-party assistance because the experience level of personnel is often low. As a matter of fact, often the collection staff does not have much experience in the commercial lending side of the bank, if any at all. This is because they frequently come out of the retail side of the bank, which does consumer and installment lending. They may even have been hired into that position because the bank was gearing up or was already heavily involved in acquiring or purchasing indirect paper from dealers that were selling larger ticket items or more expensive consumer goods, e.g., cars, mobile homes, boats, jewelry, furniture, and appliances.[1]

When seeking third-party assistance within the bank, look for someone who has good credit skills and who also may have an understanding of documentation. Better yet, if those persons have had hands on commercial lending or workout experience besides the prior mentioned skills, seek them out. Endeavoring to obtain the assistance of a third party should not be considered a reflection on the ability of the account officer. The concept of a fresh look by the third party is similar to the old adage whereby "we (the loan officers) do not see the forest for the trees." If you have access to a collection officer who can be aptly used in the particular circumstances, he or she may be better able to take the time to jointly discuss the loan with the customer, providing additional ideas for a course of action.

Business Problems

The more general ways to identify a problem loan—depending on the circumstances—as it relates to a business, are as follows:

- Change in behavior or personal habits of principals, e.g., excessive alcohol consumption, drugs, or marital problems

---

[1] As you may know, indirect paper does not pertain to a direct loan as the bank acts as a conduit in financing such items for consumer buyers, thus allowing the dealer to obtain its funds quickly rather than financing or carrying the paper. Years ago, it was more prevalent for banks to finance dealer inventory, which often involved floor planning in order to procure the retail sales paper in view of the generally higher yield the retail paper would offer the bank. The purchase of retail paper was also a source for the bank to quickly invest deposits. Many banks, however, found out that the volume on their books quickly rose, even to the point of becoming a concentrated loan level. Worse yet, many banks did not have good direct recourse arrangements with their dealers and if they did not undertake sufficient credit checks or conduct other adequate underwriting procedures, they often sustained large losses. On top of that, if they were also financing a particular dealer's inventory who was selling them paper, the risk was heightened because if the dealer sold goods out of trust and was unable to pay its debt, the bank would then also lose any additional protection it might have had from the dealer if it had guarantied the paper or endorsed it with recourse. The only substantial recovery some banks realized was from funded reserves, held out of loan proceeds to offset bad debt.

- Lack of cooperation and change in attitude; perhaps even evidence of acts of irrational behavior.
- Failure to stand by personal commitments.
- Successive changes or turnover in ownership, management, or other key personnel.
- Natural disasters including illness or death.
- Lack of management depth or experienced successors to the present management, possibly as a result of a one-man start-up owner/manager who has achieved a growth level above his or her ability to manage properly.
- Recurrence of the same old problems that were never resolved.
- Inability to make short- or long-term plans, goals, or forecasts.
- Poor or inadequate financial reporting, records, and controls.
- Entering into new product lines or businesses outside the company's expertise or making acquisitions that are not compatible with the present business or that are beyond the company's capacity to operate or finance.
- Desire and insistence to take business gambles and undue risk.
- Unrealistic pricing of goods and services.
- Negligence or carelessness in maintaining business standards or poor utilization and management of personnel.
- Slowness or undue delays in reacting to declining markets or economic conditions, or other business, economic, or labor problems.
- Antiquated, inefficient, or nonuseful plant and equipment or poor maintenance thereof, and perhaps poor financial planning in acquiring new fixed assets or making other necessary maintenance or capital expenditures.
- Loss of key product lines, franchises, distribution rights, or sources of supply.
- Loss of one or more major customers who are financially sound, especially when there is a concentration or dependence on such customers.
- Speculative inventory purchases or excess purchasing.

- Taking on substantial business orders or contracts that cannot be fulfilled or achieved because of a lack of productivity or capacity.
- Inventory that is either stale, outdated, or out-of-style; in too great a quantity, or of an inappropriate mix, or any combination thereof.

Financial Problems

Here are some general problems that become evident as the borrower's financial condition deteriotates:

- Declining bank balances, overdrafts, dishonored and returned deposited checks, drawings on uncollected funds (known as kiting).
- Heavier reliance on bank borrowings, often requested for a short term, and not being paid other than with renewals and requests for increases of new money. This could also be manifested in marked changes in timing of seasonal loan requests, and even a difficulty in meeting payroll. These requests may not have more than a single source of repayment that can be easily or realistically identified.
- An increase in inquiries from suppliers or others, requesting credit information on borrowers, especially involving requests by the borrower for special terms or expanded credit limits.

Such vendors may also call to discuss concern over a general rise in slowness of trade payments. Calls may come from new suppliers requesting credit information relative to borrower requests to grant new credit lines, whether pertaining to open (unsecured) credit or involving purchase money liens (secured purchase transactions). In these instances, be forewarned of two potential problems.

First, whenever giving out credit information on your borrower, state only your experience and check with your borrower first before giving out any confidential information. Perhaps the borrower does not want you to convey any depository information or negative facts. If so, you will have to tell the inquirer that all information is confidential and that the borrower will have to approve in writing any credit information to be offered by you. When you do not adhere to this principle, but make borrowers appear to be in better condition than they are, you may be subjecting yourself to a potential lawsuit if the supplier grants credit, based on your credit response, and subsequently sustains a loss. The same holds true when you offer any information that is partially false or untrue in order to help your own cause. On the other hand, keep in mind that other creditors may be very cognizant of the borrower's cash problems as they may have reduced or decreased trade terms or open credit limits, or even started selling only on a COD basis, or perhaps have ceased shipping to the borrower entirely.

Secondly, guard against new liens filed by vendors. Whenever new suppliers enter the picture or when the borrower requests an increase from existing ones, and you have a blanket filing on inventory, undertake routine searches of state and local Uniform Commercial Code (UCC) records (depending on your state's filing requirements) for any new purchase money liens being filed by suppliers, since such specific purchase money security interest (PMSI) could come ahead of your interests in those particular goods. However, those suppliers will have to notify you of their PMSI before the borrower receives possession of the merchandise.

Along the above lines, routine searches will often alert you to other creditors entering the picture, whether they have taken blanket liens on collateral behind you or if they have taken a specific PMSI in inventory or equipment, or an interest in other unencumbered available personal property assets on which you have not taken a lien.

Other sure signs of the borrower's deteriorating financial condition include:

- Violations and defaults under letter and loan agreements.
- Notices of insurance cancellations for failure to pay premiums. In this connection, always arrange to have premium notices come to the bank before expiration, giving you the opportunity to pay them before cancellation. Therefore, maintain a good tickler system.
- A proliferation of legal action against the company, e.g., suits, tax liens, judgments.

Follow-Up After Problem Loan Identification

There are a number of follow-up procedures that should be undertaken once a problem loan has been detected, including the following:

- Review other borrower loans, whether direct or indirect, including those tied to the relationship.
- Review and analyze both the borrower's and any guarantor's or other contingent obligor's financial statements for any available unencumbered assets. Consider taking seconds, too, in case a minimal first lien exists leaving an acceptable level of equity to encumber.
- Start monitoring demand accounts in the borrower's name more closely.

1.06 ADDRESSING AND ANALYZING PROBLEM LOANS

There are various ways to address a problem loan once it has been detected. What the loan officer does, including the depth of the analysis, often depends on the size of the credit including its size in relationship to the bank's loan portfolio and equity. The analysis may also hinge on the type of loan and any existing collateral. The analysis should attempt to determine what created the business problems in the first place. A loan officer should understand the business, plus current market conditions, and the chances of it being able to continue operating. How well does the officer understand the company and industry, and how well does he or she really understand the problem?

Workout Officers

Certainly it is the loan officer's responsibility to tackle immediately any problem loan in his or her portfolio and to inform senior management of it. Often this depends on the level the problem has reached before a loan relationship is transferred to a new officer who is assigned to the workout staff. The bottom line is: How bad does the problem have to be before it is transferred to a special workout group? And who decides on the degree of the problem? Often, a loan officer is too optimistic or will not admit to a severe problem. At other times, the loan review or audit teams complete their reviews sometime after the problem has surfaced, so the current credit rating may not yet have been downgraded. Certainly this is a serious issue many banks need to come to grips with. In this connection, and for other reasons, some banks move more quickly than others in transferring the relationship. Furthermore, some banks may have a policy to move a credit to a special workout unit while a credit is graded in the watch or criticized category (other assets especially mentioned—OAEM), while others may wait until the credit is rated substandard or has no prospects for immediate improvement.

If new officers from the workout group assume responsibility for the credit, they will have to become very familiar with the business in a relatively short period of time; they will also need to develop an immediate rapport with the company's management.

The transfer of the relationship to the workout group is advantageous because a good workout person:

- Will not personalize the problem and become emotional when dealing with the customer.
- Elicits cooperation from the borrower.
- Works hard at solving the problem.
- Can readily develop perceptive insights into the management's capabilities, the borrower's financial condition, and the limitations of the borrower whether it be management or otherwise.

Management Changes

It may then be appropriate for the loan officer to determine if the firm has plans for any management changes in order to correct the problem. The officer must continually monitor the borrower's attitude. Sometimes a good "turnaround" person will not only be able to come in and improve the condition of the business, but he or she can be of great assistance in developing the proper rapport with the bank.

The bank will have to be especially sensitive in not forcing any management change because it could be later deemed an insider under a control issue if the company files bankruptcy, or the bank could even be sued, resulting in substantial penalties under lender liability. The loan or workout officer must remember all debtors are unique in their own way. Therefore, a good banker quickly evaluates debtors on their internal financial condition, level of cooperation, and anticipated reaction.

Legal Action

Before taking any course of action, this specialist should confer with legal counsel. Together they need to undertake a discovery mission.

• For one thing, they should assure themselves that all credit and collateral documentation are in good shape. Banks often make the mistake of leaving loan documentation to others who are not properly trained, which may lead to incomplete and inaccurate documentation. For another thing, they should satisfy themselves that the credit files are sufficiently informative and that no derogatory, threatening, slanderous, or discriminatory memos or letters are in the files. Furthermore, they should scrutinize credit inquiry letter responses for false information. Problems in these areas could be raised resulting in the potential issue of lender liability in case the files were subpoenaed into court.

Courses of Action

The bank will hopefully have alternatives in dealing with the problem; it will have to decide which one is most effective in solving the problem. Here are some matters the bank may wish to weigh. To start with, should the bank continue with the borrower? As prerequisites:

- The borrowing company must be a viable entity.
- It must have unity of management.
- Management must have plans to improve operations (increase profits, enhance cash flow).

- It must have a reasonable plan to repay debt.
- It must know how any additional advances will help resolve problems.

Beyond all that, the bank may wish to evaluate the company, using the outside opinion of managers representing suppliers and customers. There are advantages and disadvantages concerning debt extension. One advantage is that it offers the debtor relief from the pressure of filing bankruptcy. Another is that it protects bank from a "voidable preference" because it takes additional collateral within the last 90 days.

On the other hand, how would debt extensions negatively impact the bank? For one thing, they may allow borrowers the opportunity to reduce their efforts to make repayment. For another thing, they may allow the borrower a way to divert funds to pay other more pressing needs or creditor obligations. For still another thing, they may give the loan officer an excuse to temporarily avoid a problem and delay possible necessary action.

Necessary Liquidation

Liquidation could be the easiest solution, but may or may not be the most effective in minimizing loss. It should be the last viable alternative in realizing any recovery on your debt; therefore, the following factors should be considered:

- Who are the potential purchasers?
- How quickly must a sale of the borrower's business or assets be accomplished and what effect will it have on existing customers? What does the sales price have to be before the bank sustains a loss? In this connection, consideration should be made of costs to be incurred, such as commissions, taxes, legal fees, surveys, fix-up costs, and expenses involved in cancelling leases.
- If the bank decides to liquidate assets itself, what will be the cost to hold and maintain such assets, e.g., security, insurance, taxes, and the cost or time value of money that could be invested awaiting the sale?
- If the assets consist of real estate, you will also have to factor in the impact of zoning, special purpose buildings, location, cash

flow, unpaid real estate taxes that would constitute a priority lien, marketability of property, difficulty in determining value, and leases.

• If the assets consist of inventory, you must remember to consider the effect of the different stages—whether raw materials, work-in-process, or finished goods versus expected sales proceeds (based on expected costs to complete or make according to firm purchase orders).

• If the assets consist of accounts receivable, remember you must get access to receivable records and notify account debtor customers to remit amounts owing directly to the bank. Consider the potential problem that you will face relative to account debtors who often devise excuses for nonpayment, such as raising defenses involving offsets for defective goods, charge-backs for credits due them, and other warranties, claims, and guarantees for the nonperformance or defective operation of goods sold to them.

• If the assets consist of equipment, consider the effect of trying to sell special purpose equipment; the cost to dismantle and move it; the possibility that it is functionally or technologically obsolete; whether it is unusually difficult to market; and the effect of any rights a landlord would have, if the equipment is located on leased property. All this also applies to inventory, too.

• If you hold a lien on all assets including company stock, it will probably be easier to sell the company as a going concern. Otherwise, you may have to sell assets piecemeal or engage in a series of sales to interested parties privately or by way of auction.

• If the problem involves fraud, or if the debtor has dissipated assets to the extent that collectibility of the loan is questionable, liquidation will be essential.

Assuming you decide to proceed, be forewarned that it is very difficult to determine the ultimate amount to be realized from liquidation of collateral such as inventory, equipment, or real estate, and especially from contracts and other intangible personal property assets. Still, a thorough analysis of values must be undertaken in order to determine the ultimate amount to be realized.

When you decide to liquidate, how will you accomplish it? First you will have to declare the loan in default and demand payment; second, you will have to pursue a judicial foreclosure by obtaining a judgment if the borrower is not willing to turn over the collateral in a friendly foreclosure procedure. This may force the borrower to file bankruptcy. However, the easiest and least expensive method of liquidation may be to arrange an out-of-court settlement.

Liquidating Trust

With larger cases, perhaps involving other bank creditors, a liquidating trust could be established by having each bank form separate companies to act as partners in the trust. This arrangement is occasionally done when the borrower and the creditors, preferably secured creditors, agree that the cost and time of going through bankruptcy is not worth it. Besides, the risk may be great to the financial institution if the borrower and guarantors raise valid defenses for nonpayment. Therefore, in order to expedite liquidation of collateral, the borrower—often including the owners who have guaranteed the debt—agrees to contribute the majority of its nonexempt personal assets along with the business assets of the borrowing entity to the trust for satisfaction of the debt and for release from any guarantees.

This arrangement is similar to a friendly foreclosure on the borrower's part, and to a friendly bankruptcy liquidation on the owner's/guarantor's part without actually filing. The banks, on the other hand, would arrange for some type of trustee or administrator to manage the liquidating trust. To be successful, the banks would all have to agree on their respective share interest in the trust, which would usually be based on their priority interest share of the collateral and amount of guaranties. Usually, the banks will share on some pro-rata percentage formula under different classes or levels of debt and collateral interests and recourse to owners/guarantors. Then, as collateral and assets are liquidated, the creditors would receive their agreed upon pro-rata shares. The trust is made up of each of the banks forming separate companies to act as partners in the trust in order to protect or shield the banks from liability, and for tax and accounting reasons.

Do Nothing or Stand Still Approach. The bank has to decide if it is going to do nothing or stand still on taking any action against the borrower, or if it is willing to risk further deterioration in the collateral or a decline in the credit. Sometimes taking no action is better at least for a while. You could be forcing the borrower into bankruptcy by taking certain quick action. On the other hand, an involuntary petition could be filed against the borrower while you are waiting to take action. Some of the other questions you must ask youself are stated below:

- Will other creditors gain an advantage if you do not take immediate action?
- If there are unsecured creditors in the picture, how will they react—will they be cooperative?
- If there are delinquent taxes, how are the taxing authorities going to react?
- Will a failure to take action be in the bank's best interests or could it prove detrimental?

The bank has to determine whether it will continue working with the borrower or not. You can do your homework by taking these steps:

1. Analyze all the factors that created the problem.
2. Develop a primary and contingent plan to deal with it.
3. Have the borrower provide information on implementing cost-cutting controls and eliminating expenses; do not get into a position of dictating in case the borrower does not make it since you could be exposed to a control issue resulting in being deemed an "insider" under the Bankruptcy Act.
4. Obtain a complete picture of all the borrower's debt, e.g., direct, indirect, and contingent, including hidden or secret obligations.
5. Determine which assets are pledged or earmarked to secure debt that should then be netted.
6. Obtain any consolidating or combining statements that make up the consolidated or combined statements as this should increase the total debt leverage position. Furthermore, these statements should furnish more details on intercompany transactions and on direct and indirect obligations on the part of each of the entities (those directly related by a parent-subsidiary relationship or through indirectly related common ownership).

7. Obtain a breakdown of all leases whether operating or finance leases. In this connection, you must obtain a total of all leases that are noncancellable and the future annual totals owed on them. Such leases represent future obligations owed by the borrower.
8. Estimate how much money the borrower needs to continue operating; to do this, obtain cash flow budgets, forecasts, and projections. The borrower will also have to prepare a proforma income statement and balance sheet for at least 12 months into the future under the worst projected conditions.
9. Estimate the prospects for repayment under the worst conditions; therefore, avoid impossible repayment terms.
10. Investigate alternate sources of funds, such as additional equity from present owners or government loan assistance programs. Perhaps new funding may be available by incurring new debt from outside sources such as factoring and finance companies, and other third-party lenders. Another alternative source is the sale of unnecessary assets, including subsidaries, affiliates, or other sundry investments. Also, consider the sale of unnecessary personal property assets and the general shrinkage of the business. Perhaps extensions, moratoriums, subordinations, and debt conversions to equity participations could be arranged with the trade or other creditors or note holders.
11. Attempt to advise the borrower on its use of funds, but do not control the borrower's actions, use, or distribution of the funds.
12. Introduce a consultant or advise the borrower on obtaining one, but again, do not force one on it or insist on using your hand-picked choice. However, review the need for a consultant and how the particular one in mind can get the job done. Good consultants offer many advantages depending on what they are used for and how they are used. For example, consultants:
    a. Provide more professional day-to-day management ideas.
    b. Develop recommendations for more time efficiency within borrowing organizations.

c. May help insulate the bank and company from legal problems and public criticism.
d. Show borrower they are truly committed in turning the business around and really mean business.
e. Provide the right source or the proper vehicle, or offer the appropriate advantage in finding a buyer and selling the company.

13. Determine working capital requirements and what absolute capital expenditures must be made in the near future.

It is imperative that the loan officer retain, or in the case of a newly assigned workout officer, establish and develop a rapport with the borrower.

The bank should document all its actions carefully; some information of a highly confidential or sensitive nature should not be placed in credit, collateral, or even loan officer working or desk files. Continued supervision is highly important as continued monitoring of the situation is critical; this includes analyzing of statements, undertaking trade and public record checks, and reviewing other vital information relative to the borrower and its operations.

The workout officer must establish a goal for corrective action and must be willing to change as circumstances change. Include contingent action plans when the primary goal cannot be achieved or no longer merits pursuit.

Support Staff

Most banks, other than small ones, have support staff within their organizations that will assist or at least address existing or potential problem credits. For example, some banks retain an on-site credit and loan review staff to conduct ongoing credit and loan reviews in order to identify problems or update the status of already identified problem loan relationships. On the other hand, certain banks accomplish this by use of traveling internal examiners.

Credit Department

In medium to large banks, a credit analyst staff is available on-site, making up a major segment of the typical credit department. Such banks may even have a separate in-house loan or asset review staff and a centralized loan operations or note and collateral department.

The general difference between credit analysts and loan review or asset revier staffs is their function. Credit department analysts often provide the full scope of credit support work to the loan officers, which includes the spreading of financial statements and the analysis of these statements along with the entire credit relationship including credit investigations and inquiry work. Analysts also perform other sundry duties, such as the completion of customer profitability, letter and loan agreement compliance checks, and loan packaging (preparation or review of loan applications including all supporting information for committee presentation). They even give special assistance to loan officers. The credit analyst may make a major contribution by undertaking a thorough analysis after receipt of statements. The loan officer generally requests the analysis. Analysts often do not have the time to analyze interim statements because of their unusual workload or because the credit department may be understaffed. In this connection, it is very important for the loan officer to make the request in a timely manner to the credit department if they need interim statements analyzed.

The manager of the credit department should also be allowed to make a judgment whether interim statements should be fully analyzed. In-depth analysis may be necessary when a possible problem in the credit is detected. Certainly, the loan officer should be the one making the request, because he or she is closer to the credit.

The credit department manager should scan all financial statements as they are received and logged in to determine whether they should be both spread and analyzed. Fiscal year-end statements should automatically be spread and analyzed whenever possible. With large borrowers, year-end statements are often audited by a CPA, or are at least CPA reviewed. CPA prepared statements are characteristically prepared in long form with accompanying footnotes to allow the analyst the opportunity for better analysis.

Also, loan officers often set the annual line of credit reapprovals shortly after the expected receipt of these annual statements in order to make a better decision before renewing the line of credit. Therefore, this is where a good credit manager and well trained analysts can make an important contribution, not only to the credit process approval but also by pointing out and furnishing facts about a bad loan, they will help the bank better address portfolio problems. This also applies to new credits being presented for the first time for approval. A good analysis may aid the bank in averting a future loss.

Another way credit analysts may be used, which many banks have not undertaken in the past other than with specialized staff, if at all, is the outside examination of borrowers' books and records. Since many banks do not have specialized personnel, whether because of cost or otherwise, to check borrower records, a very valuable service in this respect could be provided. Banks have generally maintained the right to inspect a borrower's books and records, during normal business hours, in security agreements but usually have not taken advantage of this clause.

Many banks are now finding out that a great deal more can be learned about a company's financial condition and any pending or actual problems if it undertakes on-site examination. A good on-site examination will allow the bank to really delve into the underlying makeup of the financial statements it receives from the borrower or its accountants. This examination will also allow the analysts to learn a whole new facet of credit, besides just accompanying the loan officer in a visit to look at the premises and visit with management, and perhaps briefly inspecting the collateral (just "kicking the tires").

Loan or Asset Review Department

If a bank maintains an internal loan or asset review staff, it will generally emphasize more of an ongoing credit and collateral review based on the frequent monitoring of the loan portfolio. Frequency depends on the size of loans; the credit grading classification of the particular loan or relationship; when the last review was conducted including when the credit was booked, if a new loan; and perhaps the credit concentration or available collateral. Most banks attempt to make a significant penetration in their portfolios regarding the dollar level of credits reviewed to the dollar level of the entire loan portfolio. A penetration level of 80 percent or more is very good.

The loan or asset review staff should concentrate on undertaking more of a critique type credit analysis (with short concise comments) instead of the longer traditional credit analysis often completed by the credit department (with industry studies and comparisons). This critique should include a study of the complete relationship consisting of all of the borrower's debt including related party debt. Special emphasis should be placed on reviewing renewed loans, past dues, and overdrafts. Staff may conduct updated lien searches for other secured credit interests and order more recent credit reports to assist them. Reviewers should be especially sensitive to acting as an early warning system for potential problem loans. Constant surveillance is very important in order not to lose valuable time once a problem is observed. This is also another reason why it is good to review loans within a reasonably short period of time after they are booked.

It is important that appropriate information flow from line loan officers to review staff so that an adequate review can be undertaken with current data. One way line officers can assist in the early warning identification process is for them to furnish the review staff with downgrade or potential upgrade credit memos.

Loan Review Meetings. Meetings should be conducted on a regular basis, preferably weekly. Management or executive and other senior staff members should be present along with servicing loan officers whose credits are being reviewed. The meeting may be chaired by the loan or asset review manager or other designated officer. It is suggested that loan or asset review analysts present the credits they have reviewed and give their reasons for ratings; the review should include any downgrade or upgrade of credits based on the bank's standard grading system. Then the loan officer should be allowed to defend or make comments on those credits and the findings. Officers should report what is currently transpiring on the credit, how problems are being addressed, and what is being done to improve the situation. They should also downgrade their own credits, when applicable.

Potential problem credits may also be discussed at meetings. Loan officers, with the assistance of review personnel, should prepare short reports on potential problem credits. Loans that are designated potential problems or even worse must have immediate attention. This is the time when the loan officer has to move quicklv to correct the problem or attempt to salvage the credit. He or she may have to call on the assistance of staff members.

If a bank is understaffed on the loan or asset review side, it might consider having credit department analysts evaluate the credit in conjunction with the time a review is to be undertaken which could be used in the review, thus saving employee time by eliminating the need for review staff to complete analytical work. Of course, this process must be well coordinated between the managers of the respective departments. The review staff members may also be expected to monitor exceptions they determine exist, and in many institutions they are required to furnish grade reports and projections, allocations of reserve levels, and recommendations when loans should be placed on non-accrual or charged-off.

The review staff is often responsible for maintaining a "watch-list." This list is perhaps defined differently at various institutions. It is preferable to include all "special mentioned" credits in this list, which includes examiner-criticized loans and even pass-rated loans being watched for some reason. In addition, a list of all classified loans would have to be maintained consisting of those loans rated substandard and doubtful. In some institutions the review staff works closely with the accounting department in completing and reconciling such additional reporting.

Dual Capacities. In smaller to medium sized institutions, such support staff may function in both the capacitv of credit analvsts and loan or asset review personnel.

Internal Bank Examiners

In other medium to large banks, besides having on-site credit and loan or asset review staffs depending on the philosophy of the institution, they also have a team of traveling internal bank examiners who resemble loan or asset review personnel in that they review the portfolio during infrequent visits to various banks or branches. These internal examining departments are often given different titles, e.g., asset quality control or special asset or asset review. Such departments may be located at the main bank or holding company headquarters, or even be broken up and located at regional locations if the institution is very large. In all cases, though, the examination staff usually report directly to the holding company.

Actually, many such staff members are former bank examiners, and their review procedures often resemble those used by external regulatory bank examiners. In many banks, because of economics of scale efforts, these examining staffs are completely replacing on-site loan or asset review staffs.

Internal Bank Auditors

They include within their overall general audit a review of loans, although it is more of an exception audit which may entail an examination of loan and collateral documentation. This audit function staff also usually travels between the holding company headquarters and branches. Auditors more often than not report directly to the holding company. Indeed, it appears that the auditor's role is becoming more absorbed in the loan portfolio these days. If large enough, some banks often have on-site auditors.

Loan Operations/Services (Note and Collateral Departments)

In most banks there is a separate loan operations function in order to process notes and collateral. In branch states, much of the documentation may be handled and housed at a central main office or flagship location. In small banks or branches, a small note and collateral department often exists. Particularly if part of a larger institution, the primary documentation and note processing will be undertaken at a central or regional location. By contrast, loan officers in some institutions, especially small independent banks, may process their own notes and other documentation.

The loan operations area should not only be proficient in loan documentation preparation, but also be organized to identify potential problems, especially based on the lack of documentation. Improper documentation may be identified from the ways the loan operations area functions and operates. First of all, note and collateral department personnel should be experienced, diligent personnel who are not prone to make errors. They should also act as the front line checkpoint in determining that all the bank's collateral has been furnished at the time of closing. These people should be well trained in this respect and have sufficient experience in identifying inadequate and incorrect documents as well as knowing which ones are necessary. Most banks have a checklist to follow in order to verify that all necessary documents are available at closing. Material prepared by this staff, usually on preprinted forms, must have uniformity.

Loan officers, in effect, create many troubled loans by circumventing the system, and booking loans without obtaining certain critical documentation.

Therefore, a good approval system and note department checkpoint may prevent booking without the necessary documentation. Before a loan is booked relative to a credit or collateral exception, higher officer or committee approval should be necessary, e.g., when certain collateral is not available or on hand, this could be temporarily or permanently waived depending on its importance and bearing on the credit. With a temporary waiver, a good follow-up exception system should be in place. Beyond just verifying that necessary collateral is on hand, this department should be capable of offering enhanced service by way of loan or documentation closers or processors, also referred to as closing or control unit staff, who should have the ability to determine that documentation was properly completed. These specialized support staff members are often located at a central main office or regional locations.

Their review could range from verifying security interest descriptions that may have been overlooked or incorrectly completed to a lack of determining a priority interest in collateral. A review should also include the determination of proper authorization, execution, filing, and recording of documents. This staff may even prepare more complicated material. The note and collateral department can provide an invaluable service if it can truly determine the bank's priority position on collateral before loans are booked, including active follow-up on documentation and collateral exceptions. This means personnel will often have to check public records for prior filings, recordings, and liens created by others. Indeed, this can also be important as a follow-up once a problem loan is determined. In order to properly monitor collateral, the note and collateral department needs a good tickler system or early warning system to determine when collateral may be affected by expirations and terminations. This includes knowing when lien filings and insurance policies will expire as well as knowing when insurance policies may lapse. As such, it's good to stay alert for tax liens and judgments against borrowers that could signal trouble.

Other Observations

Many banks, especially those involving branches, do not have in-house or on-site staffs to undertake continuous audits, loan or asset review, and credit analysis work. At the most, they may have a small credit staff to support the loan officers in some of their banks or branches. The shift in this direction has been a result of attempts to improve economies of scale and to generally cut overhead. Therefore, many banks have eliminated any overlap or duplication of staff functions by mainly doing away with on-site staff and leaving the review of credits, documentation, and collateral to traveling internal examiners and auditors. In addition, holding company managers have often felt, since on-site staff was under the control of and reported to local management, that they could not be as objective about credits, or recommend the necessary action, or address potential problem credits or collateral deficiencies independently enough, in case local management felt differently about the seriousness or identification of the problem.

In short, internal examiners or reviewers must be able to stand up to local management when reviewing and grading loans. To be effective, reviewers and examiners must be highly qualified and be able to identify problem loans. On the other hand, on-site credit/loan administration personnel are becoming more involved in the approval process and the day-to-day credit decision making, which seems to be an improving shift in the whole loan underwriting process.

Holding companies have also used their principal internal examining staff, located in the main or regional headquarters, to examine other banks for acquisition purposes or before acquiring closed banks or when large blocks of another bank's or holding company's stock was pledged to secure stockholder loans. Of course, as many of you bankers in the smaller, independent banks across the country know, the servicing loan officer will often have to wear all hats including that of the loan review and credit officer.

In summary, the key is to be able to properly and quickly identify problem credits in order to shore up and correct your position if possible. The larger the banking organization, the more support staff there usually is to find and identify problems whether by credit check and analysis, loan documentation and collateral review, exception checks, or other review and audit procedures. However, another key to this whole process working well is that it must be properly coordinated and organized. Moreover, appropriate people who are well trained and able to accomplish the job must be in place.

Loan Default Provisions

Now that we've introduced the players in the loan arena, it's time to describe some tools they work with. When a loan goes bad, they can turn to such tools. One is called loan default provisions.

There are standard loan default provisions in every letter, loan and security agreement. Usually, if covenant violations are not cured, waived, or amended within a specified period of time, it will trigger a loan default.

Most agreements include "insecurity" clauses, which are often referred to as a "nervous" clause. Such clauses are established to allow the bank the right to call or demand payment on a loan if for some arbitrary reason the bank feels insecure, whether because of a suspected deteriorating financial condition or diminishing value in its collateral position.

In the past, banks have found it difficult to rely on such clauses to collect on debt when they anticipated a loan default. There must be reasonable grounds for calling a loan when using such a clause. With lender liability looming at every corner, a bank must use extreme caution and be very judicious before calling a loan because a debtor suit could quickly evolve if such action on the bank's part contributes to the harm or financial collapse of the business. In the same vein, the bank could also precipitate a bad faith lawsuit by the debtor, especially when it terminates its commitment because the debtor is not clearly in default of the bank letter, loan or security agreement.

To protect itself in such instances, the bank should notify the borrower in writing that there is a problem, saying that there are grounds to call the loan and/or that there is a violation or default under the agreement that could allow the bank to terminate the loan commitment and demand payment. It is recommended that this be done first verbally with the borrower or authorized signers of debt instruments, followed by written confirmation. The bank should also undertake whatever is necessary to resolve the problem and then only terminate the relationship or commitment if it cannot settle or successfully negotiate the predicament.

1.07 REMEDIAL ACTION ONCE A PROBLEM IS DETECTED

Steps should be taken immediately once a problem loan is recognized. Your first priority should be to protect the bank's position; second, outline a plan with the borrower's assistance and cooperation to restore their financial condition to a sound and profitable operating position.

You will have to ask many questions in this entire process such as the following:

Evaluation of the Borrower

- Can you trust the borrower? Integrity and character are key ingredients.
- Is there any question that fraud may have occurred? Keep in mind that customers may resort to any means to protect themselves, depending on the circumstances, when faced with the potential loss of their business or possibility of loss of income or bankruptcy.
- Is the borrower, even if honest, capable of restoring the business to a profitable level with the proper help and guidance from yourself and others? In this connection, does he or she have the proper attitude, desire, or willingness to cooperate?

Evaluation of the Loan Officer

- Evaluate the loan officer too, especially when that person originated the loan. Look at the level of ego displayed in past credit decisions and in the handling of the present relationship.
- Is the loan officer too close to the creditor? That is, is the friendship too close to permit the officer to objectively say no to loan requests, or properly implement prudent debt restructure repayment programs, or take other necessary actions to protect the bank's best interests?
- Does the loan officer have the proper knowledge, understanding, skills, experience, or objectivity to deal with the problem quickly and prudently?
- Is the loan officer taking appropriate action on handling the account such as returning checks and not approving ODs, and is he

or she charging the customer for such action or are charges being waived?
• Is the loan officer monitoring account debtor collections, especially if loans are secured by receivables and inventory?
• Is the loan officer regularly reviewing cancelled checks to see who the borrower is paying? How else are account withdrawals being made?
• Has the officer maintained and filed all pertinent information in the credit file and documented the file properly with memos on the problem and actions being taken to resolve them? If the borrower's file is nonexistent, or if it is incomplete or very limited, or sketchy information has been furnished by the loan officer, this often speaks clearly and loudly about the loan officer.

Many times you will be able to judge the loan officer once you observe his or her actions after the loan has gone into default. Weakness may prevail if the debtor persuades the officer not to require the necessary additional and unencumbered collateral that could better secure the loan, or if the debtor influences the officer not to commence necessary legal action in a timely manner. This could not only affect the bank's chances for a greater recovery but it may even ultimately cause a further loss in rights and position versus other creditors. Another point you need to consider is that loan officers typically do not intend to become an expert in legal matters or bankruptcy law, nor do they have the time or general inclination or tenacity to work on problem credits while attempting to generate new business and service their other customers.

Other Considerations

The banker will have to consider other factors once a problem arises. These include the following:

• Who else is in the credit—lenders or suppliers? Are they secured or unsecured creditors? Will they subordinate their position regarding debt or collateral if you advance additional funds? Usually, the smaller and more homogeneous the lending group, the easier it is to deal under some creditor group arrangements.
• If there is a lead bank, does it understand the credit and always keep participants informed? The officer will have to consider the position of other creditors, too, once the loan goes into default.

1.08 MONITORING LOAN MATURITIES AND PAST-DUE PAYMENTS

Bear in mind that the objectives of loan servicing are to maintain the standards of quality established within the guidelines of the bank's loan policy and to stay abreast of the conditions surrounding the quality of the bank's loan portfolio. This requires that attention be given to the borrower's general financial condition and to the manner in which the obligation to the bank is handled. In this connection, the bank needs to establish a good follow-up program as it applies to loan maturities and past-due loans.

Review of Commercial Loan Maturities

Management should consider having a weekly maturity or coming-due report, perhaps providing a two-week or more lead time before the indicated loans will be due. This will give loan officers the opportunity to review their notes well in advance before final maturity. It is the account officers' responsibility to be thoroughly aware of the circumstances surrounding their loans and to review them for indications of delinquency. Should a pending delinquency or other significant potential problem exist, a brief analysis of the situation, together with a discussion between the servicing officer and his or her department head and/or division manager, could lead to alternative means of assuring payment. The following points should be considered in such an evaluation:

- Original loan date
- Original purpose
- Original payment arrangement and renewals
- Collateral and documentation
- Current statements and trends
- Past payment performance

A designated loan committee should review this report each week with servicing officers. It could be the committee's responsibility to review the servicing officer's decision to renew or restructure debt. This may consist of renewals and combining debt whether involving increases, no increases, decreases, changing repayment programs, obtaining new or additional collateral, or collecting and obtaining a full payment. Other discussions may center on rate adjustments or potential delinquency. The committee should suggest advice in rendering approval or disapproval relative to restructure or any other improvements in procedure where applicable, including pertinent information which might aid in monitoring, repayment, or collection.

Review of Installment Loan Maturities

Because of loan volume and the arrangements for receiving payments, installment loans are usually not closely reviewed by the account officers prior to maturity. However, it is still the officers' responsibility to be aware of the circumstances surrounding their loans, particularly those that have manifested a potential for becoming problems. Such warning signs include:

- Repeated past dues
- Unpaid late charges
- Expired or cancelled insurance

Account officers should be encouraged to discuss such potential problems with their group, with department or division managers, and with any independent managers of loan or credit administration.

Handling Commercial Loan Delinquencies

Fifteen days prior to a payment due date, for example, the loan operations/services department should provide the borrower with a billing notice. The servicing officer needs to receive a copy of the notice. This copy serves as a history of the loan and should be retained in payment date order.

Five days after the loan matures, or after a payment is due, the loan operations/services area could generate a Commercial Past-Due notice in duplicate. Both copies may then be given to the account officer as it would be his or her decision whether to send the notice to the borrower. This could be the only past-due notice that the loan operations/services area would provide unless especially requested to do otherwise.

It would then be the account officer's responsibility to collect past-due payments. The account officer could also mail past-due notices unless he or she is aware of special circumstances which would then give the option of mailing or not mailing the notice, depending on the circumstances and strategy of the bank.

Generally speaking, five days after the notice is mailed or when the loan is ten days past due, the servicing loan officer should check on whether payment has been received; if not, a phone call should be made to discuss the situation with the borrower. A follow up phone call should be made once the note becomes twenty days past due. These call dates are only recommendations; officers should use their own discretion or follow bank policy on when to make such calls. More frequent calls may be necessary in order to quickly resolve past-due payments. Also, consider the time value of money the bank is losing, as such funds cannot be reinvested as readily when payments are not received in a timely manner. It is also recommended that loan officers at least document credit files with memos, once loans become twenty days or more past due.

A master report should initially be distributed at least weekly as of a designated day, first to division and department or group lending managers and secondly separate reports should be distributed to loan officers by portfolio breakdown responsibility. These reports should list all loans that have matured or have past-due payments. Only a full payment of the delinquent amount, including interest and principal, should remove the customer's name from the list. Waivers, deferrals or splitting of full payments, or extensions, and renewals may need to be approved by higher authorities, depending on bank policy. As a follow-up, on another designated day of the following week, all past dues over a certain period should be reviewed by a loan or other special committee to ensure that the officer's best collection efforts are being made in order to maintain a system of checks and balances for the bank's best interests. Loan officers should be able to report to the committee on the current condition of their credits and the action that is being taken to collect them. The servicing officers may gain further insight into the handling of delinquencies by discussing collection strategy with other specialists within the institution.

Handling Installment Loan Delinquencies

Ten days after a payment is due, the loan operations/services department should generate an Installment Past-Due Notice and assess a late charge, as permissible under state consumer credit code statutes. These notices should be mailed directly to the delinquent parties. Notices should again be generated and mailed in follow-up intervals if the borrower has not brought the note current.

A master report should also be generated for all installment loans past due, for example, fifteen days or more. The master report should be distributed to department or group and division managers. Then reports by individual officers should be distributed to their superiors.

Some banks have opted to maintain in-house departments to collect such loans, but these departments may be more prevalent for the purpose of collecting indirect paper involving installment sales contracts purchased by the bank. In such instances, these banks may have made a heavy commitment to the buying of such paper.

In other cases, some banks may have even hired an outside firm to assist in collecting installment past dues. Usually, when outside firms are used, borrowers are instructed to send payments directly to the bank as the collection agency should not generally receive payments on behalf of the bank. The agency, in these cases, may send out notices and contact debtors under the bank's or its nominee's letterhead. These outside agencies may be allowed to work past-due accounts to the point of filing suit or repossessing collateral. Furthermore, these outside firms may have the capability of going further by taking legal action in behalf of the bank, and beyond that point they may even be used for foreclosing or executing on collateral after a judgment has been obtained. You must be particularly cognizant of the agency's compliance with the Fair Debt Collections Act when they are assigned to collect the debt as a third party. You should also check their insurance and bonding policies and the need for any indemnification agreements they may provide you when collecting debts in your behalf.

1.09 PROBLEM LOAN COMMITTEES

Consider forming a special committee for review of all criticized and classified loans. The size of the loans that are reviewed should usually be the larger ones as they relate to the bank's legal lending limit. Membership should include senior management and senior loan and credit/loan administration staff. Members should be able to assist the servicing officer in guidance and direction. By having a good cross section, you will be able to build in more objectivity. Presentations on the action taken on problem loans should be made by servicing officers with their managers or department heads present. Strategies of future action should be approved by committee members, and minutes should indicate approved future actions and necessary follow-up. The secretary should continue to bring up and record pending and carryover items pertaining to matters that still have not been accomplished and resolved.

1.10 NON-ACCRUAL LOAN STATUS

Commercial loans should be placed on non-accrual status once future principal or interest payments are deemed uncollectible and when payments are more than 90 days past due, or when the loans are both poorly secured and not in the process of collection. After this 90-day period, the servicing loan officer should generally make a recommendation to stop accruing interest. The recommendation may be made at a committee meeting, or as allowed under bank policy with management approval. Such recommendations should come from appropriate department personnel within the bank, and should first be discussed with the loan officer's department or division manager or even other designated senior officers.

If it is decided to place the loan on non-accrual, the officer should prepare a recommendation form. This same form may even be used to remove a loan from a non-accrual status. It should have space for signature approval from the officer's supervisor and any other higher level of authority, e.g., department, group, or division managers, or even the president and/or CEO in smaller banks. Once the appropriate signatures are obtained, this form should be sent to the loan operations/notes department which should in turn reverse any existing interest and prepare certain supporting documentation. After the interest reversal, copies of the Non-Accrual Memo should be sent to certain designated areas within the bank, e.g., loan or asset review, accounting, and the credit department for placement in the credit file while the original may be retained in the loan operations/notes area.

The form should include a recommendation for placing loanss on non-accrual, or recommendations for reclassifying loans to restructured status, or recommendations for removing loans from non-accrual or restructured status. An example of the non-accrual form is seen in Exhibit A.

A non-accrual asset may be restored to accrual status when none of its principal and interest is due and unpaid, or when the loan otherwise becomes well secured and is again in the process of collection, and when prospects for future contractual payments are no longer in doubt. If an officer wishes to suggest that a loan be removed from the non-accrual list, the same form should be completed and approved in the same manner as placing a loan on non-accrual status. However, ultimate removal from non-accrual status into an earning asset category may require committee approval, thus not allowing any such credit to be moved from a nonperforming to a performing status without the prior approval of such a committee, or perhaps the president and/or CEO in a smaller bank.

EXHIBIT A
Non-Accrual Memo Form

The following loans to ____________________
(Customer Name)
________________ are to be placed on non-accrual ______ or
(Customer #)
taken off non-accrual ______ or reclassified to restructured status ______ or removed from restructured status ______.

Only the following notes are to be so treated:

Note#	*Prin. Out.*	*Eff. Date*	*Acc. Int.*	*Income*	*Dec./Inc.*	*Sys. Input Date*
1.						
2.						
3.						
Totals ______						

If any accrued but uncollected interest is not fully reversed for a loan being placed on non-accrual or if all back interest is not to be paid in full before taking a loan off non-accrual, support your decision in the comments section below.

For loans on non accrual, all future payments by customer will be applied to principal first until paid in full or until taken off non-accrual. If you desire some other option, describe and support that decision in the comments section below. If restructured, report old interest rate and new interest rate in the comments below.

Completely but briefly state reasons for this recommendation as follows: (comments)

Acct. Off. ____________________ Date ______________
Dept. Mgr. __________________ Div. Mgr. __________________
Sr. Loan Off./C.E.O. ____________________

C.C.: account officer, credit file, loan review officer, loan operations manager or senior loan operations manager (original), and credit or loan administration manager.

CHAPTER 2

DETERMINING AND REVIEWING COLLATERAL POSITION AND CORRECTING PROBLEM DOCUMENTATION AND COLLATERAL

2.01 GENERAL

It is most important to quickly and properly review any problem credit and the bank's collateral position, if any, once that problem is detected. First, review all your loan and collateral documents, and make sure you have them all in your possession. This includes seeing that your note is complete and in proper form, that your security or other letter and loan agreements have been properly drawn and completed, and if applicable, that your financing and/or continuation statements have been properly filed and have not expired. Also verify all insurance coverage and make sure it has not expired. Some additional questions that you may ask include the following:

• Who is the true owner of the collateral? Who has the right to assign or pledge it?
• Does the collateral have any restrictions or has it been improperly assigned or pledged? For example, it may be in the name of a minor, pension fund, or restricted trust; or it may be in the form of investment letter or control stock, or involve certain government savings certificates that disqualify them from being taken as collateral.

- Has the collateral been located and is it all there as reported, including inventory and equipment?
- Are there any other liens including secret liens?
- What is the real value of the collateral, whether market, replacement, or book?
- How liquid is the collateral (e.g., liquid assets, like CDs, or marketable securities versus raw land)?
- How easily can the collateral be disposed of or sold? What is the market like (who, where, when)?
- What is your fidelity bond coverage in case of fraud?

If you are lacking anything at this time in the way of documentation or collateral, attempt to shore up your position by obtaining it. When there have been errors and omissions, action is particularly critical. Stock and negotiable instruments such as promissory notes should be in your possession. All this is very important because you may need the additional time to get the collateral in shape or to obtain additional collateral, before a default occurs, or worse, if a bankruptcy petition is filed. Contact the borrower immediately after you have reviewed your position and consulted with attorneys or other specialists within or outside the bank. The purpose of your visit to the borrower is to confirm any possible problems the company or individual is having and to quickly correct any deficiency or exception in your documentation or collateral position. Most borrowers do not readily admit problems; they often offer many different kinds of excuses and have optimistic opinions about the future, which may create more concerns and questions in your mind about the borrower's future.

On the other hand, do not reveal to the borrower how bad a shape your documentation or collateral is in. Instead, just explain whatever you need, e.g., missing signature or initials, an additional document or a certificate that was not previously delivered. Or, perhaps you need an updated schedule, report, or policy that was not provided. Generally, borrowers will cooperate in these instances because they do not want to do anything that would jeopardize the relationship, especially at a time when they may be getting concerned over their future predicament.

Besides particular state statutes that may govern your rights as a secured creditor, Article 9, Section 5, of the Uniform Commercial Code (UCC) covers this whole area on secured creditor rights.

If the loan officer does not have the expertise in this area, he or she should seek assistance from a collateral documentation specialist within the bank, and if that assistance is not available or is not sufficient, the loan officer will have to seek advice from the bank's outside counsel. The main thing a legal specialist or attorney can do is to determine your true legal position. The bank will then have to determine the value of the collateral from a "going concern" basis and from a hard liquidation standpoint. In this connection, it may be necessary and even to the bank's advantage to have an independent outside appraisal of its collateral by someone who is a well established, reputable expert. This is especially important when collateral consists of real estate and equipment, and often makes sense pertaining to inventory.

Again, the loan officer needs to respond immediately upon detecting a problem because further delays may enhance collateral deterioration or loss resulting in less recovery. Frequently, an outside legal specialist is brought in too late to properly assist the bank in correcting deficiencies in the credit or its collateral or in shoring up the bank's legal or collateral position.

2.02 PRIORITY COLLATERAL POSITION

To be protected, the bank must have a priority collateral position versus other third parties, whether secured or judgment creditors including tax or other liens. The bank should never rely on personal property collateral value if knowingly it went into the credit taking a second lien. Second liens may have some tangible value when taking real estate collateral, but they are questionable when taking other types of tangible and intangible personal assets, e.g., accounts receivable. Of course, this depends on the equity in the real property over and above the balance of the first mortgage, current market conditions, or whether the bank is willing or could buy out the first mortgagee's position. It would also behoove the bank to determine if it could obtain its collateral in a friendly foreclosure; otherwise it would have to seek a lifting of the stay or abandonment of the collateral while the borrower was in bankruptcy.

Collateral Perfection

A proper collateral position will also depend on its "perfection" and the bank's compliance to state statutes and in some instances, like aircraft, to federal law. This could also be important to the bank in recovering items which the borrower disposed of improperly; however, this would not apply to certain inventory that was sold in the normal course of business to a buyer in good faith.

In addition, many banks think they can restrict judgment creditors from coming in and executing or levying on the goods that secure their debt, which may not be the case. Actually, a judgment creditor may be allowed to have a forced judicial sale of the goods which the bank could not prevent, but after the sale the bank may still retain its security interest. As such, the bank should determine its position as it applies to personal asset collateral proceeds relative to whether it is limited to the 10-day rule (20 days in some old code states) under the revision of Article 9 of the UCC, as an example, regarding tangible or intangible personal property, or its rights in second generation collateral including that which has met certain segregated tests that would extend the bank's security interest beyond the 10 days. Real estate collateral must specifically comply and adhere to individual state statutes and recording rules, and usually involves taking a mortgage or deed of trust against the real property, depending on state requirements.

Perfection under the UCC is also scrutinized for proper filings in the right jurisdictions, accuracy of borrower names, and refiling regarding borrower name changes or movements of collateral into other states.

Improper Perfection

Documentation requirements, often omitted, cause improper perfection. Examples include uncompleted notes, and security and guaranty agreements. So make sure collateral is properly described as intended at the time the security agreement is executed, or this could invalidate your interest and prevent any enforcement.

Has the bank also obtained and used improper collateral documents? An example would be the taking of a trust receipt for the expected delivery (not release) of designated marketable stock certificates from your borrower or a third-party pledgor of the collateral. In such instances, a delivery letter from the securities firm committing to deliver the stock should actually be received; but because banks have been accustomed to releasing stock against trust receipts they have instead continued to also use them for future stock delivery. In addition, it is very risky to rely on the delivery of stock because it could be inadvertently sold or purposefully pledged to another creditor especially if you are expecting delivery from the borrower or owner and do not have a letter from a securities firm committing to deliver the securities.

Proper Perfection

Banks should and generally do lock up all personal assets of a borrowing company under a blanket lien filing, but if they make specific loans for the borrower to acquire goods, they may have to comply with special purchase money lien procedures. Another good reason to take a blanket lien against accounts receivable, inventory, and equipment is that the bank has a better chance of selling the goods at a better price versus a hard liquidation sale or auction price and ultimately collecting on accounts. This concerns a friendly foreclosure or lifting of a stay in bankruptcy and also applies to trade contracts or performance contracts to complete or process inventory for sale. Such contracts could even be completed by subcontracting out the work. It might be more difficult to determine if contracts can be performed while the borrower is in bankruptcy especially by third parties.

Sometimes perfection of collateral becomes very engrossed as in taking third-party leases (leases of goods by lessors to lessees, which the lessor assigns to the bank for borrowed funds). Leases are considered chattel paper, but the leased goods themselves are considered inventory to the lessor while they may be deemed to be equipment in a lessee's possession, if not a pure lease.

Perfection of chattel paper leases may be accomplished alternatively by possession or public filing. If the borrower perfects by filing, it could lose its interest to another lender who later takes possession of the original lease and advances new money in good faith. Irrespective of the bank's possession of the chattel paper lease collateral, the bank may still have to complete multiple filings involving leases, which are considered the lessor's inventory. The bank may also have to make additional filings regarding individual lessees pertaining to their use of the underlying goods as equipment in case it does not involve pure leases, and the bank desires to retain reversionary interests in the equipment based on any residual values. Also, additional filings may be necessary regarding the lessor and lessees if goods are being used and located in other states.

Tax Authorities and Liens

Debtors having problems are often impacted by federal, state, and local tax liens as a result of a rather tight and weakened cash flow condition. This is probably the worst type of float (delay in days of paying current liability obligations) a borrower can create. Sometimes it may even be done unknowingly by the borrower.

The reason for the seriousness is that government taxing authorities can file liens for nonpayment, which can quickly jeopardize the future of the business. Once creditors find out about such liens, a ripple effect can be created, and the problem may be compounded because they cease giving goods and services on credit. In addition, any subsequent loan advances made by the bank from the date of the tax lien may result in an inferior lien status of existing floating collateral coming into existence such as accounts, contracts, chattel paper, and inventory that is created after the tax lien. Banks have often sought refuge in their "after acquired" property clause, in order to retain collateral interests created after a tax lien filing, but this has not stood up very well in court.

Regarding federal tax liens, you will continue to have a priority collateral position when making advances under a prior commitment up to 45 days from the date of the tax lien or until you are notified of the lien, whichever comes first. Otherwise your position on floating lien collateral will become inferior to a federal tax lien based on collateral created after the lien is filed or the time period expires. By not moving quickly enough once a tax lien is filed, bankers often place themselves in a position where they feel a false sense of security. They need to determine if there is any written payout agreement with the IRS, or if the IRS has come to the borrower's premises and tagged the goods for sale.

If the borrower cannot work out a repayment program with the IRS, you should immediately go out to the borrower's premises to identify and protect your goods; this may involve obtaining a restraining order against the IRS. Read your daily public information or court reporter newspapers or periodicals for tax lien filings and recorded judgments. Certain state and local taxing authorities may also have the right to come on the borrower's premises and seize goods and immediately sell them once a tax lien is filed. In the latter instances, the bank may have to file quickly for a restraining order because even if you may have a prior lien on the goods and the IRS or other state and local tax authorities in turn sells them, you cannot be assured of receiving any of the proceeds. If you legally had a right to such proceeds, it may be difficult to prove on what inventory you had a priority security interest, unless you had been receiving some sort of detailed inventory listing or schedule from the borrower on a regular routine basis. Hence the need for good monitoring procedures, as is normal in traditional asset based lending.

At times, you may even be able to work out an informal or formal agreement with tax authorities to protect your collateral interest if you continue making advances to the borrower for working capital and perhaps for scheduled tax payments. In such instances, the particular taxing authority could subordinate its lien to yours for continuing to make such advances. This type of planning and action will certainly assist the bank in a problem workout situation.

Another type lien that often arises concerns the nonpayment of payroll taxes. Many bankers have unknowingly made working capital loans, but have not used "due diligence" in requiring the borrower to cut out payroll taxes if those advances were to be used in any way for payroll. In such instances, if the borrower did not make these payroll tax payments, the bank could find itself legally obligated to make them. Therefore, whenever making working capital loans, verify if any of the proceeds will be used to meet payroll, and if so, check Treasury, Tax, and Loan (TT&L) deposits to be assured the borrower has met the proper payroll tax payment on such use of funds or verify its payroll tax payment records. Another alternative is to hold out and segregate the necessary portion of loan proceeds for the amount of payroll taxes due and deposit them into your TT&L account.

Anytime you foreclose on real estate or repossess personal

property asset collateral, you are required to notify the IRS, in case a federal tax lien has been filed, within 25 days of the sale of such property. The IRS also has the right to redeem or bid-in any real estate up to 120 days from the date of foreclosure; therefore, you will have to defer the sale of any foreclosed real estate until that necessary period has elapsed in order to allow the IRS to bid or not to bid-in the property, or you could expose yourself regarding the receipt of such sales proceeds versus the agency's interest. The IRS may consent to your foreclosure before the 120-day period has elapsed when there is no equity—which they normally do not do. If you do not give notice, you may not have cleared title—IRS may then become equity owner. So always send notification. Another matter regarding real estate foreclosures is that you may be held responsible for the cost of clearing any hazard wastes on the property in accordance with pollution control authority requirements.

You need to be cautious when dealing with IRS agents. Require a subpoena before you turn over any records to them. Any information they receive from your records may be used against the borrower.

Collateral Oversight

In general, some areas where banks may have created oversight problems include instruments (notes) not being endorsed; stock or bond powers not being executed; stock that has not been delivered or is still in "street" (broker) name; and not being aware of stock restrictions under Rule 144 as it relates to the 1933 Securities Act, which could hinder the marketability and liquidation of investment letter or control stock, especially when a legend may not be evident on the certificate.

Guarantors and Endorsements

The whole area of guaranties could take up a chapter in itself regarding the rights the bank could lose and problems it could face in order to collect on them. These problems could run the gamut from not properly notifying guarantors regarding novations of debt, treating individual guarantors inequitably, not considering the importance of obtaining the guaranty of a spouse or obtaining collateral behind a guaranty, to the impact of not being able to collect on any deficiency balance after the sale of collateral because the bank impaired the collateral or because it sold it in a "commercially unreasonable" manner.

You must establish your rights under the guaranty agreement and how they directly apply to the note(s) if you have to go to court. Do not let your guaranty become stale; check any applicable state statute of limitations. If the purpose changes regarding any new debt versus what you originally obtained a guaranty for, obtain a new one. If a wife signs a guaranty thinking it is for other purposes, she could possibly raise a successful challenge or defense if the bank attempted to collect on it.

There may be an advantage of taking an endorsement—it is prima facie evidence on the same paper (promissory note). It is also clear that it only pertains to a single debt instrument and does not require a separate agreement. There are various types of endorsements. Make sure the endorsements on obligations are with "Full Recourse," thus do not accept restrictive, qualified, or conditional endorsements. An individual who agrees to be responsible for the performance of another's contractual obligation or for certain debts of others evidenced by endorsements on instruments, is considered a surety. A bank will often print an endorsement and guaranty agreement on the back of notes above where the surety will endorse the note, giving it the right to proceed against the endorser as accommodation-maker who will only become obligated if the borrower defaults.

Control of Collateral

This secondary source of debt repayment obviously becomes much more important if the borrower is starting to have problems whereby it cannot pay its debt. Banks are traditional debt repayment ability lenders, thus overall they do a good job of analyzing the financial condition and repayment ability of the borrower, but they have generally not been known to be good collateral lenders, especially pertaining to asset based collateral. Now we are not saying the bank should only make loans because of adequate or more than adequate collateral. What we are saying is that the bank should always protect itself by monitoring and controlling this secondary source of payment if possible, especially the kind that is not in its possession and not negotiable or immovable such as real estate, but which is the type that is perhaps constantly changing such as accounts, inventory, and certain equipment.

Inventory is probably the most difficult to monitor and control because it is often changing and can be very difficult to identify, depending on the type and stage of goods. Some inventory may be conducive to third-party control such as certain commodities that are better monitored by way of a public warehouse, as an example. At times, it may also be very difficult to locate inventory without third-party control. Banks have not been known to undertake a very good approach to monitoring such collateral.

Many small to medium sized banks have been lending heavily to the small to middle-sized middle-market companies without properly maintaining prudent dominion and control policing techniques to monitor their personal property collateral, whether knowingly or unknowingly. In this connection, these banks probably could have learned something from third-party commercial finance companies, often referred to as collateral lenders. The need for greater controls relative to personal property collateral has increased as banks have become more driven to compete with each other and with third-party lenders for commercial business, thus often resulting in booking credits operating on higher debt leverage and perhaps with less liquidity than was more traditional for banks to lend against in the past.

CHAPTER 3

SHORING UP THE BANK'S COLLATERAL POSITION AND PLANNING THE WORKOUT

3.01 GENERAL

Whenever a problem is identified in a credit, the bank should again look closely at the character of the borrower and its management, because this will certainly have a bearing on how the loan officer should continue handling the ongoing relationship. Implementing action regarding the relationship should also be based on the risk and size of loss exposure. This is especially important if an inadequate collateral position is detected, since the bank will have to move to obtain additional collateral from the borrower or borrowing company, or from any such related entities or third party obligors as co-signers, endorsers, or guarantors. However, you must first undertake a concerted review of all your existing collateral and your rights under loan and security agreements. During this time, you should request current financial statements and undertake a current investigation. The loan officer must reappraise and analyze the situation—maybe even more closely than at the outset of the relationship. During this whole process, your primary concern should be simply to ask, "Are we safe, and is the money good?" The answer to this question will often dictate what you do and when you do it.

3.02 ALTERNATE DEBT FINANCING

First of all, you should determine whether it is worth salvaging the relationship. It may even be in the bank's best interests to help the debtor move the debt or to obtain alternative financing. If it is not possible for the borrower to move the debt or you cannot get out of the credit entirely you should still reduce your exposure to a minimum. Under these circumstances, the debtor should certainly understand your determined interest in ending the relationship or significantly reducing your exposure. Certainly there are many ways to tighten up your present arrangements in order to move the borrower along in finding alternative financing. Here are some steps to accomplish that.

- Enforce more stringent loan agreement covenants.
- Eliminate any type of open-ended revolving credit arrangement.
- Increase interest rates when notes and commitments mature.
- Initiate the use of short-term and even demand notes.
- Eliminate and cut back on unused commitments.
- Require collateral to secure indirect guarantor obligations.

3.03 OBTAINING ADDITIONAL COLLATERAL

Early recognition of a problem loan allows the bank time to request additional collateral. Do not, however, overreact by pushing the borrower into premature bankruptcy, especially if you want more collateral before the 90-day voidable preference bankruptcy period. The character of the borrower may also affect the bank's ability to liquidate the collateral.

Extending a moratorium or forbearance on debt works to the bank's advantage. As such, the bank buys time to gain additional collateral and in turn stretches the borrower out beyond the 90-day voidable preference period.

If you take collateral for antecedent debt without advancing new money in consideration thereof and in good faith (and the borrower is deemed insolvent when you acquired this collateral interest), your security interest could not only be set aside under the 90-day ruling, but you could also lose your collateral interest up to one year from the perfection date if you are later deemed an insider by a bankruptcy court. Basically, if it can be proven that you were in control of the borrower, then you would be subject to being an insider. Therefore, the debtor or trustee may recover as a preference any assets assigned to the bank within the 90-day or one-year periods, respectively, of filing a bankruptcy petition. This Bankruptcy Reform Act ruling applies when a borrower agrees to a new or additional collateral interest, which does not involve any new money to be advanced by the bank, thus only creating a collateral transfer for existing or antecedent debt to the bank while the borrower is insolvent. This in effect, could also enable the bank to receive more than it would have if a Chapter 7 liquidation were filed.

The test of insolvency for both fraudulent and voidable preference transfers is when the debtor's liabilities exceed its assets, resulting in a negative net worth. Under bankruptcy, the test is based on total liabilities exceeding the fair market value of all assets. If the transfer of collateral is received from a third-party pledgor, assignor, guarantor, or other contingent obligor, the transfer should not be subject to any preference or fraudulent transfer. These types of transfers should only pertain to the borrower.

This is not to say that you should avoid taking a collateral interest in any collateral offered by the debtor or a third-party pledgor, even if you are aware of a pending bankruptcy. The worst that could happen is that you may have to return the collateral to the court, although you may be able to retain a portion, perhaps by negotiating with the trustee. Retaining the collateral may be more feasible and even sanctioned by the debtor, trustee, or a creditor's committee if the bank is willing to grant post-petition financing. Of course, you will have to decide if this improves the bank's position and ultimately the recovery of its debt. You may be "putting out good money after bad." If you have an unused commitment available at the time of bankruptcy filing with a provision in your documents to terminate the commitment upon default, such would be enforceable on behalf of the bank.

The U.S. Bankruptcy Reform Act defines insolvency as the inability or failure to pay debts as they mature. Under 548(c) of the Bankruptcy Act, which is the "Safe Harbor" clause, you could be protected if the bank advances new funds and it is established that this new value is given in good faith. This whole matter of the insolvency test could jeopardize your collateral position and may also apply to a fraudulent transfer of collateral under the Federal Uniform Fraudulent Conveyance Act. Basically, a fraudulent transfer of collateral to the bank, within one year of the debtor filing bankruptcy, could result in the bank being required to return the same to the court, because it received collateral without advancing new money knowing that the debtor was insolvent or undercapitalized based on the nature of its business, or could not pay its debts as they came due. The grounds under which the bank takes the collateral is the same as when the debtor intentionally acts to defraud its creditors, or when it receives less than the collateral's equivalent value in exchange, or if it was insolvent or undercapitalized at the time of the transfer, or was unable to pay its debts when due.

3.04 DEBT REPAYMENT PLAN

A strategic plan is also necessary once a credit is considered a workout or if bankruptcy becomes imminent. A debtor may try to alarm you or actually be honest about it when he says that his business is in hopeless shape, and that the only solution is for the creditors to compromise—taking a small percentage on the dollar now or over some period of time. Therefore, you must be very creative in a workout situation, such as helping the business rehabilitate by way of extensions or stretch-outs, refinancing, and perhaps offering moratoriums or other types of forbearance. You may have to arrange for equity conversions of yours or others' debt. Unsecured creditors, such as vendors, may be willing to subordinate or convert their debt to equity, especially if the bank advances new funds. They may even be amenable to taking a discount on their debt to continue allowing the business to operate. However, it usually takes a bankruptcy filing to gain such cooperation. Throughout this whole process, the loan officer must strive to retain the borrower's cooperation. He or she must not make any threats of foreclosure or other potential detrimental statements pertaining to the business because such statements could be construed as fraud if the bank had no real intent of following through.

3.05 ACTION PLANS

First of all, you need to determine whether you can work out the problem by way of a debt restructure, or the bank will have to exercise its rights by liquidating the credit due to the business's anticipated imminent failure. The liquidation of the credit will hopefully result in a greater debt recovery by not delaying action until the situation worsens while the borrower fails to salvage any assets before they are further depleted. Presuming the workout is attempted outside bankruptcy court, there will be some administrative problems that should be considered.

No matter how you're buying time, you want to use it to your advantage. When a workout is attempted outside of bankruptcy court, there are some things to attend to.

- Make sure that all withholding taxes are being paid.
- See that the borrower is paying other taxes too, and does not have much in the way of other accruals, e.g., wages and vacation pay. The Fair Labor Standards Act could be used against the bank to enjoin it from the sale of repossessed goods when employees have not been paid.
- Avoid informing the debtor which creditors to pay and which not to pay. If the debtor is having problems in this respect, it may be better to call a meeting of creditors and seek a temporary moratorium.
- Do not get trapped into schemes or questionable actions to improve your position at the expense of junior interest creditors, especially when they are extending new credit. One example of a good test would be to ask, "What would trade creditors do or say if they knew the extent or substance of your collaboration with the debtor regarding the improvement of your position over them?"
- Think long and hard before you incorporate covenants in loan agreements that could trigger an event of default or allow you to call a loan because of management changes and other company decisions affecting management. More important, do not insert a covenant into loan agreements in order to force a management change by the bank.
- Urge the debtor's board of directors to form a special committee

or task force made up of certain outside board members to work on the problem while also allowing you direct access to this group.
• Make sure your documents and agreements provide for audit rights, including the inspection of the borrower's books and records. Audit rights should include full disclosure by the debtor.

Next, you need to determine whether the present servicing officer can continue handling the relationship. Does he or she have the skill, objectivity, and time? Make sure you check the loan officer out carefully to be assured he or she has not panicked by ignoring the problem, hoping it will go away, or sweeping it under the rug by making renewals or extensions. Or even worse, that he or she was intimidated into making additional loans or advances. This would all apply even after a loan goes into default

3.06 THE FUNCTION OF THE PROBLEM-LOAN SPECIALIST

You may need a problem loan specialist with certain workout skills to take over the relationship. A fresh approach with new ideas and objectives to address the credit and its problems is often necessary, especially if the present servicing officer has developed too close a relationship with the borrower and has lost much objectivity in handling the relationship. The workout officer's skills should include being a good analyst, a skilled negotiator, knowledgeable in collection procedures, and having the ability to utilize legal counsel properly. The workout loan officer must be able to relate to and negotiate with any other creditors in the picture. He or she must also know how to get the attention of the borrower, be able to respond quickly, and use time efficiently.

Specific procedures should be considered once the credit is moved to a special workout loan department or group, which include:

- Action to ensure maximum recovery in a timely manner.
- Strict consideration of collection expense versus anticipated dollar recovery.

- Referral to and assistance from legal counsel (depending on amount of loan) to effect litigation or other debt agreements.
- Maintenance and transfer or records relating to loans cases.

On the other hand, you may perceive that the present servicing officer has a sufficient number of these qualities to continue handling the relationship. The present officer may be better held accountable for any mistakes and often has established a rapport with the borrower, which may be broken by bringing in a new officer. Naturally, the present loan officer has a better working knowledge of the borrower, its business, and industry, and may even be in a better position to still respond quickly. The present loan officer should seriously listen to and take the advice of other experienced credit officers who have demonstrated good judgment and creativity in solving past loan problems.

The loan officer needs to determine quickly the extent of the problem and devise a strategy to cure it as soon as possible after the problem is identified. If possible, the plan to correct this problem should be done in writing. First of all, the loan officer often needs to obtain additional facts and figures from the borrowing customer in order to plan a strategy which should entail psychological, legal, and financial considerations. Many officers not experienced in workouts frequently use too much supposition and conjecture in preparing an action plan. Be candid with your borrower by discussing the problem and your plan to help resolve it. Spell out clearly any available options. Do not expect your borrower to live up to things too difficult or impossible to comply with or achieve. The sign of a good workout officer is one who can negotiate and even compromise when necessary. He or she also needs the flexibility to be able to work with the borrower on a renegotiation plan as it may relate to the borrower's reorganization and strategy in operating the business in the future. The loan officer needs to be honest about how much flexibility they can or are willing to provide the borrower.

At times it may be necessary to have other officers and assistants present during meetings, especially when the borrower is represented by more than one party. This will serve to eliminate any teaming-up impact. If the borrower is accompanied by its attorney, always make sure your attorney is present. The loan officer should include a timetable and quantitative goals and objectives to resolve the problem. A primary and secondary (or contingency) plan should be developed. These plans should include the latitude of action within which the loan officer should operate, (for instance, advancing new money, restructuring debt, and strengthening documentation).

One rule of thumb is that the bank should not put out good money after bad. Loan officers at times are tempted to immediately meet the borrower's financial needs; this often is only a quick fix. Therefore, a good deal of time and effort spent by the loan officer and other bank personnel to analyze the problem and how to resolve it will serve to protect the loan officer from a rash decision to advance new money. The loan officer will need to maintain close contact with the borrower and remain alert to the situation; good timing will also be important. Another point to remember is that the loan officer should remain cool and calm throughout this entire exercise and stick to the action plan. The loan officer should not become rattled by the borrower; nor should he or she overly excite or upset the borrower. If the borrower is in a critically bad financial condition, you will have to determine how long you will be able to defer payments before taking legal action. You will also have to decide the exposure—or what might happen to your collateral—if you delay or wait to repossess and liquidate it. You need to decide, if the collateral is rapidly declining in value, what action you will take, or at what point of deterioration you will reclaim it.

Generally, attempt to work out a debt liquidation schedule with the borrower over some stated period of time. Certainly this should be a prerequisite of charging off a loan and even placing a loan on non-accrual, if interest can also be paid.

You will also have to determine what arrangements have or should be made with other creditors under some type of reorganization plan. Creditors may include trade, or other note holders, whether secured or unsecured. Such a reorganization plan would be a creditor's committee agreement and not involve a bankruptcy. In many instances, a plan will have to be worked out with them on some type of equitable basis based on the class of creditors (secured and unsecured positions). Such an arrangement preferably allows certain secured creditors to be paid some amount of money on a continuing basis while unsecured ones have to wait before receiving anything.

An agreement has to made between the borrower and creditors and should have all the appropriate provisions involving events of default, including the right to make demand and to terminate the agreement depending on whether the borrower's condition improves or worsens. Additional collection and workout techniques as follows should be considered in conjunction with any agreements:

- Offer debtors a clear choice which should determine your course of action. If they cooperate to the extent they are able, they should receive every possible consideration; but if they refuse to cooperate, the bank should take quick legal action.
- Do not let the borrower coerce you by making you overreact or compel you to make a mistake, such as convincing you to approve overdrafts or cause you to advance funds when collectability is remote.
- Institute an amortization program, specifying principal and interest payments, preferably on a monthly basis.
- Do not offer concessions unless borrowers do what they are supposed to do; for example, cutting costs and expenses, and using money from liquidated, unnecessary assets to reduce debt.
- Build goals for the borrower to achieve—goals aiming at better financial results and proper submission of prepared financial information. Consider also building in benchmarks, e.g., sales, gross and operating profits, retained earnings, working capital level, quick and current ratios and debt levels, receivables, inventory, and trade debt turnovers.
- Confer with the attorney working on the case, particularly before reaching major decisions, before contacting the debtor regarding the decision, and before making a final disposition.
- Carefully space contacts with the borrower, allowing time to respond; monitor each phase of development between contacts.
- When collection is doubtful, search for a soft spot in the debtor's armor and fully exploit it. The soft spot could be some action the debtor especially wishes to avoid.

3.07 LOAN OFFICER AND BANK ATTITUDES

Procrastination on the loan officer's part can result in a greater loan loss. Some loan officers fail to act at times because of pride; they do not like to admit they are wrong. Others refrain for fear of being fired. This is where a good internal loan review or examining team can be a great help in identifying the problem loan; this is also true of bank examinations from external regulatory agencies. Also, the bank should not use fear tactics against the officer who makes a bad loan, as officers may become even more reluctant to admit trouble. Rather, the bank should reprimand officers for *not* communicating that they have a problem. If a particular loan officer establishes a trend for making bad loans and evidencing poor judgment, he or she should be removed from this position.

Another factor which must be considered is loan officer overload. It may be very time consuming to deal with certain workout loans, which may be greatly overburdening a loan officer. The same thing can happen to a workout loan officer who handles too many such accounts.

3.08 DETERMINING THE BANK'S COLLATERAL POSITION

The collateral position is always a key factor in proceeding with a well planned debt collection. The loan officer should immediately determine if the collateral is really available or is obsolete or deteriorated, resulting in a greatly diminished value; this can only be accomplished by inspection. At times, there is a lack of documentation or follow-up, or the failure on the officer's part to act when he or she is the first to realize they have a problem loan on their hands. Yet this is actually the time when loan officers should move quickly so as not to lose any valuable time in working toward correcting the problem.

Obtaining Additional Collateral

When your collateral position is inadequate or the loan is unsecured, look for ways to obtain more collateral. In most circumstances, this will be an advantageous course of action. But it won't always be feasible. Other creditors for example, can have negative pledge agreements or clauses in their loan agreements that a default would trigger when the borrower pledges or assigns collateral to another party.

There are definite procedures one must undertake to obtain additional collateral and shore up the bank's position. Many times a banker will only verbally discuss with the borrower what additional collateral may be available. The banker may even go to the borrower's premises to "spot-check" the collateral without taking a thorough inventory, and may neglect to seek out additional collateral.

Know what type of collateral you really have and its true value. Seriously consider trading off more time to your borrower regarding debt repayment in order to obtain money—good collateral—which could temper any ultimate loss. You should also consider the impact of any capital gains or losses the borrower may sustain and the impact on its financial condition in case you decide to liquidate certain collateral or when offering more time to repay debt in exchange for additional collateral. Be aware that the debtor will often bargain for substantial concessions before offering security or additional collateral. Also, remember that transfer of collateral to your bank may be attacked as a preference under the bankruptcy code.

Categories of Collateral

There are various categories of collateral, including real estate, equipment, and intangibles.

Real Estate. Do not be timid about taking a lien or security interest in any collateral. Look at the long-term value; watch single-purpose or limited-use collateral such as certain buildings which may not be useful to others. Seconds are often not beneficial pertaining to personal property assets but there may be more realizable value on real estate. If you take a second deed of trust or mortgage on real property, make sure the first is not in default; check on whether intervening liens have been recorded. Make sure you also have a right under a deed of trust or mortgage, to any assignment of leases, rents, income, and proceeds. Your borrower and its tenant or lessee should execute an acknowledgment agreement that requires payments or proceeds to flow directly to the bank as assignee. It is also prudent to take any available assignment of leasehold interests your borrower has when it is renting real property under a long-term lease. Your borrower/tenant should execute a mortgage or deed of trust and collateral assignment to the bank for such an interest which should be recorded in the land or deed records. Also, obtain an acknowledgment of the assignment from the owner when possible.

Equipment. If you have a blanket lien on equipment, obtain a listing of all equipment. Also, obtain a depreciation schedule reconciling existing equipment from the time you originally acquired your lien, reflecting in it (by item and type) all additions, deletions, retirements, depreciated amounts, and net book values. Next, go out and inspect all equipment and match it against your updated lists and reconciliation schedules; you may also have to obtain an independent appraisal. If possible, during your inspection procure a listing of all serial numbers or other identification markings regarding collateral.

With leased equipment, make sure you have listings, identification markings and serial numbers just in case the lessor has not filed a financing statement. Such leases may be considered conditional sales contracts subject to the Uniform Commercial Code (UCC)—disguised leases, in other words—rather than deemed true or pure. You may rightful obtain a valid first-lien security interest in this collateral. In this connection, make sure you attach all these equipment listings and reconciliation schedules to your security agreement to validate your collateral interest. Of course, with certain equipment you will have to perfect a specific lien, perhaps under state statute such as under a certificate of title act pertaining to vehicles, boats, trailers, and mobile homes. A federal lien act may address aircraft and railroad cars; check admiralty law relative to first preferred ship mortgages.

In conclusion, your inspection and audit is important in order that you do not overlook any additional collateral you may be able to take.

General Intangibles. Another often overlooked area is general intangibles. While most banks do include blanket-lien language in their security agreements and financing statements, they have not really given much attention to this category because it was in fact intangible in nature and of questionable value, if any. Banks have often not realized that when the company has certain general intangibles, it might be necessary to comply with specific assignment procedures before a legal collateral interest could be obtained.

As an example, let us say the borrower is a manufacturer of a particular fiberglass sailing boat that started to win many races around the country. The bank may have taken a blanket lien including general intangibles when the company was first organized. Now, because of the success of this particular sailboat, the patent of the molds, patent application, and construction rights to this particular sailboat have become very valuable. But the company has not shown any value for the patent and rights in its financial statements. As a matter of fact, let's say an entry for general intangibles was not even reflected in financial statements. Besides filing under the Uniform Commercial Code, to further perfect lien rights the bank must undertake appropriate filing procedures with the U.S. Patent Office in Washington, D.C. Thus, the bank may have missed the opportunity to complete perfection of its interest in this potentially valuable intangible.

The same thing applies to a book publishing company which may have the right to assign agreements it has with authors, including copyrights of books, periodicals, or other publications. If the bank has neglected to follow specific filing procedures with the U.S. Copyright Office in Washington, D.C., it could lose certain assignment rights to this material.

One more example of taking a valuable general intangible could involve a garbage business which has obtained a valuable dumping site in a large city where such sites are rare. In effect, the right to use this site may prove very valuable to this garbage business or any other third party that has a right to use this land for garbage dumping. While the bank may have taken a blanket lien on all general intangibles and may even have included dumping rights—even going as far as to take an assignment of the company's leasehold property rights for use of this land and record it in the deed or land records of the county where the site is located—the bank may still not have gone far enough. Actually, the bank would need to obtain the proper approval and acknowledgment from the city or other governing body that had the right to assign such rights to the dumping site.

These are only a few of the many examples of overlooking or improperly perfecting a collateral interest in intangibles. You should also consider the importance of receiving much more detail regarding the particular intangible, such as obtaining copies of certified plans, specifications, drawings, and other designs.

By having a lock on the particular intangible along with a general blanket lien on all company assets, you will certainly boost the bank's ability to realize a greater return as the business could probably be sold for a bigger lump sum as a complete package, based on its intrinsic value

Assignment of Landlord's Interest in Lease. Another valuable intangible often overlooked by the bank is the lease involving the property from which the borrower operates. If the bank has an assignment of the lease, it will be in a better position to sell the business as a going concern along with other assets in case it has to take over collateral. By having the assignment, the bank could move in another tenant to take over the business and assume the debt without removing the assets, which obviously would save the bank a good deal of money. Such an assignment is very important with certain types of business loans, such as a pizza restaurant which has large ovens built into and attached to the real estate.

We want to emphasize that we are not just talking about taking an assignment of your borrower/tenant's leasehold interest. In addition, we recommend that you take an assignment of the lease by having the landlord acknowledge and approve your stepping in based on curing any defaulted payments and allowing the bank to in turn sublease the premises to a third party acceptable to the bank. This third party will usually be another entrepreneur who will continue operating a similar business from that location and may often be assuming the debt. If the bank only takes an assignment of the tenant's leasehold interest and does not obtain landlord approval, it may not be able to move another tenant into the premises.

Obviously, the best time to obtain the landlord's cooperation is when the initial lease is being negotiated with your borrower. If you seek the landlord's cooperation once the lease is in force, the landlord usually will be uncooperative. To persuade the landlord, you must show some definite benefit to allowing you the right to step in and negotiate a new lease.

Another concern you should be aware of is that if you do not obtain the landlord's consent, and your borrower later defaults and you attempt to remove certain equipment and fixtures from the premises, it may be very costly and difficult to undertake—even if you have a waiver from the landlord to remove any goods. Often there is a clause in the lease that if damage to the premises occurs during such a removal, whoever is responsible will have to cover it.

Therefore, getting back to the pizza ovens for a moment, not only would it be expensive to remove them (because of the difficulty involved), but the bank may incur additional cost if movers damage the premises when removing the ovens. The lesson? When a business has fixtures attached to the real estate, it may not only be expensive to remove them, but chances of damaging the premises upon removal may also prove costly.

Therefore, in such cases, the bank needs to place a high intangible value on the assignment of a landlord's interest in the borrower's lease. Moreover, the bank should ask the landlord to execute a waiver as to any landlord lien that could be created against the borrower's personal property assets on the premises in case of rental default. This could be accomplished in the same document as the lease assignment. It will also be very important because the transfer or sale of any inventory, equipment, or fixtures will have to go hand in hand with any reassignment and sublease of the premises to a new tenant who may assume the original borrower's debt.

Insurance Proceeds. Another valuable type of intangible could be realized in the form of insurance proceeds. We will address both hazard insurance and life insurance.

Hazard Insurance. This represents insurance coverage pertaining to the assets of the business. Whenever banks loan money secured by business assets, they should require the borrower to obtain insurance covering the value of these assets, naming the bank loss payee. Fire and extended coverage gives that protection. Of course there are other types that may be applicable under the circumstances. Consider having the borrower add the necessary type depending on its location and the overall risk and exposure in its business and the collateral being insured. You must read the policy and any endorsements closely in order to understand clauses pertaining to the coverage. You want to have answers to many questions such as:

- Is the coverage under an umbrella policy?
- Does coverage fluctuate periodically, such as with inventory because of its constantly changing value, or is it fixed?
- Is coverage limited to certain locations?
- What is the co-insurance clause which not only has a bearing on the amount of insurance, but on any penalties for lack of replacement value coverage?
- What is the grace period for nonpayment of premiums?
- Will the bank be notified before any cancellation?
- Is it necessary to have flood insurance?

On occasion, banks have found themselves in a vulnerable position because a policy expired, or was canceled for nonpayment, and sometime thereafter a fire destroyed the premises. These banks were negligent in their follow-up on insurance coverage. The bank should make sure it has a good tickler system and long-form endorsement coverage that offers prior notice of policy expiration and an opportunity to cure premium payment defaults, if necessary, within a certain grace period. Another thing banks must be alert to is whether the insurance board in your state allows the insurance company the option to cancel insurance for reasons other than nonpayment of premiums under certain notification requirements. Finally, always check on the rating of the insurance firm according to *Best's Insurance Guide* to see whether it meets your requirements.

Life Insurance. Banks should always determine the necessity of obtaining life insurance on key individuals of a business borrower in some acceptable amount, naming the bank as assignee. This could prove to be a valuable intangible because any policy proceeds paid against the debt could temper the bank's exposure in view of the loss of a key company official.

With the advent of the 1972 revision of Article 9 of the UCC, proceeds from such policies would automatically flow to the bank if the policy were owned by the company and the bank had properly perfected its interest in such general intangible collateral, unless the policy had been directly assigned to a third party, which was acknowledged by the insurance company. Therefore, we still recommend that the bank arrange for a direct assignment of the policy because even if you were properly perfected under the Code, another lender or creditor could come ahead of you—even if it entered the picture later—by obtaining a direct assignment from the insurance company. Also, always make sure you hold the original policy or a certified copy to protect you against cancellation without you first being notified. Also, attempt to arrange for notice of nonpremium payment in case the policy owner defaults on it.

Most policies purchased at the request of the bank are term insurance, which is the least costly. But, bear in mind that the amount usually decreases in face value every year so your underlying protection regarding any payment of proceeds will concurrently shrink.

Third-Party Collateral. Do not overlook obtaining additional collateral from third parties related to the entity. Often, the best type of collateral backup may be from third-party guarantors who are already contingently liable. In such instances, attempt to obtain collateral that will secure their guaranty. This could be most beneficial in case the guarantor is not directly affected by the debtor's subsequent bankruptcy filing, i.e., not personally heavily relying on income from the business or not in jeopardy should the business collapse. The guarantor is also not greatly at risk when the guaranty is not substantial compared to the borrower's financial condition and debt, and because the guarantor should not normally be forced to file bankruptcy, too. This would also apply to company guarantors as long as they are clearly a separate entity, as identified by the court. Therefore, if the guarantor does not file bankruptcy, you should not be legally stayed from proceeding against it. From a practical standpoint, you should be able to receive some sort of debt recovery from a guarantor who still has more than enough assets and cash flow to meet its own debt obligations, notwithstanding the fact that it may raise numerous defenses against the bank to relieve it of its guaranty.

Debt subordinated to the lender can provide support, too, if it is tied to the guarantor's obligations. First, consider the underlying cushion that subordinated debt provides the lender regarding getting paid first. Regarding subordinated debt, you are reminded that what is discussed herein are private subordinations directly agreed to by the guarantors or other interested parties in a closely held company. This is not a discussion of subordinated debt involving larger public companies as such will surely engross a contest of positions regarding creditors in any Chapter 11 proceeding.

Beyond subordinated debt itself, you may be able to obtain additional collateral, if as any example, such debt is owed your guarantors. First of all, have the guarantors turn over any instruments taken for this debt and hold them in your possession as collateral behind their guaranty; next have them assign both the note(s) and any collateral interests taken from the company to secure such debt against their guaranty.

3.09 PLANNING THE WORKOUT

Planning for the workout is significant in the ultimate repayment and collection of the debt. The degree of the plan and control the bank implements over the credit depends on the respective situation.

Still, temper your behavior. For example, do not cause a customer to have a mental breakdown or any other debilitating problem that could affect their well-being. Do not overact by calling the loan too quickly; you must gain or continue your efforts to retain the borrower's trust. Be sensitive to the borrower's situation. Only seek enforcement as a last resort. Once it has been determined that the borrower can no longer meet debt payments on schedule, the bank should consider the following steps:

- Initially, arrange for an interest rate decrease or moratorium (deferral of interest payments) for awhile if psychologically the borrower will cease payment because he or she can't see a way to reduce their debt. This should not be a concern when you control the payments of collateral proceeds; for example, when remittances by account debtors flows directly to your lockbox or to an account at the bank.
- Then apply all payments to principal including any interest received, without informing the borrower of placing the loan on non-accrual (when interest no longer accrues). Attempt to keep the principal safe; then try to recoup your interest. You may even have to forgive interest entirely to make changes in the terms and conditions and debt structure in order to keep the principal safe.
- The loan officer should also examine notes for allowable legal and other collection costs. He or she should project an image of being firm but fair and always maintain themselves in a calm, poised and professional manner.

Borrowers often show definite states of mind while dealing with them in a workout situation. Initially, the borrower may refuse to acknowledge the problem; this represents a state of denial. Borrowers who get beyond the denial stage may start showing anger as they come to grips with their problem; at this point, they will often seek to blame others for their problems. Next, they may enter the depression stage as they start blaming themselves for their problems. Borrowers should next be ready to take action; this is when you will have to be ready to negotiate with them and even be willing to compromise your debt position if necessary. At the time the borrower seeks restructuring demands, renegotiate loan agreement covenants that will build in goals to improve the health and financial solvency of the business.

Check and monitor the company's progress closely; you may even require the borrower to provide monthly budgets and "turnaround" plans with achievement dates built in for you to monitor. The company may have to take more drastic action to survive, such as dumping inventory at a discount, or it may have to sell nonessential assets. It may have to take drastic cost cutting measures. Furthermore, it may have to start leaning on the trade or fall behind on other obligations, although this is a dangerous practice especially if it is already slow or past due. In this connection, do not get in the middle of enforcing or even strongly recommending such action because it could be construed as control if the borrower later enters bankruptcy or files a lender liability suit against the bank.

Dealing with Guarantors

If the bank is highly dependent on the success of the company for debt repayment, loan officers should not press guarantors too hard for repayment once debt becomes past due. Do not overreact when a company borrower becomes past due; also do not collapse any guarantors who are doing a respectable job of operating the company; instead, compare the risk of taking premature action versus allowing the company to operate without moving against the guarantors who work in your favor. Indeed, they may go out of their way to pay the bank back with corporate funds in order to protect themselves. In contrast, in other cases where the loan was granted to a start-up business or solely on the financial strength of the guarantors (involving a company with limited finances), perhaps you should put pressure on the guarantors once the debt becomes past due.

Some borrowers are honest and attempt to meet a sensible repayment program; if management is cooperative you have a chance to workout the debt. If management is agreeable to a reasonable debt restructure—including new or amended agreements and perhaps providing additional collateral, or inclined to offer new guaranties—this reflects a cooperative attitude.

In contrast, other borrowers are less cooperative, even dishonest; obviously their management is defensive. The uncooperative, or their attorneys, use many different tactics to evade repayment. In these cases, you will probably have to consider taking legal action quickly. The uncooperative may be hopeless, what with little or no income and no available assets. As such, it is not worthwhile to take any expensive legal action other than obtaining a judgment, unless some third-party obligor has sufficient assets to go after.

With certain cooperative borrowers, a suspended judgment makes sense. In these cases, a borrower may be agreeable to execute an agreed judgment in hopes of buying time to repay the debt. As such, the bank should not record its judgment so long as the borrower remains in compliance with the terms and conditions of this agreement. Should the bank find it necessary to record the judgment because of nonperformance and default by the borrower, it would then have the right to execute or levy on nonexempt property owned by the borrower.

Recommendations on Handling the Workout

- Initiate the best possible repayment program from any and all resources of the borrower and any guarantors or other surety parties; this may require offering concessions on interest and longer principal payback terms. Although you may offer a longer payback, place the debt in a short-term note with a monthly amortization repayment program that will result in a balloon payment at maturity. This should at least result in a scheduled debt reduction.

- Review offering debt extensions which may be enough consideration for taking new guaranties.
- Take additional collateral even if such action is later deemed a preference; always act in good faith when taking additional collateral by providing some form of consideration even if not monetary.
- Assist your borrower, if possible, in methods of liquidating all unessential business assets or collateral, and apply all proceeds to the debt. If other creditors have a lien or collateral interest in certain assets, you must be cautious about this particular liquidation because lien positions may control who gets paid first. Such action could force your borrower to file for bankruptcy. Consider tax impacts on your borrower when liquidating assets, too.
- Build in performance standards on a monthly basis in new or amended letter and loan agreements, perhaps using stair step formulas and ratios
- Include other deadlines for the borrower to complete certain actions or goals which should be part of a new or revised business plan it submits. If these deadlines are not part of any written

agreement, follow up with a letter of understanding confirming what was agreed upon and when it should occur. However, do not let the letter extend to any direct control of the business in view of a potential lender liability suit.

- Help borrowers arrange for moratoriums with trade creditors; this may be arranged on existing obligations, but not on future trade debt that the borrower incurs according to bankruptcy law.
- Assist borrowers to move loans to another creditor when you seek to terminate the relationship.
- If you have no guarantors or secondarily liable parties, then work with owners and any board members; if a family business, attempt to work with all members, especially those active in the business.
- Do not control the company; instead, remain aloof enough to prevent yourself from being deemed an insider under the Bankruptcy Reform Act or from being named in a lender liability suit.
- Do not harm debtors by your actions, as this could be deemed "inequitable conduct" resulting in a "lender liability" suit.
- Make sure all factual information, reports and interviews are properly documented and there is nothing in such data that could jeopardize the bank's position. Remember, such documents could be subject to a subpoena, if needed as evidence in a lender liability suit.

When other banks participate in the credit, the first rule is that nobody gets bought out first. If there are any tacit agreements or ethical considerations with other banks or if there are any agreements to buy a loan back, the original lender should seriously consider buying the debt back even if not in written agreement form in view of potential suit by such participants. You may be able to negotiate buying the debt back at a discount, so keep your options open.

If you are the lead or agent bank, always keep the other participants informed when taking appropriate action—conflicts of interest may arise if your bank has extended other debt to the borrower such as secured debt, giving you an improved collateral position, which may not even have been intentional on your part. Always work with the bank group in accordance with the requirements pursuant to the participation agreement—this is the originating bank's responsibility.

3.10 ADVANCING NEW MONEY

Making new money advances should be based on management performance and compliance with its own goals; too many banks advance new funds based on management's plans to resolve the problem based on overly optimistic proformas and projections to perform in the future. Also, do not expect to be the last to put new money in the business and the first to be paid. Furthermore, do not put additional good money after bad.

If you have to advance new funds shortly, attempt to have management obtain "stand still" agreements or interest and principal deferrals or moratoriums from other creditors. Further, attempt to have junior or second-line creditors agree to cancel interest and even be a party to putting new money up as part of the overall plan. Alternatively, they may have to agree to a conversion of old accrued or unpaid interest by converting and accepting interest-bearing notes or even accepting the cancellation of such interest in full as part of the overall plan. Furthermore, have vendors also accept a moratorium on their payables or even consider having them accept a conversion of their accounts to subordinated debt behind any new money advances. In a nutshell, always attempt to strengthen your overall position when you have to put new money in the business.

Also, always consider the time value of money when you are negotiating repayment of your debt; it may be worth compromising some to obtain money now which you in turn could reinvest versus waiting and trying to obtain more in the future. Money or collection value may also be diminished by delays in collection during some holdup or even the occurrence of a bankruptcy. Therefore, the bank should consider the discounted present value factor of money and the compounding effect based on taking a compromised settlement immediately, which is the time value of money approach.

Solvency of the Borrower

Another very important area to consider before advancing new money is the solvency of the borrower in order to protect against a voidable preference under the Bankruptcy Reform Act or fraudulent conveyance under the Fraudulent Transfer Act. Therefore, obtain a current balance sheet or trial balance statement prepared by the borrower's outside accountants because evidence of solvency at the time of advancing new money should refute any claim by the debtor or trustee that the borrower was insolvent at the time of the advance.

Such statements will give more validity to those opinions under testimony, even if these statements are not audited. Make sure the borrower signs the statements as being true and correct before you accept them; this serves as a minimizing effect in case the debtor or trustee claims that the statements were false. If the company admitted that the statements were false, the principals could be prosecuted both on civil and criminal charges for obtaining loans on false and misrepresented information.

Keep in mind that the test for insolvency under the Code is not a negative book net worth, but is based on total debts exceeding the fair market value of assets. Therefore, on the one hand the bank may be able to show the borrower is solvent because of fair market values exceeding current book values, which may be supported by independent professional appraisers.

A higher fair market value may be easy to show in a growth or inflationary economy, but it may easily go the opposite way in case of a recessionary economy or in a depression as evidenced in the Southwest for the past few years. In such latter cases, the fair market value may be the liquidation value which could very well be below the book value of assets.

Under these circumstances, the bank needs to make sure it receives statements properly prepared using Generally Accepted Accounting Principles (GAAP) and that the borrower certifies to the effect that it was not insolvent or undercapitalized to the point where it could not pay its debts as they became due at the time of the issuance of the new statement unless by obtaining additional debt or capital or through the liquidation of a substantial amount of its assets.

Bear in mind that this may still not matter as knowledge or reasonable cause to believe that the borrower is insolvent may be immaterial to a court as the lender is no longer protected if it relies on false or fraudulent financial statements while the debtor is actually insolvent.

The question of insolvency may become a moot point if the bank takes additional collateral, thus any contemporaneously granting of new purchase money could be given in consideration for the additional collateral. Also, any excess advance on a borrowing base formula, such as, receivable and inventory lending, where that portion of the excess is reduced by account debtor remittances or collections from inventory sales within 45 days of the advance would not be considered as a preference relative to an improvement in position under an exception to preference rules.

Make sure in this regard that your security agreements give you the right to apply collection proceeds from receivables against debt in any manner you deem suitable.

Also, be aware that a court may give certain intangible assets much more hidden fair market value than what is depicted on the borrower's financial statements, thus increasing the chances of solvency. This may even include noncancellable leasehold interests the borrower has access to over a long term. If the bank determines that the borrower is insolvent at the time of the issuance of financial statements, and if the owners or any friendly parties have loans to the borrower which they would be willing to convert to capital, this could meet the test of becoming solvent, which would then allow the bank to advance new money without being exposed to the insolvency risk.

CHAPTER 4

DEFAULT: REPOSSESSION AND FORECLOSURE

4.01 GENERAL

If your primary workout plan cannot be accomplished, you must move quickly with a contingency plan. First, consult with your attorneys and other specialists regarding your collateral position since it may be time to move for foreclosure if your borrower is not performing or you are not confident that the company can comply sufficiently with your primary plan. Worse, prospects for continued operations may be remote.

Second, obtain the proper approval internally, whether it be by senior or management staff or by committee. Seeking approval before demanding payment is a good habit. This will protect against any unreasonable or capricious action on the officer's part; it can also discourage action taken because of a personality conflict.

Consider the human element. Calling a loan may make you nervous or even scare you. Calling a loan is a big decision because it can easily result in forced liquidation and bankruptcy; it is a real test of banking ability to recover money while salvaging a customer in the process. Do not make demand on any formal commitment unless there is a clear and obvious "event of default" under the note or other agreements.

Always give ample notice to direct or contingent obligors before demanding payment as evidence of good faith. Also, give the assignor or third-party pledgors (who may not be the borrower) and the debtors, or other third-party obligors appropriate notice.

If you had a formal commitment in place, you may have an advantage when the borrower sells the collateral outside the normal course of business without your consent. This could continue your security interest in the goods, now in the hands of a third-party buyer in case they have not yet paid your borrower. Without a formal commitment in place, your collateral interest would not secure advances made after the earlier of 45 days after the sale or the date you find out or receive notice of the purchase. Furthermore, future advances made by the bank after the sale would not be affected under a formal commitment, if such were made involving a commitment that was signed before the unauthorized sale or transfer of the goods.

Liquidations may be carried out by a number of means; for example, collateral repossession or foreclosure; assignment for the benefit of creditors; bulk sale; general court receivership; a Chapter 7 liquidation filing; or a liquidation plan presented while in a Chapter 11 reorganization.

Undertake a "friendly foreclosure" whenever possible, without forcing the borrower into bankruptcy. If you have taken any additional collateral in order to strengthen your position, wait at least 90 days from when it was taken before commencing foreclosure because such action could precipitate a bankruptcy. Therefore, any collateral taken within 90 days of a bankruptcy for antecedent debt would be deemed a "voidable preference." As you begin to think of seriously stepping in and repossessing collateral, have your own plan of action for recovery and means of disposal. Do not overlook anything. Generally, security and other agreements should be written to give you the right to have the borrower assemble goods at its location for sale or liquidation, which has to be undertaken in accordance with "commercial reasonableness" rules of the Uniform Commercial Code (UCC).

Usually, the bank's loan and security agreements allow it to enter the borrower's premises during normal business hours in order to locate its collateral and may even require the borrower to assemble or marshall it for turnover to the bank for sale or place it on one particular location accessible to the bank. Of course, the bank should not breach the peace to obtain such collateral. If you undertake the sale of foreclosed collateral, you will have to be cognizant of selling it in a manner consistent with commercial reasonableness.

The idea is to get possession of your collateral peacefully. You may have to obtain a sequestration order to pick up goods if the borrower is uncooperative—do not breach the peace to reclaim the goods, or the borrower may be able to raise a valid defense, or worse, you could lose a lawsuit. Once you obtain control of the goods, audit and count them—separate them, if necessary. Also obtain possession of accounts receivable records based on default if you have taken a collateral interest in them; do this by letter with the borrower's approval of surrender.

Use "due diligence" in protecting the collateral while under your control. Be especially alert to the possibility of sudden deterioration due to lack of proper maintenance. Security and loan agreements will also often provide for the right to pick up collateral records or even to have someone stationed at the premises to receive or collect collateral proceeds or remittances if collateral consists of accounts, contracts or chattel paper.

You may have to hire guards to protect and preserve collateral. Perhaps you'll have to move goods to another location, although your agreements should give you the right to not only have the borrower assemble the goods on its premises, but also let you sell them there. At any rate, do not interfere with the borrower's normal business, even though your agreements should allow you the rights and remedies of preserving your collateral.

Get in touch with an auctioneer who will be selling the assets, if necessary, very quickly. Move quickly in repossession; this way you can beat other creditors to the punch.

After you determine the collateral value, perhaps with the assistance of an appraiser, then sell the goods in a private sale. If you find a private independent buyer, you should comply with the federal "Bulk Sale Act" when you sell certain assets. If this compliance becomes too difficult to adhere to, you may have to guarantee the sale and title to the goods for the buyer.

If you are unable to accomplish a bulk sale or cannot guarantee title, you may have to undertake an auction sale to sell the goods and bid them in yourself for ownership in order to convey a clear title to some other party. A public auction may be a last resort, depending on your ability to successfully sell the goods to a private party. Always determine the best course of action to obtain the most in recovery.

And when you have taken accounts as collateral, send notices to account debtors to remit amounts due directly to the bank; send them sufficient evidence of your collateral interest, e.g., copies of security agreements and other documents. Account debtors often ignore requests and find many excuses to evade payment. Liquidating your collateral takes some common sense and know-how–do not get caught in a "commercial unreasonableness" sale pursuant to the Uniform Commercial Code. Remember, during this whole time you will have to think, plan, and remain calm.

When the credit has deteriorated significantly and the bank decides against bailing out the borrower, the bank should prepare itself for a bankruptcy. The bank should first determine if the borrower is in default under the terms of any agreements before it cuts off advances or calls its debt. You will then have to determine your contractual rights and appropriate notice requirements before attempting to foreclose on your collateral.

Precautions

Before you undertake closing the loan or taking the above action to repossess or foreclose on your collateral, think through and consider the following:

- Ensure that documents are in order. If vital documentation or collateral items are missing, you as a secured lender may have a very bad bargaining position since effective realization upon the collateral may be difficult and expensive. So, never let yourself be in that position to begin with. When finalizing the loan, review all collateral documents, making sure your package is complete. If you signed the loan pending receipt of certain items, make sure you follow up to obtain them.
- Consider the many possible default issues before the loan is consummated, especially weighing the best and easiest method to dispose of collateral.
- Areas of particular concern may include intangibles such as trademarks, trade styles, patents, and various types of contingent agreements and the ability to foreclose on them. Therefore, even if you have taken a security agreement and filed a financing statement on general intangibles, always perfect an interest in these items

specifically in order not to face any problems later in foreclosing on your collateral. Many intangible items require stringent adherence to unique and specific collateral perfection procedures. This is particularly important when having to comply with the requirements of involved third parties. In many situations, a contractual arrangement with the third party may be the only real protection.

• Another area concerns the landlords of borrowers who are acting in the capacity of tenants and operating their businesses on leased real property. The prudent secured lender will pursue obtaining a landlord lien waiver which should include the right to enter the premises to pick up collateral. Also, you should obtain curing rights or the right to pay per diem rent or even the right to assume, assign and sublease the premises in case the debtor defaults on the lease. Write into the waiver that you not only have the right—as the secured lender—to assemble and pick-up the collateral, but also to hold an auction sale on the leased premises.

• Carefully obtain access to accounts receivable and executory contract records when they are part of the collateral. Access provisions should always be built into security and loan agreements. Such provisions may often require agreements with third parties.

You should be aware even when your collateral package is adequate and well-documented that your rights can be substantially modified in a bankruptcy case. Here are three major concerns.

- You may be stayed from proceeding against the collateral.
- The debtor or trustee may be able to use your collateral during the pendency of the case.
- Your rights as a secured creditor may be altered or modified under the plan of reorganization relative to a Chapter 11 case.

4.02 SETTING OFF ACCOUNTS

The right of a bank to set off an indebtedness against general unrestricted deposits of one of its debtors (a depositor) may arise from one or more of the following conditions.

- Maturity of the debt which is now past due.
- Insolvency of the debtor/depositor.
- Possibility of repayment of the debt has been substantially impaired so that the bank may accelerate an indebtedness under any applicable acceleration clause. This conclusion is based on good faith estimates, stemming from factual evidence.

The reasoning behind the right of set-off for insolvency or pending insolvency is that although the debt has not matured, there is no other equitable way in which the debt, or any part thereof, could be recovered.

Often, the further problem of dishonoring a check drawn by the depositor on the account upon which a set-off has been made will arise. Whenever an account has been set off, the bank should immediately give notice to the debtor/depositor that the set-off was made, thus preventing the debtor from writing any more checks on the account and alleging that they had no notice. Without proper notice to the borrower, the bank could be setting the stage for an action of wrongful dishonor. In one case, the court held that the bank was not permitted to decline payment of a check on the grounds that it had charged back an unpaid note against the borrower's account, which it had discounted for the borrower. The bank, in so charging back the note, had not taken the necessary steps to obtain a full recourse endorsement by the borrower on the note. The lesson? This case indicates that banks must be very cautious when setting off an account.

Certain procedures, depending on the particular type of transaction (e.g., a note that has been discounted or a note that has been made directly to the borrower/depositor) must be followed. The bank should comply procedurally with any particular language used in any instrument relative to the transaction.

Check your own state statutes on whether or not you will be required to automatically comply with a writ of garnishment being served on your bank by another judgment creditor, without first allowing the borrower/depositor due process under the law. Due process would require the bank to first notify the debtor and give it the opportunity to be heard in a court of law before the bank honors a garnishment. Also, this would prevent the property (cash deposits or equivalents) from being arbitrarily taken without a hearing. In such instances, do not freeze or set off the funds in the borrower's account without first promptly notifying this depositor. Such garnishments, though, are usually valid based on an existing recorded judgment against the depositor.

You can set off accounts prior to a bankruptcy, but it will be measured under the 90-day preference test from the date of filing for any improvements. This means that any amount in the account at the time of set-off that exceeded the amount in the account 90 days prior to the bankruptcy filing has to be remitted back to the court. Also, a transfer and assignment of depository accounts by a debtor to a creditor within 90 days of the filing of a petition in bankruptcy may cause a voiding by the bankruptcy trustee. A preference will, therefore, cause a transfer to be voided under the following conditions:

- A transfer of the bankrupt's nonexempt assets.
- A transfer made by the bankrupt within the 90-day period to or for the benefit of a creditor.
- A transfer for or on account of an antecedent debt.
- A transfer while the debtor was insolvent.
- The transferee obtains a greater reduction of its debt than some other creditor of the same general class.

Set-Off and Bankruptcy

Once a bankruptcy is filed, the bank will be stayed from setting off any accounts. The stay is not only automatic, but it remains in effect until the court annuls, terminates, and modifies, or conditions the stay or the case is closed, dismissed, or converted to a liquidation bankruptcy; or the property subject to a lien is abandoned or transferred with court approval. Therefore, you are prohibited from taking any act against the property of a person filing a bankruptcy petition, and that prohibition includes set-offs under a consensual (contractual) lien granted in a depository agreement or any other instrument, or by way of any other pledge agreement.

The bank should become more cautious about not exposing itself to lender liability, especially as it pertains to formal commitments and the setting off of certain accounts. Banks will usually set off accounts when they think a workout plan cannot be achieved or a pending bankruptcy is imminent, even though they may have to remit a portion of the funds back to the court because of an improvements test.

Setting off against certain accounts or dishonoring certain checks may create further problems for the bank. As an example, you may not be authorized to set off certain restricted accounts entailing a trust or other fiduciary capacity, or accounts for federal or other local governmental body obligations. Also, depending on how the bank's signature cards or other account or security agreements read, you may not be able to legally set off two-party or multiple-depositor accounts when each party has not agreed to such action. Parties in affiliate businesses, for example, may not have agreed. Always obtain a contractual agreement regarding a right of set-off besides relying on your general banker's legal right of set-off because this may give you a priority position ahead of other secured creditors or federal tax liens.

A contractual right of set-off can be easily handled in a boilerplate covenant of your security agreement form that should be executed by the pledgor of the funds or account, whether owned in the name of the borrower or a third party.

If the borrower is not the owner of the account, make sure the third party pledging such accounts receives proper consideration or defined benefit for such action.

As an example, if either direct or indirectly related affiliate corporations are on joint accounts together and only one is the borrower, obtain a resolution from the nonborrowing affiliate authorizing it to pledge the account with evidence in the resolution indicating the benefit and consideration that the affiliate will receive for pledging their undivided interest in such funds.

There has been an abundance of case law on the subject of "equitable" set-off by a bank of a borrower's general deposits (as distinguished from a deposit for a "special" purpose of which the bank has or should have knowledge, such as a trust account), when a debt is owed to the bank by the depositor. The following are hypothetical cases whereby a bank could face an improper set-off proceeding.

ABC Company, owned by Mr. Jones, owes the bank a total of $200,000 involving two notes of $100,000 each. Account balances in the company account are nil; worse, the account has often been overdrawn lately. Mr. Jones admits the company is in deep financial trouble. He helps prop up the company by borrowing $100,000, secured by certain real property he owns. Proceeds of this personal loan are then deposited directly to the company account. Immediately thereafter the bank decides to set off its debt to the company by debiting the company's account for the $100,000. In the eyes of certain courts, the bank may have improperly set off the company account. The problem arises because these new borrower funds did not enter into the company account in the normal course of business. Instead, the bank should have considered having Mr. Jones pay off or buy one of the company notes with the proceeds of the personal loan if its intent was to reduce its debt exposure.

Similarly, a situation could arise where a good-faith borrower, who is close to bankruptcy, comes in and gives you a third-party check to pay off his debt. Instead of taking the check and returning the note paid, have the borrower deposit the check and in turn debit his account. Then send the check for immediate collection. In the meantime notify the borrower by letter that you will be setting off his account to pay his debt.

4.03 PREPARING FOR IMMINENT BANKRUPTCY

To prepare for a forthcoming bankruptcy, the lending officer or special assets officer should first confer with counsel and go over the following matters:

• Prepare for hearings which will be forthcoming upon the filing of a bankruptcy under a Chapter 11 whereby the borrower is seeking a "debtor in possession" status and is attempting to use proceeds from your collateral whether or not a cash collateral account has been established.

• Plan a defense against preferences relative to the debtor or trustee recapturing or recovering prior debt payments, set-offs, and collateral improvements.

• Review possibilities for obtaining "adequate protection," pursuant to bankruptcy law, regarding future hearings in this respect by analyzing liquidation values of unencumbered assets, including potentially being able to provide substitute collateral protection.

Do not forget your contingent obligors such as guarantors who provide a source for additional collateral.

• Evaluate the extent the debtor may require or want to continue utilizing your noncash collateral, e.g., inventory, machinery, equipment, or real estate. Your attorney should request the bankruptcy court for an "indubitable equivalent" in accordance with bankruptcy law, of rental proceeds, wear-and-tear cost, or monthly depreciation value.

• Prepare for hearings on the debtor's claim of need to use all or part of the cash collateral account, if one is established. Unless the debtor, probably under the advice of its counsel, has opened sufficient accounts with noncreditor banks, it is a foregone conclusion in a Chapter 11 reorganization that the court will most likely require and permit the use of the account by the debtor while providing the lender "adequate protection" in the form of substitute collateral.

If you have done your homework, with the assistance of your legal counsel, you will stand the best chance for successfully contesting or limiting use of cash proceeds or of obtaining the most optimum source of substitute collateral among the debtor's unencumbered assets. This is not to say that you may accept a second, perhaps on real property with a fair amount of equity in it. A prepared, secured bank lender will also promptly petition the bankruptcy court to maximize its recoveries especially pertaining to trading or working assets involving cash collateral sources restricted to prepetition interests, such as inventory and accounts receivable. A prompt petition would also be applicable for wear and tear or depreciation for the debtor's expected use of noncash collateral such as real estate with improvements thereon, machinery, and equipment, especially vehicles and rentals regarding leased premises.

4.04 ACTION AGAINST PERSONAL PROPERTY AFTER DEFAULT

To begin with, we need to define *default*. Default officially occurs once loan payments become late or past due, or if the borrower violates or defaults under any of the terms or conditions of the loan contract and/or covenants of any security and loan agreement(s). If the debtor falls behind in making payments when due, and you do not take action to demand payments, this could nullify your rights to demand payment in the future under a default clause. Furthermore, it is not unusual for a bank to accept late payments on a regular basis, which could be construed as a waiver against declaring a default against the borrower for subsequent late payments. When you engage in this tolerance policy, you must notify the borrower that strict compliance is necessary to avoid default when you resume a strict posture. With the next late payment, you can demand payment under this default clause—a demand you should make without reservation.

Default clauses themselves should be spelled out in notes, and in security and letter and loan agreements. As a matter of fact, it is not inconceivable that because you have so many covenants and events of default in your documents that the borrower was in default the moment he or she, or company representatives executed the loan documents. Most banks can probably act more quickly than waiting for default to occur by making demand under their insecurity clause, often referred to as the "nervous" clause. The key in relying on this clause is that you must have a very good reason for calling the loan and you must act in good faith truly believing that performance or the payment of the debt is seriously in jeopardy. When demand is made under the insecurity clause, the burden of proof that the bank did not act in good faith is with the borrower. Still, the bank should be very cautious in using this clause because of the proliferation of liability lawsuits these days.

Default: Repossession

At the time of default you will generally have the option of taking possession of your collateral, if you do not already hold it, either privately or through court proceedings.

Consider having your security agreement give you flexibility by allowing you the right to enter the borrower's private premises for repossession, although this will most likely not allow you to go into closed or locked premises. Check with your attorneys on whether you can take such action in your state.

Incidentally, once you repossess collateral, especially vehicles or aircraft, immediately take an inventory of the contents. If you find personal contents, hold them and contact the borrower right away. The borrower should come down and execute and acknowledge receipt of the items in the inventory list evidencing return of these personal items before you release them, thus relinquishing you of any liability. If you are holding aircraft, the equipment that is removable is considered subject to the Uniform Commercial Code (UCC), while the aircraft itself is under a Federal Aviation Administration (FAA) lien. Therefore, proceed to take an inventory of such equipment and hold onto any you feel you have an interest in if you have properly complied with filing requirements.

According to the UCC, personal property collateral is broken down into two categories—intangible and tangible. Intangibles include accounts receivable, chattel paper, documents, instruments, and general intangibles which is a catch-all for any collateral that cannot be properly defined or which is truly an intangible asset. Tangible assets not only include inventory and equipment, but also farm products and consumer goods.

The bank needs to closely determine its position regarding the collateral class before it takes action to repossess or sell any. This also has a bearing on its rights as a secured party. With most types of tangible collateral, the bank generally has a right to repossess it after a loan default, then to sell it and sue the borrower or any contingent obligors for any deficiency. Regarding intangible collateral, the bank should have a right to collect on the unpaid amount, and still sue for any deficiency, or to sell such debt and/or collateral to an outside party

4.05 SALE OF LOANS, COLLATERAL, AND CHARGED-OFF DEBT

Do not overlook your right to privately sell collateral or to even sell existing debt, secured by the underlying collateral, to an outside party. This often has to be done at a discount.

Over the years, there has been an increase in the secondary market for the purchase of loans, including troubled or problem debt. More recently, security investment firms and other independent investors have been buying loans from financial institutions and the Federal Deposit Insurance Corporation (FDIC). Purchases vary depending on the term of the credit; its seasoning (how long it has been paying), whether the loan is in a performing or nonperforming status; underlying collateral (its quality, type, margin, marketability); and whether there is a recognized market for the collateral. Do not overlook this national market or even local markets for bad debts that have been charged-off, too.

Local collection agencies and attorneys have always purchased charge-off debt, but now an expanded market encompasses problem loans that are still live debt. You should realize that the discount on charged-off debt will probably be higher than on live debt. Also, if you want to sell charged-off or bad debt, the longer you wait, the more stale it becomes. Chances of recovery become more remote. And the older the debt, the greater chances of it reaching a statute of limitations point in time, thus eliminating the legal opportunity of collection. As such, check your state's statute of limitations.

Selling loans may also apply to the sale of good quality loans, typically arranged under a participation agreement. It is frequently easier to sell a government guaranteed portion of a note to an investor who may be able to arrange for a security-backed debt instrument to be sold in the secondary market, based on the guaranteed portion of the debt, e.g., Small Business Administration (SBA) and Farmers Home Administration (FmHA) guaranteed loans.

Sellers of loans, on a nonrecourse basis, may be any type of financial institution including commercial banks, thrifts, insurance companies, or any other type of third-party lender. Buyers of loans may also be these same types of institutions, but may also include nonfinancial corporations, pension funds, money market mutual funds, and private investors. The same parties that have acted as buyers at one time are probably doing more selling these days, especially in view of the problems the thrift and banking industries are encountering. In this connection, bankers and attorneys are having to deal with the complexities of the uncertain impact of the Glass-Steagall Act and certain securities laws; competitors are making the accusation that banks, companies, and other financial institutions that sell loans are acting in the capacity of investment bankers. The bankers' defense includes the fact that they deal in loans and have a right not only to originate them or sell participations in them, but to also continue servicing such loans; this has always been a natural outgrowth and operating function of commercial banking. Most of the sellers to this point have been money center banks, but more regionals are now entering the playing field.

Sellers of loans recognize the need to improve their liquidity positions and enhance equity, thus improving capital adequacy through improved retained earnings including a higher return on assets. Sellers are also looking to purge portfolios for better diversification and quality in addition to reducing risk. Of course, there are a number of factors which a seller must consider. These include:

- Market conditions.
- Various loan terms such as stripping (selling maturity segments of loans), although such could be construed as involving recourse transactions according to regulatory standards.
- Present and anticipated yield on loans.
- Other existing terms and conditions.
- Collateral considerations.
- Asset management considerations.
- Impacts on the bank's portfolio because of securitization loans.
- Sales contracts and negotiating selling terms.
- Servicing and administering requirements of sold loans.

Sellers are finding it more difficult to sell problem loans because buyers are looking for good quality without collection difficulties and also with a fair investment return. Certainly, the whole idea of selling loans allows the bank to make more loans and turn over its portfolio more times. This should improve bottom line profits, especially if the bank participates out the bulk of the loan and if it has received a fee of some type for making the loan in the first place.

Selling loans is something banks have always been able to do but have not done to any great degree because they have traditionally maintained the loans on their books. Banks are now becoming more involved in this quasi-investment-banking activity as a means to remain competitive and retain financial strength in view of the difficulty of competing, especially in the world of deregulation. On the other hand, there may be instances of banks wanting to buy loans for various reasons including excess liquidity, a desire to make a shift in their income-producing assets for purposes of mix and maturity, and an interest in proper asset-and-liability management. Buying loans could both reduce overhead costs for banks and improve efficiency, even though loan yields could be less. However, the majority of loan buyers these days is probably in the segment of non-bank companies. Buyers must do their homework, acquire loans from reputable sellers, and be astute in analyzing the credit they buy, just as they would with any other investment or money market debt instrument.

While problem loans are more difficult to sell, there is a sophisticated market out there for them. Problem loan buying transactions may entail asset swaps or sale/purchases involving securities or cash by related companies; or they may be straight cash sales to unrelated entitites. There are definite analysis considerations that should be undertaken by buyers. Usually a discounted cash approach is used by the buyer. This includes discounting the future cash flow of the loan, (i.e., principal, interest, fee payments, distributions from business and asset sales involving foreclosures or liquidations, securities distributed in a restructure, or other cash outlays or payments due buyers) less costs relative to loan administration. Buyers usually use a higher discount rate based on risk than do sellers. Bankers, as sellers, tend to discount at current money market rates (such as prime), resulting in higher present values of such loans as compared to discounted values determined by buyers. Some buyers equate the discount that *should be* paid for troubled credits to what *is* paid or *has been* paid for secondary issues of junk bonds. Of course, each loan case will be unique to itself; this is the reason for differing discount rates.

4.06 REPOSSESSION OF CONSUMER GOODS

At times it may be more difficult to repossess consumer goods than other classes of collateral. It may become more difficult when the goods can be easily moved, hidden, or retained behind locked doors or premises.

Check your own state laws on repossessing consumer goods,

such as vehicles that may be towed off by repo agents. Also, examine your own state laws regarding penalties against debtors or collateral owners who may have concealed collateral or who, under oath, have not revealed where collateral is located, including any penalties to defraud creditors by selling or improperly disposing of it.

Legal Steps in Repossession

The initial step in repossession is to advise the customer in writing (one copy certified and one regular mail, with a copy for the file) that satisfactory arrangements must be made within a specific time (usually 10 days) to cure the default. Often customers realize the seriousness of their delinquency at this time, and that they will have to deal with the bank. When no response is forthcoming within the allotted grace period, a formal notice of the acceleration of maturity should be sent to the customer, giving the debtor another 10 days to repay the debt in full. This is called a demand letter. Some banks only send one demand letter when the borrower is in default, rather than taking the extra step of offering the additional time. Exhibit B is an example of a demand letter.

In your letter, only quote a net payoff and any late fees actually earned, if dealing with an add-on or discounted installment note. Assuming that the customer still has not responded to the bank's letters at the end of these two periods, repossession should commence.

Repossession Procedures

Some states still allow creditors to repossess collateral without judicial process, provided it is done without breach of the peace. Other states mandate due process. Check your own state statutes in this respect. Your bank's installment loan, collection department, or even charge-off/recovery department should maintain a list of reputable recovery agencies that adhere to the letter of the law.

Once you have taken repossession, send another letter (certified with a copy for your files), notifying the borrower of your intention to sell the collateral. Again, a grace period of at least 10

EXHIBIT B
Demand Letter

Date ________________

Certified Mail

Return Receipt Requested

Name ____
Address ____
City, State and Zip Code ______________________________

Dear :

The promissory note dated ________________ payable to ABC Bank in the original amount of ________________ has a balance of ________________ which remains due and owing. Demand is hereby made upon you for the payment of such amount.

By giving this matter your prompt attention you can avoid the possibility of incurring the additional expense of court cost and attorneys' fees that may hereafter be assessed by a court in the event that it becomes necessary to file lawsuit for the collection of this balance.

Please contact the undersigned either by telephone at the number listed above or in person at 12345 Mason St. within 10 days from the date of this letter to arrange for the payment of this amount.

Yours truly,

(Account Officer)

c.c. Via Regular Mail

days should be given to the debtor,[1] indicating the earliest date the collateral will be sold unless fully redeemed by the debtor.

If perchance this date comes and goes and you do not sell the goods shortly thereafter, cover yourself by again notifying the debtor that you are still holding the collateral and are attempting to sell it under a private sale arrangement. Indicate that you have no further obligation to inform them of such a sale, but that as long as you are holding the collateral without having a letter of intent or contract with specific closing dates from a buyer in good faith, they may redeem the collateral at their option. Indicate in this letter that if they redeem the collateral that they will also be responsible to pay for repossession and legal fees, including storage.

If an add-on or discount installment loan, proceeds from the sale should then be applied to the net balance, including all repossession fees. Monies realized in excess of the debt balance and other charges from the proceeds of the disposition must be returned to the borrower. When the collateral sale is finally settled, either publicly or privately for the highest possible price, the debtor should be sent a final letter advising him or her of the disposition of the collateral and any deficiency remaining on the balance of the debt. If the bank is still carrying the loan on its books, any deficiency should be charged-off and the account should be turned over to the charge-off/recovery or loan reclamation department for any follow-up.

The whole process of repossession may make the bank more vulnerable to litigation. To minimize your exposure, always document your actions and obtain legal advice in or outside the bank. Seek assistance should circumstances become questionable or out of the ordinary.

4.07 RIGHT TO RETAIN COLLATERAL IN SATISFACTION OF DEBT

Consider your right to retain the collateral in satisfaction of the debt. It may be worth your while to accept it in satisfaction of the

---

[1] References to debtor include the owner or owners of the collateral and any contingent obligors.

debt based on the margin of value in the collateral after any prior debt reduction and the current worsened financial condition of the borrower. This may also apply to goods that are presently depressed in value and which could be worth more in the future if you hold onto them. Check your own state law in this connection.

Indeed, you may be given this right by the debtor if, after default, he or she or a company representative executes a letter giving up debtor rights to the collateral in satisfaction of the debt. You may even be able to send a certified letter, and if the debtor does not reject your offer within the allowable time, you may be able to legally retain the collateral in satisfaction of the debt. Under such circumstances, you should realize that you legally may not have any right to pursue further action against the debtor for a deficiency (if the balance of the debt including interest and repossession charges still exceeds the net proceeds received on the sale of the collateral). If the debtor rejects your retaining of the collateral, then proceed with the normal foreclosure to ultimately obtain and sell it.

4.08 REPOSSESSION AND SALE OF PERISHABLE GOODS

If the collateral consists of inventory, your rights will vary when the goods are perishable—for example, certain types of commodities, fresh meat, vegetables, fruits, and certain other food products. You will be allowed to immediately repossess and sell such goods upon default without notice to the borrower. In such instances, you do not have to even repossess the goods, but you may make arrangements for a third party to pick them up; this third party may either buy them or deliver them to another party for sale. Of course, in these situations you have to have a cooperative borrower who allows such third parties onto the premises.

This is another reason to consider the advantage of having issued warehouse receipts when lending on commodities or other perishable goods because it not only offers you third-party control via a public warehouse arrangement, but allows you the right and ease to pick up and sell the collateral quickly without debtor interference or intervention. The only real concern in such instances is to make sure you have complied with all the commercial reasonableness tests although such sales when made in recognized markets normally meet the Code's requirements. Of course, if a bankruptcy petition was filed, this would stay you from taking any of the above actions; a pending bankruptcy prompts you to sell goods fast.

In another exception, if perishables are customarily sold on a recognized market on a given day at recognized daily market prices, you have the right to immediately pick up the goods and sell them without giving the borrower notice in either instance. This pertains to commodities, farm products, and livestock (e.g., grains, cotton, and cattle). Whenever there is a recognized market on which to sell the goods, it is advisable to proceed with such sales in that market rather than sell them on your own, because if you sell the goods for less on a day the recognized market prices are higher, the sale could be deemed not to be "commercially reasonable."

4.09 REPOSSESSION AND SALE OF OTHER GOODS

If the collateral for a business loan consists of equipment (e.g., machinery, rolling stock, or office equipment), consider repossession upon default by the debtor, but do not breach the peace. Therefore, if you are unable to pick up the collateral without a confrontation, such as breaking and entering private property, then go through ancillary action by a court of law for a writ of sequestration to obtain the collateral. To be entitled to obtain a writ, however, you may have to establish facts that will lead the court to believe the borrower will hide, destroy, dispose of or sell it, without your permission to prevent you from repossessing it. If you do not have good enough supportive or factual information that the debtor will take such steps, you may be opening yourself up to countersuit. Even if you do succeed in obtaining the writ, the time delay, expenses and court costs could greatly affect your return once you gain possession of the equipment and sell it. In addition, if the borrower wins a counterclaim against you for such action or for wrongfully securing the writ, it could cost you a lot more in the payment to them for damages including attorney's fees.

You may be able to render the collateral unusable if you cannot pick it up, or if it is too cumbersome to reassemble (if it has been broken down), or if it is just too difficult to pick up, such as heavy machinery or equipment. The cost of moving it may be prohibitive. Then there's the need to have it disassembled and assembled. Worse, storage runs up bills. Therefore, make sure your security agreement has a clause allowing you to render the equipment unusable. In addition, the clause should require the borrower to not only allow you the right to dispose of it on their premises and to disassemble and reassemble it, if necessary, but to move it to a designated place of your choice that would be reasonably convenient for both parties. Hopefully, this can be accomplished with the borrower's cooperation. For if you have to take court action to foreclose on and repossess it, physically disassemble or reassemble it, and then move and store it yourself, it may be too costly an undertaking.

When the borrower is uncooperative and unwilling to assemble the collateral, a court may grant you an injunction compelling the borrower to assemble it and turn the equipment over or make it available for you to pick up. In these instances, consult with your attorney and outside professionals who are familiar with the equipment because you need to take the most prudent steps, especially when you only want it temporarily unusable in order to obtain access so that you might sell it.

The writer had an experience in this connection regarding a drilling rig that secured a loan involving a company that went into bankruptcy. We petitioned the court for an abandonment of the rig, which was quickly granted because the borrower had entered a Chapter 7 liquidation proceeding. The rig was located on leased land. So besides arranging to keep the lease current, we were allowed to have a guard watch over it until we could move it. We had to break the rig down and truck it to a yard owned by another private party. Then we had to undertake cleaning and painting. Despite advertising in trade journals to obtain private bids, we were unsuccessful because of the age and limited drilling capacity of the rig. Finally, we sold it in parts at a public auction, and what remained we scrapped.

The bottom line was that we only received a few cents on the dollar for the rig after all our expense versus the large market and replacement appraisal values we had in the file from a third party when the loan was originally granted.

If you do sell equipment such as drilling rigs, make sure you will obtain the highest return based on whether you sell it as a whole unit or in parcels. Thus, attempt to obtain values both ways and put it out for bids based on these two alternatives. Finally, make sure you contact all other second lien or inferior lienholders that you know who may have an interest, whether they have notified you of their interest or not in order to cut off their rights prior to the sale, unless they want to buy out your debt position.

If you can procure the equipment, you may be able to sell it at a private or public sale, in whole or in parcel parts. Whatever way you decide to sell it, comply with the Code's "commercial reasonableness" standards. Your decision to sell the equipment at a public auction or by private sale should hinge on a number of factors. For starters, you must evaluate the type of collateral and how it may be sold. In some situations, such as with vehicles, it may be easier to sell them on a private bid or offer basis—besides you often realize more. You also generally can obtain more by selling a company as a going concern when you have a lien on all assets including the stock.

But a different approach may be necessary. As an example, if a company is going out of business shortly because of pending or inevitable bankruptcy, then an auction or public sale may be the best way to realize the highest return.

The writer has taken this approach on a department store that was going out of business. All the goods were tagged and ready for a closing sale with the cooperation of the borrower. One advantage that a public sale offers is that you may be able to buy in the goods yourself for the amount of debt when you feel the bidding process is not realizing enough.

However, you cannot do this in a private sale unless it is the type of collateral sold on a recognized market or subject to standard price quotes that are widely distributed. Of course, in a private sale you do not have to take the first available offer. Also, just because you held onto the goods hoping that a better price could be obtained by a future sale, this will not necessarily make the sale ultimately "commercially unreasonable" in case you do not realize a better price.

Still, be cautious in your approach. In a private sale, take the best price and do not wait too long to sell.

If you decide to hold the equipment in anticipation of a market turnaround, it is recommended that you take the equipment in satisfaction of the debt, especially if there is a good chance it may return more than the outstanding debt. In some cases, you may only be giving up a right to a deficiency, which may not be very much if the borrower is financially insolvent or the guarantors or other contingent obligors are basically judgment proof; that is, where there's very little chance of getting anything out of them because they have very limited resources or income or free or unencumbered assets.

There are some advantages in taking the collateral for debt satisfaction, e.g., you may save considerable time and money, rather than going through any long drawn out legal action.

The process is also simple; all you need to do is notify the borrower that you are taking the collateral in satisfaction of debt. Of course, you must notify any other creditors having an inferior (second, third or other junior) lien. If you receive an objection from any of these parties within 21 days, you will have to proceed to obtain the collateral by foreclosure according to the Code. Check for any state exceptions to this rule and regarding cases where you have a security interest in or hold goods that could be construed as being consumer goods.

The writer was involved in another situation in which the borrower's scrap-iron operation was going out of business. Thus, the bank held a public auction on the borrower's premises. Acting in a spirit of cooperation, the scrap-iron operator included certain equipment that was saleable. But this did not draw high enough bids to let certain pieces go. By selling some of the goods at a public auction and selling the balance privately, though, the bank realized the highest return.

If you buy in the equipment at a public sale, this will allow you to take over ownership or title to the collateral from the borrower or a third-party assignor—besides cutting off any other second or inferior lien creditors having an interest in the collateral.

However, make sure the sale has been conducted in a "commercially reasonable" manner based on a well-defined procedure to adhere to the Code. Remember, the importance of giving reasonable notice of the sale to the debtor and any other party who has met public notice filing requirements or who you know has a security interest, even if that entity has not filed a financing statement. At a minimum, you must inform them of the time and place of public sale or the time after which private sale is expected to take place. A reasonable notice is at least 10 business days.

After giving notice, you can sell the equipment "as is" or after any preparation or processing. Decide whether the preparation or processing will create or add to the value before incurring such additional expense, or if you will net less if you decide not to go forward. However, minimal repair and maintenance, such as cleaning and painting, is recommended in order to comply to a "commercially reasonable" sale. You may also sell the equipment in whole or piecemeal; you may sell for cash or by way of a contract of sale.

Above all, sell it for the most optimum return, which will benefit both you and the borrower by decreasing the debt.

Next, you have to determine how to apply the sales proceeds. If you received cash, first apply it to all expenses in taking, storing, or holding the collateral including any preparation, processing, cost in selling goods. In addition, cover any legal or court costs you have incurred. Then apply the balance of the proceeds to your debt. If there is anything remaining, you have to remit it to any inferior lienholders who have properly given you notice and evidence of their security interest before you disburse any remaining sale proceeds to the debtor. If these other so-called creditors have not complied with this requirement, you can ignore them. If there are any funds remaining after all this, they would go to the debtor unless you had taken title or ownership to the equipment in satisfaction of the debt; if you did not and the borrower still has a deficiency, you would be able to sue him or her for the deficiency.

4.10 LIQUIDATION OF INTANGIBLE PERSONAL PROPERTY

Beginning with accounts receivable, you should realize that you are dealing with open, unsecured trade credit. Upon default, you have the right under the Code to notify account debtors to remit payments directly to the bank in satisfaction of the borrower's debt.

Make sure this notification is written right into security agreements, so you can implement notification even before the borrower defaults. You have to furnish account debtors with evidence of the borrower's assignment of their accounts by way of copies of security or other loan agreements.

If account debtors do not pay the bank directly after such notification, the bank may undertake collection procedures against them, which could go as far as moving for a restraining order and obtaining an injunction regarding payment. Such expenses could also be netted against any account proceeds the bank receives.

You should still have a right, based on the borrower's debt obligation with the bank, to sue the borrower for any deficiency after applying the net proceeds of such a sale or collection of proceeds to your debt. On the other hand, if you receive over and above your expenses and the balance of your debt including accrued and unpaid interest, you must remit this excess back to the borrower. Personally, the writer has never found this latter situation to be the case. As a matter of fact, every time I have placed account debtors on notification, especially when the borrower was imminently facing bankruptcy, I received a minimal response and only a few cents on the dollar. Even the threat of legal action against account debtors did not produce any better results.

Chattel Paper

Accounts receivable are not the only type of intangible personal property. Chattel paper, consisting of loan instruments and documents, often involves conditional sales contracts or leases. Such obligations typically have underlying security behind them.

Therefore, you may have a complex situation to deal with

involving chattel paper after default. First of all, if you hold a note or chattel paper (endorsed) and the payee has been meeting its payments and you have sent them an estoppel letter that insulates your position (which they have acknowledged and returned to you without raising a defense), this would be ideal. In this enviable position, you generally will be considered a true holder. This would place you in the borrower's shoes for taking any action necessary for subsequent nonpayment by the payee or obligor.

However, banks often do not go to such lengths. At times the borrower will have difficulty paying on its debt, especially when a payer stops paying on its obligation. This is another reason why the bank should hold the chattel paper in its possession, as then it will hold the necessary documents to follow up with payers or other makers. If the bank is not receiving payments directly from the payers or obligors, it then has to send evidence in the form of copies of the assigned documents to them.

When the payers or obligors fail to respond (and still owe back payments), then the bank needs to repossess or foreclose on the underlying collateral securing the borrower's debt. The bank can again sell the collateral and possibly sue both its borrower and the payer or obligor if the latter has defaulted under its contract or lease with the borrower.

Do not forget to notify all interested parties and other known lienholders of any sale.

Promissory Notes

Dealing with promissory notes can be somewhat similar, yet more complex. One advantage in dealing with promissory notes is that they are negotiable and may be sold or transferred. On the other hand, for all practical purposes you cannot conduct a public sale of negotiable instruments. This also applies to CDs and publicly traded stocks and bonds, which are also negotiable instruments, as they are all considered securities under Securities & Exchange Commission (SEC) laws. Furthermore, it is very difficult to place a value on promissory notes depending on their terms, the financial condition of the obligor, and the underlying collateral to the note.

This also makes it more difficult to have a "commercially reasonable" sale, to comply with the Code, because you have to determine the proper value of the instrument. The best thing is to support values of any existing collateral behind the note with independent appraisals, if necessary, and sell the note reasonably soon after taking the highest of a number of offers. Don't forget to give consideration to a lower full cash payment sale versus a higher term payout sale in view of the time value of money. You may decide to hold the note and continue having the payer remit payments directly to the bank.

If the payer is unwilling or unable to pay, you will have to proceed with the same action as stated above, regarding chattel paper, in that you will have to repo or foreclose on the underlying collateral and in turn sell it.

Again remember, you have to notify all interested parties of a sale whether it's the borrower regarding the promissory note or other interested parties relative to the underlying collateral including known inferior lienholders. You will also be able to sue the borrower for any deficiency or possibly the payer for a default under the note obligation.

Warehouse Receipts and Bills of Lading

Another intangible area is documents of title—warehouse receipts and bills of lading. The issuance and possession of those documents controls the underlying merchandise. After default by the borrower, you may either sell the document of title to the goods in a private sale, after giving reasonable notice to your debtor, or use your documents to take possession of the goods which in turn will allow them to be freely sold.

Your action should depend on the situation. If there is a recognized market for the merchandise—which is often the case because warehouse receipts usually represent title documents for commodities—it is better to take possession of the goods and sell them in that recognized market at current prices. This also applies if the borrower is nearing bankruptcy. By having the goods under third-party control in a public warehouse, it offers the bank quicker and less troublesome access to the goods.

Certificates of Deposit

CDs, issued on other banks, are easier to deal with than other intangibles. In these instances, you should contact the other institution by letter or submission of a draft that was executed in blank by the borrower when the loan was originated.

If the debtor executed a draft, fill it in before sending it to the other institution in order to obtain the collateral proceeds at maturity, in case of loan default. This draft procedure is similar to the use of a stock power when liquidating negotiable securities. Of course, besides holding the CD in your possession, hopefully you had sent the other institution an agreement or letter, subordinating their interest in the CD. The other institution should have acknowledged and returned this agreement or letter to you before you proceeded to disburse loan monies to the borrower. In this letter, the other institution should have indicated that it had no interest in the CD or that its interest is subordinated to your interest. The letter should also evidence their agreement not to take the CD as security while your interest is in force, and that they will not set-off against it for any reason. If you did not take this precaution, having possession of the CD alone may not fully ensure your access to the full amount. After default, notify the borrower that you are cashing in the CD.

Stocks and Bonds

The last intangible area we want to cover is publicly traded stocks and bonds. If the borrower defaults, it should not be too difficult to sell listed securities that are sold on recognized markets, but it will be more difficult to sell unlisted, closely held or private stock and to realize much value. The attempt to sell securities in the public market without having been registered could be in violation of SEC laws. Unless you're able to go through the difficult process of registering the stock—which may not even be possible—you will have to undertake a private sale. One alternative is to obtain a repurchase agreement upon approving the loan from an interested party, such as a stockholder or even the company itself.

As a final thought about collateral, once you have repossessed or foreclosed on it, consider the necessity of continued use. Consider cases when you are dealing with certain types of equipment or machinery, especially a plant operation. By shutting a plant down or leaving it idle, you could be jeopardizing the future value of the collateral by lowering it. In one such instance, the writer was involved with a bankrupt gasoline processing plant which we had to temporarily shut down. We had to spend money to, in effect, not let it dry up. The longer the plant would have been shut down, the greater the risk of it being frozen or locked up, and or the more difficult it would have been to start it up again and get it running well. Fortunately, the bank soon found a buyer for the plant. Therefore, protect yourself under such circumstances. In fact, build in such protection as a legal right in your documents.

At other times when you are involved with a large debt involving a number of other creditors, the borrower's attorney may call a meeting of the creditors or confer by letter with all creditors. Basically, the borrower may offer the creditors so much on the dollar for the collateral, including other assets of the business based on its estimation of the liquidation value. This represents a compromise settlement of all debts in lieu of the borrower filing bankruptcy. On one hand, it may appear that you will be a loser based on the offer. But, you have to analyze the possible cost of having your attorneys work on the case through to the point of bankruptcy and the possibility of realizing less on the assets if they are later sold under a forced bankruptcy liquidation sale (including legal fees).

4.11 LESSONS TO LEARN IN PREVENTING PROBLEM LOANS

Some of the caution signs that may protect you from problem loans are as follows:

- Lenders need to be cautious about being lured into lending small amounts at first to borrowers which may even be repaid, and then becoming overly committed later based on larger loan requests which are *not* paid.
- Bankers typically act very slowly in liquidating collateral which has often deteriorated.
- Equity capital is often not raised soon enough to assist or alleviate a problem.

• The borrower and banker are characteristically and frequently not on the same wave length as the risk looks different to the banker than to the borrower who will not admit to himself the company has a real problem.
• The loan officer may not know his or her customer and business.
• The banker must be able to carefully analyze the problem, evaluate alternatives, and prepare a plan of action, and then be proficient in monitoring the progress toward the planned objective.
• External factors: The banker must constantly be aware of the changing economic climate locally and even nationally, and monitor the borrower's position within the marketplace; he or she needs to keep abreast of changing laws and regulations within the banking industry along with any unforeseen circumstances, e.g., natural disasters or events that could impact the business.
• Internal factors: The banker needs to know the impact from competition on the borrower's business; he or she needs to be sensitive if the borrowers are losing their objectivity, indulging in bad habits, or perhaps becoming careless in managing the business.
• The bank must move quickly to protect its rights once a bankruptcy is filed. Do not make it easy for those who file a petition.

Some of the ways that the banker may prevent future problem loans include the following:

• First of all, the loan officer should have adequate training and experience in the type of loans he or she will be granting and servicing; if there is a lack thereof, officers need to be given ample time to obtain training before being allowed to extend such loans independently within a bank approved lending limit.
• The banker should always determine whether all the five *C's* of credit have been met, e.g., character, capital, capacity, conditions, and collateral, and that they know the borrower is capable of managing a business profitably.
• Officers should thoroughly analyze and investigate the company, principals, management, and market—good background checks in these respects are important.
• Newcomers and veterans should employ sound credit fundamentals and principles and always obtain the assistance of other

experts when necessary; therefore, the loan officer should not be careless in granting and documenting the loan and not be timid about seeking advice.

• Good loan officers always know and monitor how loan proceeds are going to be used to benefit the business.

• An officer always knows the borrower's primary source of repayment and as a cautionary measure he or she will arrange for secondary and tertiary sources of repayment.

• Good loan officers know the sufficiency of their collateral, including its current liquidation value, sources to liquidate it, and ability to dispose of it

• A good loan officer makes sure the loan is documented properly and does not use the wrong forms, and makes sure that no blank spaces in documents remain, that new documents are drawn, and that existing ones are initialed properly by corrections.

• A good loan officer verifies that the signers, if a corporation, have the authorized capacity to execute documents, and that the appropriate acknowledgments are provided and completed.

• Servicing loan officers make sure that documents are properly recorded and filed in the right jurisdiction(s).

• A good loan officer knows when filings expire and when proper names are missing or spelled incorrectly, and can spot when collateral and legal descriptions are inconsistent in documents.

• Careful loan officers do not forget the loan once it is booked—they will continue to monitor the relationship, e.g., periodic reviews of financial information; periodic plant visits including exams of the borrower's books and records, if necessary; periodic visits with management to review plans and objectives; and periodic credit and trade industry checks. This all may take more time and effort, but certainly to be a successful lender it is necessary. This whole process may also be rewarding as a good source of new and continued business.

General Procedures in Maintaining Safe Loans

The loan officer also needs to undertake a number of the following precautions in maintaining a safe loan portfolio:

• Never request collateral, a guaranty, or an endorsement you do not need, but once you do, do not waive the requirement or wait to the next maturity.

• Never wait until the "next time" or until the next maturity to raise a rate which is justified now.

• Do not gamble on the stock market by making or continuing to renew loans on thin margins or by anticipating the price will increase, especially pertaining to those loans that are undermargined by security values and involving those borrowers who have virtually no financial substance or supplementary means to repay their debt.

• Never make a business loan on the strength of personal endorsers or guarantors, and if you do, do not fail to evaluate their financial statements as thoroughly as you would the statements of a borrower, including their reasonable ability to repay all personal debt, plus any other debt they endorse or guarantee or for which they are contingently liable.

• Keep in mind that business loans are generally paid from three sources: the conversion and sale of assets to cash; from earnings or other capital sources; and from rollover of debt to another creditor.

• Always control the loan or credit relationship or it may control you.

• Beware of link financing, i.e., account balances placed in the bank to induce you to make the loan but which do not secure the debt and which are generally not in the borrower's name and which could be quickly and easily moved.

• Never make or continue to carry a loan against the assignment of accounts receivable without considering the risk of offsets, sales returns, allowances, credits memos, backcharges, concentrations, financially weak account debtors, or fictitious accounts; also remember to monitor collections.

• Always control ODs and uncollected funds approvals as carefully as you would control your new loan approvals, and focus on ODs and potential kiting patterns as frequently and regularly as you do on past-due loans.

• Never forget in lending to contractors that retainages and surety bonds are for the protection of the owner or prime contractors and not the bank—and that mechanics' and materialmen's liens and bonding company subrogation rights may come ahead of the bank's rights and claims on a job.

• Beware of lending against particularly heavy or specialized equipment on the merit of its cost value to the borrower, especially equipment that is used in a volatile industry.
• Be cautious, judicious, and even suspicious—the best defense against problem credits is a good offense and sense of circumspection. Have regular meetings with your borrower, its accountants, and other representatives—this could prove to be a real offensive advantage.
• Know your borrower. There is no such thing as a good loan to a bad manager. Special attention must be given to those companies that are experiencing exceptional growth, either from within, or by way of acquisitions. Many problems in this area are the direct result of inability of management to grow with the company. Adequate management depth is always necessary with any growth business.
• Once a problem is detected, a good loan officer takes timely action; a good loan officer is not reluctant to obtain legal counsel; does not fail to review his or her own portfolio constantly, and seeks help within the bank to do so, especially regarding potential problem loans. Mature officers admit when they may have a problem.

4.12 USE OF ATTORNEYS

When confronted with difficult decisions or situations, there may be a natural tendency on the part of loan officers and other bank personnel to call on or consult with an attorney. Lawyers should be used to make legal decisions, while the bank should have or develop the ability of loan officers to make sound business decisions. To do otherwise is unwise and costly. However, in situations where there is substantial risk, it is better to consult an attorney and pay a fee than to proceed improperly and possibly pay a larger fee later. Lawyers should be called for assistance when necessary to protect the bank, but whether an attorney is used or not, it is the responsibility of bank servicing loan officers to make sure that all their loans and supporting papers are properly prepared, executed, and recorded.

CHAPTER 5

BANKRUPTCY

5.01 GENERAL

Bankruptcy generally results because of continuous losses that deteriorate a company's financial condition to the point where it is unable to meet its obligations. In extreme cases, it may result from massive fraud or for other unusual reasons. The presence of a substantial amount of public debt can make it very hard to keep the problem out of a bankruptcy court. Before you force a company into involuntary bankruptcy, consider the risks the bank will run.

- Legal and accounting expenses.
- Raising of defenses on the part of the borrower.
- Potential exposure to lender liability lawsuits.
- Damage to a going concern, (e.g., customers lost, employees quit; the company's inability to liquidate assets at market values, and the vendors' refusal to extend trade credit).
- Risk that the court will make your loans inferior to other creditors (known as equitable subordination).

The bank will spend money and time, whether the borrower moves into a Chapter 11 reorganization or a Chapter 7 liquidation (voluntary or involuntary) where the borrower may lose complete control of the business operations.

5.02 SETTING OFF BEFORE BANKRUPTCY

If you have any reason to believe the debtor is going to file for bankruptcy, consider set-offs of any of its accounts, even if such is later deemed a preference. You will retain the right to set off against prepetition deposits and debts.

If a bankruptcy petition has already been filed, consider freezing the individual borrower's accounts, but do not charge these accounts as such charges may be deemed a preference and also be in violation of the automatic stay. There have been a lot of decided differences in cases pertaining to whether a bank may proceed to place a freeze on a debtor's account without sanction of the court once a stay goes into effect. This is another reason why it is a good habit to have contractual security interest language in your account cards, depository, and security agreements. As such, it can protect you against the challenge of the trustee for these funds which would then represent contractual and consensual security to the bank.

Business Accounts

Be extremely cautious before setting off accounts of a business, because certain funds may represent restricted balances or checks may be for restricted purposes. If payroll checks are being drawn on any of the borrower's accounts, they have a priority right ahead of any security interest right you may claim in the accounts. Setting off against such accounts could make you very vulnerable to a greater legal attack and retribution, not only on the borrower's and trustee's part, but on the individuals whose checks bounced.

The debtor's attorney will often recommend that it open a new bank account at another bank once an "order for relief" is entered. The debtor would then deposit all post petition deposits to such an account. Such an account would normally be out of the reach of the secured lender relative to its request for a set-off regarding prepetition debt.

Improvements Test

If you have set off against any of the debtor's accounts, such will be measured under the Bankruptcy Act's "improvements test" during the 90-day voidable preference period prior to the date of bankruptcy filing. Improvements to your bank's position because of such set-offs over this period will be subject to recapture as a preference. To determine this dollar amount of improvement to be returned, calculate the insufficiency between the outstanding loan and the debtor's aggregate funds on deposit at your bank, as of 90 days before the bankruptcy filing date, or the earliest date within the 90-day period that a set-off was made. Next, compare that initial insufficiency, if any, with the actual insufficiency on the date the set-off was initiated. To the extent the actual set-off insufficiency is less than the one on the 90th day, the difference ("improvement in position") may be recovered by the debtor or its trustee. An example may be helpful:

Let us say the 21st day prior to filing, the bank reduced its debt exposure from $2 million to $1 million by setting off against the borrower's accounts, compared to a hypothetical set-off on the 90th day prior to filing, which would have reduced the exposure from $2 to $1.7 million—or $.3 million. Thus, the $.7 million difference in set-offs between those dates is the actual improvement that the debtor or trustee should be able to recover.

In order to improve your set-off position without being penalized under the improvements test, consider these points. For starters, you have to know that you have a problem well in advance of a bankruptcy, or at least 90 days before any filing. Next, you need to know the patterns of the cash levels in accounts. This study probably has to be well developed before a bankruptcy filing. In conjunction with this you need to know all about any business cycle.

Other than understanding a business subject to cycles, it is fairly easy to determine consistent declines and growth. The problem credit will most likely be the one involved in business declines.

In this connection, observe when the borrower's account is at its peak, and set off at that time.

However, this may not get you the most money, depending on the debt and balance 90 days before filing. To the extent the account balances for the past 90 days have exceeded outstanding debt, the potential for full recovery could be good. Of course, with a weakening financial condition, this is unlikely.

If per chance, the present account balances are substantially higher than 90 days ago, the set-off will probably result in a bankruptcy filing with a probable return to the debtor or trustee of the improvement as seen in the example above.

If you do not set off, the bankruptcy court may treat the debtor's account as cash collateral for the benefit of the bank as of the filing date. This may be beneficial to the bank if it already had a contractual collateral interest in the debtor's operating accounts. For the debtor to then use such cash collateral account proceeds, it would have to seek permission from the bankruptcy court and in turn provide the lender with adequate protection.

Improvements Tests of Floating Lien Collateral

Creditor attorneys contend that there should not be a preference if creditors receive payment from their own collateral proceeds, i.e., collection of assigned-account debtor proceeds which is applied to the borrower's debt.

However, the same improvements test applies to the recapture of floating lien collateral, such as, receivables and inventory.

The calculation of collateral improvement under the 90-day voidable preference rule is similar to the set-off account recapture rule. Basically, the net exposure at the 90th day prior to the bankruptcy filing is compared to the improvement, if any, at the time of filing. If on the filing date, the creditor's position had been improved, that collateral improvement will be subject to the recapture rule. As an example, 90 days before bankruptcy the borrower owed the bank $2 million, while inventory and receivable collateral totalled $1.5 million, thus leaving a collateral insufficiency of $.5 million 90 days before bankruptcy. At the date of filing, total debt had been reduced down to $1.5 million. Assuming the collateral position still totals $1.5 million, the debtor's attorney may claim, pursuant to the improvements test, that the bank's lien position should be set aside to the extent of $.5 million. In other words, in view of the bank's improved debt to collateral position, the bank's lien may be limited to $1 million.

The improvements test could go back one year if you are deemed an insider in accordance with the Bankruptcy Reform Act. The insider rule applies anytime it is proven in court that the bank was in control of the borrower's business financially, or by way of stock or management control, including knowing that the borrower was insolvent during this one-year period. Extension of the preference recovery period for such an extended period of time is possible if the debtor's attorney can prove the bank's control of the debtor. While the Bankruptcy Reform Act does not clearly define "control," it does offer numerous examples, e.g., lender/director board members, voting stock control when substantial company shares are held as collateral (20 percent or more), control over what checks are paid and disbursements are to be made to other creditors. Unlike the 90-day preference presumption of insolvency, under the one-year insider preference period, the burden of proving insolvency and control rests with the debtor.

5.03 OTHER CONTROL ISSUES

Regarding control involving the issue of equitable subordination, the debtor will have to prove that by virtue of that control that the lender allegedly had over the debtor, the lender inequitably derived a benefit to the detriment of the other creditors of this particular debtor.

Onerous provisions in secured loan documentation pertaining to default and rights and remedies could also raise the issue of control, which may even be enhanced when you have tied up assets of an owner/guarantor to secure the company debt, as this would naturally give the lender a good deal of possible power and at least a strong psychological influence over the owner.

The key is not necessarily *having* this power, but *exercising* it to your advantage and to the detriment of the debtor. Therefore, the debtor's attorney possibly can prove control, based on how the lender exercised that power.

Should the debtor prove both insolvency and control, all debt payments made by the borrower and any set-offs against accounts or of collateral improvements received for the full year prior to the bankruptcy filing date may be recoverable by the debtor or trustee. So do not throw caution to the wind. Control may be more evident when the bank's misconduct regarding influence on a debtor (who is unable to pay its obligations from current assets) results in harm to third parties, thus heightening the risk of the bank being in control of a financially distressed debtor. Risks of control include the following:

- Subjection to the one-year preference period under the bankruptcy code whereby the transferee (the bank) will be considered an insider.
- Being joined in suits against the debtor on the theory that the lender "aided and abetted" in the alleged violation, thus being subject to the Racketeer Influenced and Corrupt Practices Organization Act (RICO).
- Being subject to "equitable subordination" under the Bankruptcy Reform Act. Again, if the bank as a secured lender is deemed in control of the debtor's operations, it will have a duty to deal fairly and impartially with the borrower and its unsecured creditors.
- Being faced with suits by trade creditors on a joint venture, fraud, or other theory whereby a direct recovery from the bank is sought rather than equitable subordination.

One interesting area of the control issue that may arise is the tort of willful and malicious lending of money. In this connection, you could face a tort under the following scenario.

As an example, let us say you loan money to a holding company—which is nothing more than a shell—to buy an operating company. Thus, the parent's only real asset is its ownership in the operating subsidiary that has intangible personal property and tangible personal and real property assets. In turn, you take an assignment of all the subsidiary's assets, while payment of the parent's loan is completely dependent on upstream dividends from the subsidiary to the parent. Under such an arrangement, you have placed the burden of debt repayment on the shoulders of the subsidiary, together with assigning all its assets to secure the parent's debt. Therefore, what is the consideration to the subsidiary for actually assuming the obligation secured by its assets?

Thus, the bottom line is that if the subsidiary files bankruptcy down the road, its own creditors (such as the unsecured trade) may be able to convince the court of your bank's gross inequitable conduct which could result in the bank debt being equitably subordinated to the subsidiary's other creditors' debt.

Worse, if you actually put the loan in the subsidiary's name, a court could easily trace the liability to its balance sheet without any proportionate increase on the asset side, thus obviously from a prima facie standpoint not evidencing any benefit or consideration to the subsidiary relative to the loan proceeds.

A slightly different scenario may be applicable if, as an example, the seller carried back a note from the holding company for a partial amount of the sale which was in turn secured by the stock of the subsidiary company. In such instances, the bank should work towards an intercreditor agreement from the parent company's seller. If consummated, the intercreditor agreement should provide, among other things, that the seller holding the pledge would not exercise the stock voting powers for the purpose of placing the subsidiary into involuntary bankruptcy while any debt was still owed to the bank. Nor would it join in a petition or file its own petition to place the company into bankruptcy. Such agreements are not unusual in a sale involving a leveraged acquisition such as this one. Even if you were unable to prevent the seller from forcing the subsidiary into bankruptcy because of defaulting on its debt, with the intercreditor agreement having been executed by the seller prohibiting such action, the bank would have good cause and probably a valid claim for damages against the seller for taking such action. Whenever you have an intercreditor agreement, and you proceed to repossess or foreclose on your collateral and in turn liquidate it, make sure you comply with a commercially reasonable sale. The sale may often be challenged by other creditors.

Another way a lender can become entrapped and become subject to an equitable subordination is reflected in the following example.

Let us say the owner of Company A also owns the controlling interest in Company B which is free of bank debt, but has substantial unsecured trade obligations. The debtor, Company A, needs to borrow additional funds for its survival as it is struggling.

So the owner agrees to sell its controlling interest in Company B to the minority owner. However, to acquire ownership of the remaining stock the minority owner has to be willing to encumber all the assets of the company to the lender for the seller's additional debt.

Now, while the minority owner receives consideration in the form of the additional shares, Company B itself does not receive any benefit while pledging all its assets.

In such a case, if Company A eventually fails and the lender repossesses or forecloses on Company B's assets—forcing it into bankruptcy—the unsecured creditors of Company B may have a valid claim of equitable subordination against the lender of Company A.

Bulk Sales

One more area where a question may arise is whether the above transactions were subject to the Bulk Sales Act since acquisitions may be accomplished by acquiring assets or stock. If there is no bulk sales of business assets but only stock acquisitions, then these laws do not apply.

As a lender, you may be better off with an asset acquisition, rather than with a stock acquisition. A "bootstrap" stock acquisition (i.e., one in which the borrower does not put up any money, but rather accomplishes the acquisition entirely on the basis of debt financing) may allow easier identification of insolvency based on a balance sheet net worth test versus the fair market values of acquired assets being higher than book values, which could be transposed into the value of the new company under an asset acquisition.

If you finance an asset acquisition, you must give bulk sales notices to inventory creditors and other parties of interest regarding inventory items and other goods for sale or lease. There are no bulk sales requirements pertaining solely to sales of equipment. If equipment is part of a sale involving inventory, then it is subject to the "Bulk Sales" Act. Other creditors, as a rule, do not generally respond to bulk transfer notices, which should make this task even easier.

In assessing the question of control, a risk-reward ratio should be determined. As a general rule, control and the appearance of control should be avoided unless a substantial benefit can be obtained or a material risk avoided.

5.04 PROOF OF CLAIM

Once a bankruptcy has occurred, always file a "proof of claim" with the court even if not required, as this will assure and verify that your claim is of record.

For larger debts, have your attorney review and file the document; always list your claims and the value of any collateral. Make sure it is properly completed and signed. Attach appropriate evidence of your collateral interest, such as a security agreement or note which evidences the bank's collateral interest and required writings on which your claim may be founded. File within the proper time frame, depending on the case. Generally, no fee is charged for filing a "proof of claim."

Remember to include other allowable costs, for example, the attorney's fees (if the loan is determined to be oversecured), the outstanding debt, and the unpaid interest. The only time in the writer's opinion when you will not have to file a proof of claim is in a Chapter 7 "no assets" case where your claim is unsecured. A standard form for a "no asset" case is seen in Exhibit C.

EXHIBIT C
No Assets—Do Not File a Claim

United States Bankruptcy Court

For the ________ District of ______________
Manchester, Missouri

In re:

Debtor's Name(s) Case No. _________

Debtor

Social Security Number(s)

ORDER FOR MEETING OF CREDITORS AND FIXING TIMES FOR FILING OBJECTIONS TO DISCHARGE AND FOR FILING COMPLAINTS TO DETERMINE DISCHARGEABILITY OF CERTAIN DEBTS, COMBINED WITH NOTICE THEREOF AND AUTOMATIC STAY

EXHIBIT C (*Continued*)

To the debtor, his creditors, and other parties in interest:

An order for relief under 11 U.S.C. Chapter 7 having entered on a petition filed by (or against)
Name of Debtor(s) (Address)
of
whose lawyer is (Name, address, and phone)
on (Date), it is ordered, and notice is hereby given, that:

1. A meeting of creditors pursuant to 11 U.S.C. 341 (a) shall be held at (Creditors Meeting Address) on (Date) at (Time) o'clock P.M.
2. The debtor shall appear in person (or, if the debtor is a partnership, by a general partner, or, if the debtor is a corporation, by its president or other executive officer) at that time and place for the purpose of being examined.
3. (If the debtor is an individual) (Date) is fixed as the last day for the filing of objections to the discharge of the debtor.
4. (If the debtor is an individual) (Date) is fixed as the last day for the filing of a complaint to determine the dischargeability of a debt pursuant to 11 U.S.C. 523 (c).

You are further notified that:

The meeting may be continued or adjourned from time to time by notice at the meeting, without further written notice to creditors.

At the meeting the creditors may file their claims, elect a trustee as permitted by law, (if appropriate) designate a person to supervise the meeting, elect a committee of creditors, examine the debtor, and transact such other business as may properly come before the meeting.

As a result of the filing of the petition, certain acts and proceedings against the debtor and his property are stayed as provided in 11 U.S.C. 362 (a).

(If the debtor is an individual) If no objection to the discharge of the debtor is filed on or before the last day fixed therefor as stated in subparagraph 3 above, the debtor will be granted his discharge. If no complaint to determine the dischargeability of a debt under clause (2), (4), or (6) of 11 U.S.C. 523 (a) is filed within the time fixed therefor as stated in subparagraph 4 above, the debt may be discharged.

The date of the Discharge Hearing will be announced at the 341 meeting of creditors.

EXHIBIT C (*Concluded*)

If it appears from the schedules of the debtor that there are no assets from which a dividend may be paid, creditors will be so notified and given an opportunity to file their claims. Unless the court extends the time, any objection to the debtor's claim of exempt property (Schedule B-4) must be filed with 15 days after the above date set for the meeting of creditors. (Name) of (Address and phone) has been appointed interim trustee of the estate of the above named debtor.

YOU ARE HEREWITH NOTIFIED, pursuant to 11 U.S.C. 554, 11 U.S.C. 363b, and 11 U.S.C. 102, that the trustee may sell all nonexempt property of the estate in which there is equity for the estate and may abandon all property that is burdensome to the estate. Any creditor who desires a hearing on such action must file a written request for hearing with the Court before the conclusion of the meeting of creditors above referred to; otherwise the trustee's action will be deemed approved and granted.

P ____ pages	Requests for copies of Petition (P), Statement of
S ____ pages	Affairs (S), Schedule A (A), and Schedule B (B)
A ____ pages	should be sent to the Clerk of the Court. Enclose
B ____ pages	payment of .50 per page. The number of pages
	is indicated at left. Address appears below.

Dated __________ of (Name of Clerk) United States

Bankruptcy Court and Courthouse Address

In order that your proof of claim is complete in every respect, make sure it includes these details.

- Claimant's (bank's) name with proper authorization given to bank officer signing the document and acting on behalf of the claimant.
- Amount of indebtedness and interest owed, including any allowable attorney's fees the bank has incurred.
- Consideration granted the borrower for debt evidenced in the form of a promissory note.
- Attachment of letter, and a loan or security agreement.
- Indication that no judgment has been rendered on this claim.
- Indication that the amount of all payments on this claim have been credited and deducted for the purpose of making this claim.

• Indication that this claim is not subject to any set-off or counterclaim.
• Evidence that the undersigned bank officer on behalf of the bank claims a secured or unsecured interest based on above points, e.g., promissory note, letter or loan, or security agreement.

These are the basic requirements of the proof of claim's contents besides the above mentioned items. As a matter of practice or depending on state requirements, mail two copies of the proof of claim with a cover letter to the bankruptcy court of the jurisdiction handling the case, requesting the filing of your claim and the return of one stamped copy evidencing receipt of the claim. A sample copy of a proof of claim is illustrated in Exhibit D.

EXHIBIT D
Proof of Claim

United States Bankruptcy Court

For the ________ District of ____________

In re*

Case No. ________

Debtor*

PROOF OF CLAIM

1. (If claimant is an individual claiming for himself) The undersigned, who is the claimant herein resides**
(If claimant is a partnership claiming through a member) The undersigned, who resides at**
is a member of , a partnership composed of the undersigned and
of** and
doing business at**
and is authorized to make this proof of claim on behalf of the partnership.

Note: Penalty for presenting fraudulent claim. Fine of not more than $5,000 or imprisonment for not more than 5 years or both-Title 18, U.S.A., 152.
* Includes all names used by debtor within last 6 years.
** State Post Office address.

EXHIBIT D (*Continued*)

(If claimant is a corporation claiming through an authorized officer) The undersigned, who resides at**
is the of
a corporation organized under the laws of
and doing business at**
and is authorized to make this proof of claim on behalf of the corporation.

(If claim is made by agent) The undersigned, who resides at**
, is the agent of
, of** , and is
authorized to make this proof of claim on behalf of the claimant.

2. The debtor was, at the time of the filing of the petition initiating this case, and still is indebted (or liable) to this claimant, in the sum of $
3. The consideration for this debt (or ground of liability) is as follows:
4. (If the claim is founded on writing) The writing on which this claim is founded (or a duplicate thereof) is attached hereto (or cannot be attached for the reason set forth in the statement attached hereto).
5. (If appropriate) This claim is founded on an open account, which became (or will become) due on , as shown by itemized statement attached hereto. Unless it is attached hereto or its absence is explained in an attached statement, no note or other negotiable instrument has been received for the account or any part of it.
6. No judgment has been rendered on the claim except
7. The amount of all payments of this claim has been credited and deducted for the purpose of making this proof of claim.
8. This claim is not subject to any set-off or counter-claim except
9. No security interest is held for this claim except

(If security interest in property of the debtor is claimed) The undersigned claims the security interest under the writing referred to in paragraph 4 hereof (or under a separate writing which (or a duplicate of which) is attached hereto, or under a separate writing which cannot be attached hereto for the reason

EXHIBIT D (*Concluded*)

set forth in the statement attached hereto). Evidence of perfection of such security interest is also attached hereto.

10. This claim is a general unsecured except to the extent that the security interest, if any, described in paragraph 9 hereof is sufficient to satisfy the claim.

(If priority is claimed, state the amount and basis thereof.)

11. This claim is filed as a(n) (unsecured) (secured) (priority) claim.

$______________
Total Amount Claimed

Claim Number
(For Office Use Only)

Name of Creditor:______________
(Print or Type Full Name of Creditor)

Dated: Signed:______________

Comments (Use this space for additional information):

5.05 OTHER BANKRUPTCY CONSIDERATIONS

Depending on the circumstances and the type of bankruptcy that is being filed, always review the statement of affairs and schedules the debtor submits to the court. Also, review the debtor's plan if one has been submitted. Next, you and/or your attorneys need to review your loan documentation, including credit and collateral files, to determine how you should proceed with handling the case. Make sure you have completed the proper internal forms and checklists, which is covered in more detail elsewhere, in order to monitor your cases. Much of the factual information on cases may be found in notices from the bankruptcy court.

Next, you should make a comparison of the most recent debtor financial statements, including schedules and any tax returns you have in your credit files, against the statement of affairs and schedules or plans as submitted by the debtor to the court with its petition.

In this connection, you need to look for inconsistencies and discrepancies, such as assets appearing on the statements the bank holds, while not being revealed in those submitted to the court. In those instances, debtors could have misrepresented their position to the bank or possibly sold assets between the time your statements were prepared versus the ones submitted to the court.

If you can prove false financial statements were submitted to you, it would be grounds for an exception to discharge. If the debtors sold assets, they would have to prove where and how the proceeds were received and used. When the debtor used the proceeds to pay another debt within the last 90 days, this could be voided as a preference by a trustee.

Check for the value of any collateral you hold as indicated in the bankruptcy schedules; if you do not agree with the value, state what you believe is the value and your basis for it. If the collateral consists of goods, verify the insurance coverage.

After reviewing all these matters, it may then behoove you to call the debtor's attorney in order to correct any omissions, discrepancies, inconsistencies, or differences that can be easily resolved. This may pertain to listing collateral that was not included, or if it was included, it more than likely was given an incorrect value. Thus, perhaps amending the schedules or plan regarding these differences can be accomplished.

Should the attorney refuse to make an amendment, have your own attorney file a motion of objection or complaint.

If you can resolve any differences with the debtor's attorney and have already filed a "proof of claim" yourself, you can always prepare for the first creditors' meeting yourself, unless you think you will be more comfortable having your attorney present. Your attorney may be better able to serve you if you have any valid reasons for contesting or objecting to the bankruptcy.

Also, check on any exposure you could face during the debtor's insolvency proceedings limiting your perfected security interest up to 60 days after the commencement of any insolvency proceedings or expiration of your filed financing statement, or 60 days after any confirmation of a plan. Make sure that a debtor's Chapter 11 reorganization plan explicitly preserves and continues the lender's perfected security interest and that this is acknowledged. In addition, if the debtor's place of business is moved or it moves your collateral to another county or state, file a new financing statement in order to retain priority over other creditors or subsequent collateral purchasers.

Bankruptcy matters are handled by federal courts in the jurisdiction where the debtor's principal residence (domicile), or principal place of business is located. Furthermore, the debtor must have had this residence or principal place of business within that federal judicial district for either six months preceding the filing of the petition, or at least for the majority of that time versus any other judicial district, within the preceding six months.

Creditor Meetings

The first creditors' meeting will usually be held within a few weeks or up to several months after a petition is filed, depending on the caseload.

When you attend the first meeting, always prepare a set of questions to be answered by the debtor. You may find yourself limited for time because of the heavy caseloads in many courts these days, so you better be ready to take advantage of whatever time you have.

Ask basic questions that may disclose a discrepancy in the borrower's response to questions versus what was reported in schedules, which could result in an objection to discharge of the case because of possible fraud, thus continuing the borrower's obligation to make payment. If the debtor admits the collateral was and still is being used for purposes other than what was authorized under the security agreement or than that which was intended when the original loan was granted, the bank may be warranted in requesting adequate protection from the court. This protection may come in the form of additional collateral, or a larger payment, or shorter payout of its debt.

Also, determine if a fraudulent conveyance has occurred whereby the debtor may have transferred or conveyed certain assets improperly within a one-year period of filing bankruptcy. This may be determined if your collateral is in another party's possession or sold to them, not in the ordinary course of business.

Further, question the debtor on previously submitted statements pertaining to assets disclosed and values, along with details on income and expenses. Always verify and check debt to individuals, especially those being exhibited (ostensibly owed to family members) to determine if figures are not only real but accurate. Inaccurate amounts could result in an objection to discharge of the case or at least allow for a possible larger distribution to creditors.

If goods are not disposed of or used in the ordinary course of business or sold on an arm's length basis without fair consideration, or assets are not replaced in appropriate or equivalent amounts, investigate what has happened.

If you feel the assets acting as your collateral have been improperly disposed of, conveyed, transferred or are missing, or may have disappeared for one reason or another, you may file an adversary action to deny the debtor a discharge in bankruptcy or at least prevent a discharge of the debt secured by those assets. Therefore, if a debtor attempts to transfer this property with an intent to hinder, delay, or defraud its creditors during the one-year period after filing bankruptcy, this would be grounds for not discharging the debt. This is similar to a fraudulent transfer under the federal Fraudulent Transfer Act.

The best place to begin your investigation is to determine whether any assets were transferred to family members or trusts.

Test of Solvency

You may be exposed to the 90-day preference period under the Bankruptcy Reform Act in view of the fact that the code permits the debtor to seek the return of all payments made to unsecured creditors during the 90-day period immediately proceeding the filing date based on a balance sheet test of solvency. Insolvency, based on a balance sheet test, exists when a company's debts, including its contingent liabilities, exceed its assets at "fair valuation." If it is deemed the debtor has virtually no assets to pay its debts or the business cannot continue operating and is insolvent, the case should be moved to a Chapter 7 after which time a discharge should be granted the debtor. A sample "Discharge of Debtors" form is seen in Exhibit E.

There is a sequence of creditor meetings that is normally followed in accordance with Section 341 of the Bankruptcy Reform Act:

- The date and time of meetings are usually set by a clerk or U.S. trustee. This is provided creditors through a standard notice by the clerk or trustee. The notice is sent to all creditors of record as furnished by the debtor and to any other interested parties who have generally made ample advance requests for such notices.
- Meetings are normally conducted by appointed trustees to such cases. The format for Chapter 7 and 11 cases are usually the same. However, Chapter 7 meetings are usually shorter and attended by fewer creditors because naturally these are straight liquidation cases often leaving very little recovery potential for the creditors.
- Regarding Chapter 13 cases, which is a general payout arrangement by individuals or proprietors with their creditors, a standing Chapter 13 trustee, appointed by the bankruptcy court, may generally handle all such cases as a routine matter of course. The debtor's statement or proposed repayment plan will be scrutinized by creditors who attend the meeting. These creditors will be given the opportunity to object to any of the plan's provisions. Negotia-

EXHIBIT E—Discharge of Debtors

United States Bankruptcy Court

For the ________ District of ____________

In re:

Name of Debtor(s)* Case No. ________

In appearing that the persons named above have filed a petition commencing a joint case under title 11, United States Code on ____________, that an order for relief was entered under Chapter 7 and that no complaint objecting to the dis-

EXHIBIT E (*Concluded*)

charge of the debtors was filed within the time fixed by the court (or that a complaint objecting to discharge of one or both of the debtors was filed and, after due notice and hearing, was not sustained, it is ordered that

1. The above-named debtors be and they hereby are released from all dischargeable debts.
2. Any judgement heretofore or hereafter obtained in any court other than this court be and it hereby is null and void as a determination of the personal liability of the debtors with respect to any of the following:
   (a) debts dischargeable under 11 U.S.C. 523;
   (b) unless heretofore or hereafter determined by order of this court to be nondischargeabe, debts alleged to be excepted from discharge under clauses (2), (4) and (6) of 11 U.S.C. 523 (a);
   (c) debts determined by this court to be discharged under 11 U.S.C. 523.
3 All creditors whose debts are discharged by this order and all creditors whose judgments are declared null and void by paragraph 2 above be and they hereby are enjoined from commencing, continuing or employing any action, process or act to collect, recover or offset any such debt as a personal liability of the debtors, or from property of the debtors, whether or not discharge of such debt is waived.

Dated __________

BY THE COURT

____

Bankruptcy Judge

----

* Include here all names used by Debtor(s) within last 6 years.

tions will often be encouraged by the trustee to obtain an immediate solution and approval of the plan.

• Questions at meetings are usually closely controlled and are often not allowed by noncreditors who attend. At the first meeting, questions pertaining to anticipated or pending litigation are generally not allowed, including depositions of debtors. Often nothing happens unless someone objects. However, the debtor is under oath and the meeting is held in order to give creditors an opportunity to ask questions of the debtor.

• Questioning is often directed to the debtor-prepared Statement of Affairs and supplemental schedules and often involves their accuracy and validity.

Debtors are usually allowed three basic choices in responding to questions: they may reply in complete detail; or they may refuse to answer the question in which case a ruling may be made whether the question is appropriate and should be answered or not. If the ruling is in favor of the creditor and the debtor still refuses to answer the question, legal remedies may be used to obtain a response to the question. Even if the ruling to a negative response to answer the question is in favor of the debtor, the creditor can still pursue a response through legal proceedings, which then may have to be addressed at a later date under a different hearing.

The third response to any questioning of the debtor may be by "taking the fifth amendment," which is rare. When it does occur, it is often anticipated, based on the facts of the case, especially when the debtor may be subject to criminal violations. These instances will normally be referred to the U.S. District Attorney's office and the FBI, if they are not already involved in the case. Thus, debtors in these situations may be subject to investigation and ultimate prosecution by the U.S. Justice Department.

Chapter 11 Meetings

Oftentimes, there will only be one meeting of the creditors regarding Chapter 7 and 13 cases while there may be numerous meetings involving Chapter 11 reorganization cases.

These additional Chapter 11 meetings often go on to allow participants the opportunity to question the debtor regarding progress and results in preparing a plan of reorganization. Creditor meetings vary in different states and districts.

In respect to individual borrowers, you should also press for reaffirmation of the debt when feasible, especially when the borrower holds collateral it needs, and when collateral has questionable or rapidly depreciating value, making it difficult to liquidate. When possible, arrange for the borrower to voluntarily turn the collateral over to the bank in case it rescinds its reaffirmation agreement within the 60-day rescission period.

Collateral Protection and Plan Rules

When a business borrower moves into voluntary or involuntary bankruptcy, you need to determine how to be assured the collateral is protected and cared for. This becomes paramount in the case of collateral exposure, deterioration, or imminent liquidation.

To gain access, the bank must petition the court to lift the stay in order to have the collateral abandoned to it. Or, the bank may opt for a court order to repossess goods. An automatic stay goes into effect from the time of the bankruptcy petition filing, not from the time you are notified. This creates an automatic lien enforcement, which means you cannot do anything with the collateral from the time of filing until the court lifts the stay.

The bank may also have to prove the risk and exposure to the collateral to reclaim it. Therefore, at the first hearing it could be to your advantage to move for an abandonment of the collateral when you believe the debtor cannot continue operating, or when you will be substantially exposed by a loss in collateral value as it may deteriorate or at least continue to depreciate while the borrower retains it. Otherwise, the borrower may legally be able to retain possession of the collateral under an extended stay while it continues operating as a "debtor in possession." Furthermore, you may be faced with a "cram-down" plan presented by the debtor that may be accepted by the judge (this plan has to comply with special "cram-down" rules).

It may become incumbent on the bank to arrange for security or guard service, once it takes possession of certain goods. A bankruptcy trustee may move to upset your lien position if there is a contention over improperly perfected collateral. The bank can move for a lifting of the "automatic stay" so it can foreclose or repossess its collateral for various reasons, e.g., a debtor in default who is not meeting payments.

Such rules are generally designed to induce all classes of creditors, whether secured or unsecured claims or capital note holders, to accept a plan—voluntarily. Under certain conditions, a reorganization plan may be confirmed, despite the dissent of creditors. However, the class of various creditors should have a bearing on the outcome of the plan, based on their respective positions, without forcing a judicial "cram down." If this judicial power must be invoked, the general requirements on which a plan may be accepted are that "it does not discriminate unfairly, and is fair and equitable with respect to each class of claims or interests," according to creditor makeup.

Unsecured Creditors' Committees

If you are an unsecured creditor, you may have to decide whether you should serve on the official unsecured creditors' committee, assuming you are one of the seven largest unsecured creditors involving a Chapter 11 reorganization plan. The seven largest creditors typically include one or more bank lenders. According to the Bankruptcy Reform Act, the seven largest unrelated creditors of the borrower are entitled to be named to the committee. In fact, banks are often strongly encouraged to join such committees based on the perception that it is a good source of potential future financing of debtors in possession, especially those who continue to use bank collateral. Besides being perceived as having mature financial and business judgment, banks are also perceived as being understanding. Being on this committee entitles the lender to expense reimbursements, to have a vote in the choice of legal counsel, and to use accountants and other outside professionals chosen to represent the committee.

Membership on a committee also entails responsibility. As a committee member and an officer of the bankruptcy court, you will represent all classes of unsecured creditors—not just your own bank's interests.

Before you join any committee, however, make sure it is to your advantage and that your interests are compatible with other unsecured creditor committee members. When it is not in your best interests, decline to serve and go it alone.

It probably would not be good to serve when the majority of the committee would constantly be advocating positions that you would not support or vice versa. If you decide to serve, consider the time commitment as well. If this does not fit your schedule, based on other priorities and commitments, pass up the responsibility.

5.06 INITIATING A PETITION

Creditors can initiate an involuntary Chapter 7 against an individual or business debtor. They can also initiate an involuntary Chapter 11 case against a business debtor. Debtors themselves can file voluntary petitions. For creditors to force a debtor into bankruptcy under either of these two chapters it must be shown that:

- Creditors' claims in the aggregate are at least $5,000 greater than the value of any security, and
- If there are 12 or more creditors, at least three must agree to force bankruptcy, or any single creditor can force bankruptcy when creditors total 11 or fewer.

Moreover, creditors filing involuntary petitions under Chapter 11 must show that the debtor is generally not making payments as they become due, or that a custodian has been appointed for, or has taken possession of, the debtor's property within 120 days of filing. Nonprofit corporations are not subject to involuntary petitions.

Before getting into various bankruptcy cases, there may be instances when the bank may not necessarily have to charge off the debt because a debtor has filed bankruptcy. This usually applies to borrowers who continue to pay their debt in a timely manner.

The author handled an oil production operator which filed bankruptcy under a reorganization plan. The operator continued to pay the bank, which had all the oil well collateral and runs tied up, while he paid only minimal amounts to the unsecured creditors, despite owing them a substantial amount in excess of the bank debt.

Those creditors finally settled for a small percentage on the dollar. But the bank was paid out in whole.

Thus, the bank never had to charge off the debt, and the bankrupt was finally discharged. The oil company came out of the Chapter 11 after six years.

Also, if the debtor exempts the collateral and reaffirms the debt, the bank may not have to charge off the debt.

5.07 BANKRUPTCY CHAPTERS

The following sections contain information on several bankruptcy chapters, ranging from Chapter 11—which aims to reorganize businesses—and, permitting continued operation, to Chapter 7 liquidations.

Chapter 11

There may be numerous reasons to force a workout credit into bankruptcy including the following.

- In a Chapter 11 of the Bankruptcy Code, dissenting creditor groups may become more cooperative when bound by a plan or reorganization.
- If the debtor is subject to a substantial and burdensome real estate lease, the lease could be rejected and any resulting damage claim limited while the company is in bankruptcy.
- By being placed in bankruptcy, it may be easier to get the business sold or liquidated, especially when the borrower is insolvent. Benefits to a senior secured creditor such as the bank may include the fact that most of the losses will most likely be incurred by junior creditors.
- There is a securities registration exemption while a company is in bankruptcy and "safe harbor" protection from antifraud laws for those soliciting to acquire the business in good faith.
- The automatic stay allows debtors to use, sell, or lease collateral while awaiting a plan, and prevent disruption by other creditors.
- The amount and risk of claims against the lender during the workout period should decline once the debtor is in bankruptcy.
- New credit can be extended by the secured lender with a priority over an intervening lien while the debtor is in bankruptcy, e.g., a

partly completed construction project with intervening mechanics' liens filed.

• Transfers of the debtor's property may be recovered, based on laws involving preferences and fraudulent transfers.

Various other means to preserve the company's status quo and promote equality while in bankruptcy should be present.

Once a Chapter 11 is filed, the automatic stay goes into effect. The borrower may continue operating the business, pending an entry of an order for relief, which is the order placing the debtor in bankruptcy. Therefore, the debtor may continue to acquire, use, and dispose of property as if the case had never commenced. However, filings jeopardize normal operations. Vendors often stop furnishing supplies and creditors cut off advances.

The period between the time of filing the bankruptcy petition and the time this order is issued is considered the "gap" period. Debts created by the borrower during the "gap" period and in the ordinary course of business will still be treated as prepetition debts.

The one action you may take as a secured creditor during this waiting period is to petition the court to appoint an interim trustee to operate the business, based on the necessity of preserving estate property or preventing loss. If a trustee is appointed, the debtor can still regain possession of its property by posting a bond. Also, if a trustee is appointed and an involuntary petition is later denied, the petitioning creditors can be held liable by the debtor for any damages resulting from the trustee taking over and operating the business.

The bank's collateral other than cash may be sold, used, or leased by the debtor or trustee in the ordinary course of business without notice to the bank. Only if such noncash collateral is going to be used outside the ordinary course of business should the debtor notify you, thus allowing you the opportunity of a court hearing regarding such use of collateral.

Additionally, sale of the collateral, whether or not in the ordinary course of business, can be free and clear of your lien without your consent if one of the following conditions can be met.

• When the sale is authorized by the bankruptcy court.

• If the sale price exceeds the aggregate total of all the encumbrances.
• When you are forced by a court to accept cash satisfaction of your lien based on legal and equitable proceedings.
• If your claim is subject to a valid dispute such as a legal discrepancy of your collateral interest.

Initially you should file a claim. Your claim may be disputed while you will be stayed from liquidating any collateral or your claim may remain in a contingent status, in whole or in part, which is more apt to occur in Chapter 11 filings. Once you have determined the type of claim, make a decision early on how to deal with it. Remember, you do not have to file a Proof of Claim, if your claim has been properly listed by the debtor in its schedules, unless your claim has been scheduled by the debtor as disputed, contingent, or unliquidated.

Therefore, our advice is to always file when in doubt. Basically, the law allows you to file a Proof of Claim at any time before the date on which a "disclosure statement" is approved by the court.

In a bankruptcy reorganization—which is what establishing a Chapter 11 is all about—the debtor or trustee files a plan which attempts some type of compromise of the business's total indebtedness. Typically, certain unprofitable assets will be sold and the proceeds distributed among creditors. The healthy or potentially profitable segments of the business will continue to operate. The purpose of a reorganization is to retain the debtor as an on-going economic entity capable of generating income from which the creditors' claims have a better chance of receiving repayment than they would from a straight Chapter 7 liquidation. The debtor may even be allowed to sell certain assets, while in bankruptcy, to continue operating. One valuable asset that may be sold is any unencumbered executory contract where adequate future performance is assured.

One decision of great significance during the pre-plan period is that concerning the management of the Chapter 11 debtor.

Old management under an 11 will remain in control unless one or more parties of interest (creditors or others) convinces the court to replace management with a trustee.

Like everything else under the Bankruptcy Reform Act, leadership should be scrutinized and weighed cautiously and diligently. Obviously, if management has questionable character or a poor reputation, this should be an automatic reason for replacement. What may be harder to determine is their incompetence or lack of ability which may have led them into this trouble to begin with.

On the other hand, even the most competent trustee may require sufficient lead time to grasp the inner operational workings of the business and to adjust to the debtor's business and industry. Also, if the business entails too great a specialty, the trustee may never fully understand it.

If the court and the creditors understand the debtor's weaknesses and faults, perhaps with the proper committee supervision and oversight by the court, it may be better for the company to leave the existing management in place, rather than attempting to make too many changes which could prove disruptive.

Before you leave managers intact, make sure they are cooperative and willing to adjust and make changes and that they are responsive to your advice and communication. The writer has seen too many management teams continue the same old lifestyle of overspending and imprudence. Meanwhile, the corporate financial condition became critical. Sadly, these managers never recognized reality or accepted the fact that the company was close to being—or virtually was—insolvent. Seeing such a psychological pattern, this banker refused to extend post-petition financing to the bankrupt debtor in possession.

If you are convinced that the present management or the trustee may be able to get the business back on its feet, and that its future, if properly restructured, is bright, your bank and/or creditor's committee should consider extending post-petition financing. Make sure that the new money is loaned with reasonable assurance of repayment and supported with adequate margined collateral, and that any new advances will maximize recovery of any outstanding prepetition debt. Then, any new debtor in possession of post-petition financing should be worth the risk.

For a Chapter 11 reorganization plan to be accepted by a judge, it must be approved by two thirds of all of the debtor's creditors. If one half of the number of all classes of creditors, which make up at least two thirds of the total, can agree to a plan, the court will impose acceptance of the plan upon any dissenters.

Any filing of a petition under a Chapter 11 acts as an automatic stay against creditor foreclosures or repossessions. Debtors have to list all assets and liabilities in a disclosure statement.

If no trustee has been appointed, the debtor has the exclusive right to file a plan of reorganization within 120 days of the bankruptcy filing. In addition, the debtor has another 60 days to obtain acceptances of the plan. Thereafter (180 days), or if no plan has been drawn up by the debtor after the initial plan period of 120 days, creditors, stockholders, or other third parties of interest, (usually under committee agreement) can file their own proposed plan. On the other hand, when a trustee has been appointed by the court, a committee or other parties of interest may file as soon as they want from the date the trustee is named.

Extensions to file a plan may be authorized by the court for good cause. All creditors have a chance to vote on the plan. It is during the development stage that the various official and unofficial committees may have a positive impact on the plan terms and on future viability of the debtor. Management of the debtor or trustee should meet frequently with the committee concerning the changes it is making, along with its accomplishments in reaching goals.

A primary goal should be to work out and complete the plan as soon as possible for its acceptance by all the interested parties. Perhaps that will entail a great deal of negotiation. Keep in mind the advantages of working out such a plan quickly. Speed is to your advantage in several respects.

• It should improve the time value of money (shorten the time of tying up loan funds in an unproductive manner).
• It should cut down the expense of ongoing litigation, not only in money but time and effort, especially if the delay in the acceptance of the plan drags out over months and/or even years.
• To the extent a class of creditors is impacted adversely by a plan (to which they do not agree), they may be forced to accept the proposal ("crammed down") if they will not receive more than what they would have in a Chapter 7 liquidation, provided no junior creditor class receives anything without the approval of that senior class.

As an example, if the unsecured creditors do not approve the plan, they may have to accept a "cram down" order by the court; thus, they may get only whatever property remains after the debtor remits all payments due to secured creditors, based on the "absolute priority rule" under the Bankruptcy Reform Act. Therefore, it seems to be better to accept a reasonable amount, e.g., $.90 on the $1.00, while permitting a $.10 on the $1.00 distribution to a junior class of creditors, such as subordinated debenture holders, or capital note holders, which represents quasi-equity, or another equity class, for their prompt plan consent, thus reviving the debtor. This is not to say that total surrender to the unreasonable demands of junior creditors is acceptable, not only in the particular proceeding at hand but in other cases as well. However, remember that good common sense and judgment in negotiations is important for a fair compromise for all sides. Also, the circumstances of each case should have a bearing on the direction you take.

Take care to make the plan workable. One way to do this is by presenting the maximum perceived benefits to all parties whose acceptance is required in accordance with the Bankruptcy Reform Act. It is important to consider the obstacles; get all the parties of interest together by notifying them, presenting, and working out the proposed plan with them, and then soliciting and obtaining their consent. This may be particularly difficult where public debentures are held in street names or when Eurodebentures are involved. In accordance with bankruptcy creditor committees, requiring a 90 percent acceptance from a broad spectrum of creditor classes is probably expecting the impossible. Depending on the circumstances, a 66.66 percent approval vote from committee members may be the best you should require. Always attempt to structure the plan with viable alternatives, especially since creditors often have different views and interests in what they would like to see. Even members of the same class of creditors disagree with each other.

Some banks or other long-term institutional lenders often give up front-end cash payments for a potentially greater payout through equity appreciation, and/or for long-term debt positions. Others, such as unsecured trade creditors, may opt for a maximum amount of up-front cash.

By offering creditors alternatives—such as a combination of

packages that may include an early payout if they are willing to take a discount, or a larger offered recovery if they are willing to stay with the credit including the potential of possible full recovery—negotiations and approval of the plan may be easier. Keep in mind that the plan generally should not be too generous with front-end cash, or it could become too burdensome on the debtor, eventually forcing the debtor to again seek relief in the bankruptcy courts when the industry or business cycle experiences a slight downturn.

The plan must distinguish the differences between an interim (temporary) and final plan, and how the workout will affect the bank's position, particularly in these respects. Also, consider the following:

- If the bank's debt has matured or has been called, the agreement on the method of extension must be addressed, preferably in an additional letter agreement.
- Exact negotiations must be spelled out so that the bank may not be equitably estopped to assert an event of default.
- The final plan should spell out the reorganization or recapitalization relative to debt restructure over a long-term period which will allow the debtor reasonable prospects of business survival. The proposed operating plan and the debt restructure may require review by an outside investment banker, auditor, or consultant to be sufficiently "valid" to achieve creditor acceptance.
- Consider security laws and other potential problems in soliciting consents to a plan that is agreed upon outside of court. On the one hand, you may find it difficult to work with public debt holders as dissenting holders of public debt cannot be bound outside of the bankruptcy court. On the other hand, you may find it easier when dealing with closely held companies involving guarantors.

And when debt securities are being issued as part of the plan, compliance with the Trust Indenture Act may be necessary.

Be forewarned that if you do not finance the debtor in possession, the bankruptcy court may allow a new lender to enter the picture, even to the extent they may be given new collateral (in whole or in part) out of your potential source of other collateral. Hopefully the new lender will give you some form of adequate protection in the form of other collateral and/or cash equivalents.

One advantage of extending new credit is that it often can be conditioned upon the debtor's meeting previously established financial conditions. Such conditions should also call for a matching of new funds by other interested parties or creditors and for concessions on the part of other creditors. Concessions could consist of give-ups, stretch-outs, moratoriums, freezes, or subordinations on debt and collateral.

Misuse

A Chapter 11 debtor in possession may exercise certain powers (that is, to avoid certain things) through the trustee on behalf of the estate. Thus, the bank could be subject to a voidable transfer of collateral received prior to the filing of the bankruptcy petition. This normally results under the voidable preference rule whereby the debtor transfers its property within 90 days preceding the bankruptcy to a creditor involving antecedent debt while the borrower was insolvent, thus allowing the creditor to realize more against its debt than it would have received in a Chapter 7 liquidation if the transfer did not take place. Most transfers of the borrower's assets within the 90-day window will, therefore, be obviously closely scrutinized and thus avoided in bankruptcy.

This same voiding rule of transfers will reach out up to one year prior to a bankruptcy if the creditor is deemed an insider and against debtors if they are convicted under a fraudulent conveyance of property.

A fraudulent conveyance under Section 548 of the U.S. Bankruptcy Reform Act may be applicable if transfers of the borrower's properties were made with an "actual intent to hinder, delay or defraud" creditors, or if the transfer was for "less than its reasonably equivalent value," while the debtor was either insolvent, unreasonably undercapitalized, or when the borrower intentionally incurred debt beyond its ability to make repayment.

Another area that the bank must be cognizant of is the misuse of control that may prejudice other creditors—an area referred to as "equitable subordination." In instances where a violation is committed by the bank, its claim may be moved to a lower priority class of creditors. Several occurrences should be evidenced before the bank's claim would be equitably subordinated. The bank could be found guilty of inequitable conduct resulting in injury to other creditors, or perhaps it could be proved that the bank creates an unfair advantage for its benefit over other creditors. Or, perhaps there was collusion between the bank and the debtor to take unfair advantage of other creditors. There have even been cases where some unsecured open account creditors conspired with the debtor by taking notes and collateral for their obligations (and reduced their debt), knowing that the borrower was close to insolvency—while other unsecured creditors were not included in the renegotiations.

In addition, when the bank asserts a domineering and controlling posture over the borrower at the expense of other creditors, its debt position could be relegated to an equitably subordinated claim. This occurs mostly when the bank obtains additional collateral. Furthermore, if the bank is deemed in control of the borrower's operation, it could be found in violation of any one of a number of security laws, committed by the borrower. Indeed, banks have faced class action suits for allegedly injuring stockholders based on allegations they had control over the borrowing company prior to filing for bankruptcy.

Furthermore, the bank can be held liable to the borrower itself for detrimental control, resulting in damages to the company, for improper conduct or interference with its business affairs. To avoid being held liable, the bank must not act in bad faith by using its loan agreements to control the company to the latter's detriment, thus arbitrarily or purposely implementing certain controlling covenants and events of default.

Adequate Protection. The court must look closely at the issue of adequate protection as it reviews petitions by creditors and others regarding the lifting of automatic stays.

In fact, the court will not lift a stay unless the debtor can "adequately protect" the creditor's collateral in accordance with the Bankruptcy Reform Act. Adequate protection becomes significant when it is determined that the collateral has declined in value below the debt it secures. In these instances, the court either must lift the stay or insist that the debtor provide adequate protection from falling collateral values (such protection could be periodic cash payments or additional liens on unencumbered properties).

The court can approve adequate protection in the form of a replacement or an alternative lien, or can require that periodic payments be made on your debt during the case, or give you what is called an "indubitable equivalent" by giving you an equivalent in replacement collateral or equivalent cash for the loss of giving up your original collateral.[1]

When the debtor in possession seeks to sell the bank's collateral free and clear of its lien, the bank should in turn seek adequate protection. More often than not, this protection can be provided by having the lien attach to the proceeds of sale.

When the sale is imminent, the secured party usually must be notified, and it may bid on the property. If the bank obtains the property based on being the successful bidder, it has to offset its security interest or lien against the property at its bid price. However, the bank cannot offset its indebtedness secured by other collateral based on the purchase or bid price. Should the purchase price of the property exceed the specific debt it secures, the bank will be out the balance it pays over the related debt.

Relief from an automatic stay should be forthcoming if certain conditions can be met by the bank, which has a blanket lien on all the assets of the business, and can prove that:

- There is no equity in any of the personal or real property assets, including the collateral, during the time that debt far exceeds the liquidation value of such collateral.
- There is no prospect that the debtor can successfully reorganize within a reasonable period of time.

Exhibit F is an instruction format that may be used when presenting information to your attorneys in order to file a motion for relief of stay with the court.

The reorganization question allowing the debtor to continue operating may be the most difficult to deal with because this could become a somewhat subjective matter which often needs some amount of time to be worked out.

The only problem you might face is when the court still defers relief from the automatic stay (by giving you an unsecured claim with a super priority), despite the fact that you clearly show that the protection is inadequate. Banks have really faced a dilemma in recent times regarding adequate protection as authorized by the

---

[1] It is very questionable that many lenders or other creditors are receiving "indubitable equivalents" these days based on the cases the writer has analyzed.

EXHIBIT F
Instructions of Motion for Relief of Stay

To: (Name of attorneys and Address)

1. Provide an accurate and complete legal name of the debtor(s) whether individuals, partnerships, or corporations et cetera. Also, include domicile or principal residential address if an individual(s), or executive or main office street address if a business.
2. If you plan to proceed against any contingent obligors, i.e., co-makers, endorsers, and guarantors, relative to making demand and suit, please furnish their most current addresses.
3. The aggregate balance on all debtor loans including a breakdown on each particular debtor loan, reflecting those secured, cross pledged and unsecured as of the date of this notice is as follows:

A. Principal Balance of Debt $ ____________

$ ____________

(use other side if necessary) $ ____________

$ ____________

Total $ ____________

B. Interest through ______, is $ ____________

______, is $ ____________

______, is $ ____________

______, is $ ____________

Total $ ____________

C. Per diem from and after is $ ____________

$ ____________

$ ____________

$ ____________

D. Advances use for accruals, i.e., payroll, taxes, insurance etc.
$ ____________

E. Available escrow balance $ ____________

F. Amount of any escrow deficiency $ ____________

G. Late charges accrued $ ____________

H. Attorney's fees incurred to date $ ____________

4. The amount that would be necessary to bring total debt owed current $ ____________

EXHIBIT F (*Concluded*)

5. Non-monetary defaults including events of default under notes, security and loan agreements.
A. Date of default
B. Events of default
C. References to specific clauses, covenants, events of default in documents and agreements which have been violated.
6. Payment history
A. Dates of latest payments
B. Dates of requests and demands for payment
7. Your best estimate of given collateral values
8. Detail description you want repossessed or foreclosed
9. Names and addresses of other lienholders of debtor's assets and what they specifically have or hold as collateral including position, i.e., first or secondary liens, purchase money security interests, subordinations etc.
10. Any particular circumstances or situations lawyers need to be privy to, i.e., collateral abandonment, skip, lapsed insurance etc.

Name of Bank ____________________________
Name and Title of Officer ____________________________

courts because what they have received has been nothing as to what was expected, or for that matter, had any comparable value to what they had prior to filing.

Now, what if you seek relief, but because you have failed the improvements test, your position is exposed to a preference? In such circumstances, consider working off the preference by advancing post-petition financing. As an example, for every dollar that you advance to the debtor, you should be entitled to a credit, dollar for dollar, against any potential preference return of funds to the debtor. When a borrower files a Chapter 11, always compare the collateral values you show and the dates of such collateral values against the values and dates the borrower lists in its initial filing schedules. In particular, watch for significant differences and the reasons for such, and whether any damage or rapid deterioration has occurred. If such differences are prevalent, investigate to see if they are justifiable. Any improprieties—purposeful damage, destruction, or sabotage involving the condition of the collateral—could be grounds to deny the borrower's request for discharge. Or, the court can dismiss its proposal to continue operating under Chapter 11 protection.

If the borrower moves into a Chapter 11 proceeding, the court may allow it to continue operating as a debtor in possession or the court could appoint an independent outside trustee to operate the business, which could be determined based on the creditors' election.

On the other hand, an interim trustee will not ordinarily operate the business, but will take possession of all the debtor's property including bank accounts, and will continue to collect receivables and contract proceeds.

The Bankruptcy Reform Act does not allow for a prepetition floating lien to attach to property acquired once the bankruptcy petition is filed. Therefore, the borrower may continue to operate with these assets now owned by the bankruptcy estate.

However, proceeds acquired by the debtor after bankruptcy, but attributable to collateral acquired prior to bankruptcy, may still be deemed cash collateral and should remain subject to the bank's prepetition lien. On the other hand, a court hearing could side with the debtor by reducing the bank's interest in such cash proceeds, such as with post-petition costs incurred by the debtor in processing inventory which in turn enhanced the value of the prepetition inventory sold after the bankruptcy filing.

Cash Collateral

As defined by the courts, cash collateral is actually the working capital proceeds from inventory sales and leases, including contract rights that may have been converted to cash proceeds, e.g., checks, payments by sight drafts, or noncash proceeds such as accounts, contracts, chattel paper, and notes. Section 363 (a) of the Uniform Commercial Code defines cash collateral specifically as:

> Cash, negotiable instruments, documents of title, securities, deposit accounts or other cash equivalents whenever acquired in which the bankrupt estate and an entity other than the estate have an interest in including the proceeds, products, offsprings, rents, or profits of property subject to a security interest as provided in Section 552(b) of this title, whether existing before or after the commencement of a case under this title.

Banks, on the other hand, generally use the term *cash collateral* for actual cash proceeds or their equivalent already held in a restricted capacity or bank controlled account, while the courts use the term generically to define all the classes and types of cash collateral. Of course, the bank could have a lien on all such generic collateral, besides requiring the proceeds to be deposited in a cash collateral account.

The bank may be requested to extend post-petition financing. It has to determine whether to provide such financing, based on hopefully realizing a greater recovery. Worse, it could only be just putting good money after bad. If the bank's debt is not fully collateralized, it may be more amenable to advancing post-petition funds if the bank receives an enhancement in its collateral position.

When the bank does not expect any additional collateral, it would still have to decide whether it is in its best interests to assist the debtor to remain in business by making post-petition advances, anticipating that the debtor's financial condition will improve, thus, hopefully allowing the debtor to pay more on its debt than it could if the collateral were liquidated. Also, the bank should receive a security interest in "after acquired" collateral for the consideration of extending post-petition financing.

Financing after the Petition

If the bank decides to proceed with post-petition financing, it needs to build in some requirements in the agreement to its advantage. Here are some suggestions:

- Control all cash collateral proceeds through a lockbox.
- Obtain a lien on all hereafter floating collateral, including cross collateral interests in other assets owned by the borrower or from third parties, with priority over most administrative expenses.
- Make sure your pre-filing rights are not altered, and obtain a confirmation of payment on all obligations, as you could be negatively affected by additional orders from the bankruptcy court, and by subsequent filings of reorganization plans by the debtor or others.
- Receive adequate financial information and schedules, or any other such reports to continue properly monitoring the borrower's financial condition and collateral position.

• Require a condition in the agreement that your post-petition financing be paid in full if another lender enters the picture. If you lend post-petition money against certain collateral and you cannot obtain a lien on all the debtor's interests, make sure such financing will be paid in full under the plan as protection against the debtor obtaining additional financing from another lender who may take other assets as collateral which could prime your bank's lien with a senior or equal lien under Section 364(d) of the Bankruptcy Reform Act.
• Make sure you receive adequate time and means to permit you to liquidate your collateral under any lifting of the stay.
• Attempt to build in a cushion of collateral coverage or a borrowing base ratio or formula for future advances. If the borrower falls below such levels because of operating losses or the collateral declines in value, attempt to build in protection, namely by a clause that lifts the automatic stay (under Section 362 of the Bankruptcy Reform Act) so that you may quickly obtain your collateral in order to gain the maximum recovery.

If you had a priority lien on all the debtor's assets before the filing, you may not feel comfortable enough to participate in any type of plan, and only seek relief from the automatic stay or seek adequate protection if you have no other choice.

Generally, the trustee or debtor may not use any cash collateral that was generated prior to a prepetition filing, although in view of the frequent urgency to continue operating and lack of other available funds, the debtor will often use this cash collateral—without authority—to meet operating expenses.

Therefore, when the bank disagrees with the debtor's use of collateral proceeds, the debtor will frequently petition the court for an order allowing it to use such funds even over the objection of the bank.

After a hearing, the court may authorize the debtor to use the prepetition cash collateral, but only if the secured lender is adequately protected as required under the Bankruptcy Reform Act.

Most courts have held that a guaranty from a third party, which was in place at the time of bankruptcy filing, will not be considered adequate protection, which should prove beneficial to the bank.

If the value of the collateral exceeds the debt and continued operation does not eliminate the equity cushion, that equity cushion alone may be adequate protection.

Furthermore, if the collateral is inventory, for example, and the debtor demonstrates that the inventory level will be maintained by way of continued purchases of materials and goods for sale, the bank's prepetition position may be considered adequately protected if the bank is also offered a post-petition security interest in after acquired inventory, which is sufficient to replace the prepetition level of inventory.

While this whole matter could be a major problem in a Chapter 11, it probably would not be one in a straight Chapter 7 liquidation.

Apparently, a lot depends on the bank's agreement with the plan to allow the borrower to continue operating in bankruptcy and what benefit it is to receive. If the determination is made that this is in the bank's best interests, thought needs to be given to making an agreement, subject to court approval, that would make operating funds available to the debtor.

This could take the form of an agreement allowing the debtor to utilize cash collateral, or an order permitting the debtor to borrow money, or a combination of both. Therefore, some of these cash collateral problems can be avoided if an arrangement can be made, prior to bankruptcy between the lender and borrower for all proceeds from secured property to go directly into a special segregated account which the bank refers to as the cash collateral account and over which the bank alone has control. This means that while deposits from account proceeds may be deposited and credited to this account, the bank may make any draws or debits to this account which are in turn usually disbursed and credited to the borrower's unrestricted operating account. This approach should further protect the bank as the court may be less likely to allow the debtor access to these segregated funds when the debtor is attempting to seek authority to use the cash collateral account.

Practically speaking, if there is just one secured bank creditor in the picture, the only realistic source of funds for a financially depressed debtor is usually from the prepetition bank creditor who may not be fully secured but which may be willing to go along with continuing the operation in hopes of realizing a greater recovery.

On the other hand, a creditor, secured in excess of the debt, may have no basis to object to such an arrangement.

Even so, the court generally encourages negotiations between the debtor, the secured bank lender, and unsecured creditors, subject to court approval regarding the establishment of a cash collateral account.

When no agreement is reached, the debtor often seeks approval from the court, over the objection of the bank lender and other creditors. Once a borrower enters Chapter 11, it cannot continue borrowing money against its assets without court approval. Furthermore, the court would have to approve the terms and conditions of any future borrowings as well.

If another lender is the primary secured creditor and your bank is an unsecured creditor, you have to scrutinize any court order authorizing new borrowings to be extended by the secured lender and any so-called adequate protection provided. In addition, examine any approval to allow the debtor's use of cash collateral. If you are an unsecured creditor and believe that such an order will enhance the secured lender's position at your expense (e.g., by granting a post-petition lien to an existing secured lender), object to such an order on the grounds that it will reduce the assets available to unsecured creditors, in case of either a liquidation or plan of reorganization. Accordingly, you should also object to any such authorization or provision, even if your request is likely to be denied. Here again, the court encourages negotiations between the debtor, the secured lender, and other unsecured creditors, although it makes the final determination; and if approval is granted, the court is the final authority on setting the terms and conditions of the new debt. However, as a secured lender you will not be forced to extend any new credit to the debtor if the proposed terms and conditions are not accepted by the bank, thus certainly giving you leverage and a distinct advantage.

Relief from Automatic Stay

The bank, or any other party of interest, may move for the court to end the automatic stay, allowing them their rights to repossess or foreclose on collateral. The stay can be lifted if you establish that the collateral in question is not necessary for an effective reorganization and that there is no equity in the asset(s). While the equity question may not be a difficult issue, the court will usually require the bank's collateral (e.g., after acquired accounts receivable and inventory) to remain in use for the borrower's operations.

If the collateral was taken as secondary or as an abundance of collateral and is separate from the general operating assets of the business, chances are the court may not require it to be used in the business in an ongoing manner.

On the other hand, if the debtor can show that the property is essential to continue operations or that there is equity in the property, the stay will remain in force, provided the secured bank creditor is given adequate protection. Keep in mind that as a secured creditor, you have an interest in the collateral only up to its value, while having merely an unsecured claim for any deficiency between this value and the total of the debt. The secured lender's collateral position that existed at the time the petition was filed cannot be decreased. If an equity cushion existed at the time of bankruptcy filing, the right of the secured creditor to ultimately realize fully on its secured claim must also be preserved by the court.

One form of relief the court may offer is to continue the stay for a definite period of time, and thereafter to allow it to terminate, based on its determination that while there is present equity in the property, the property will deteriorate over time. A stay may also be terminated for causes other than lack of equity and the necessity for reorganization, for example, failure on the part of the debtor to properly retain insurance on the bank's collateral or evidence that the collateral is being wasted or overexposed, or allowed to deteriorate, spoil, or be contaminated.

To obtain relief from the stay, at least one hearing is required by the court. There should be an initial hearing, which must be held within 30 days from the filing of the pleading seeking modification of the stay. If a hearing is not held within that time, the stay may be lifted.

If the court does not terminate the stay following the preliminary hearing because it is satisfied that the trustee or debtor may be able to justify continuation of the stay, the court may order the stay continued pending a final hearing that must commence within the next 30 days. Therefore, the final hearing must commence within 60 days of the creditor's motion. The two hearings may be combined into a single one. At the creditor's request, under certain emergency circumstances, the court may lift the stay.

The creditor seeking modification of the stay has the burden of establishing its debt and security and any equity therein. On the other side, the debtor or trustee has the burden of proof on all other issues, including the necessity for reorganization and adequate protection.

Consequently, the bank must be prepared to offer evidence of the value of its collateral. In complicated and involved cases, especially when you have not been monitoring the collateral or obtaining frequent updates on values by way of internal or outside reports, schedules, appraisals, or inspections, proving the value of the collateral may require considerable time and expense. If the bank does not believe there is any equity in the collateral, it certainly has to present credible evidence, establishing proof of the value. This may entail hiring certified appraisers, inspectors, or other experts to locate, identify, and appraise the goods.

This is another reason why you should maintain good and updated records of values on all collateral, whether it consists of accounts receivable, inventory, contracts, or chattel paper, instruments, equipment, machinery, or real estate. In this connection, always attempt to obtain serial numbers and identification markings for better identification.

If it can be proven that the bank (as secured lender) can be adequately protected, the court may give it something beyond an administrative claim for any damages caused by the stay's continuation. Thus, the bank may be entitled to additional compensation in the form of a super priority unsecured claim for any damages including the expense of administration. To get the super priority, you must insist on adequate protection.

There are certain exceptions to an automatic stay. Some are listed below:

- Commencement or continuation of criminal actions against the debtor.
- Commencement or continuation of any enforcement of a judgment by a governmental agency to enforce its regulatory or police powers.
- Collection of alimony, child support, or maintenance.
- Action to perfect an interest in property to the extent that the trustee's powers and rights are subject to such perfection.
- Any act by a lessor against a debtor to take possession under a

nonresidential real property lease which has expired; this will also apply to proceedings on a forcible suit to obtain possession of the real property.

• Criminal action against the debtor for passing bad checks in accordance with statute violations.

• Commencement of other filings, namely, the taking of appropriate steps by mechanics and materialman claimants to protect their liens by recording such without risking a violation under the automatic stay.

• The imposition of nonmonetary restrictions on debtor companies under the Occupational Safety and Health Act (OSHA).

Disclosure Statements

Before any plan may be submitted to creditors and other parties of interest, the one(s) submitting the plan must submit a disclosure statement which first has to be approved by the court. The disclosure statement is the document that accompanies the plan of reorganization and discloses information about the debtor and the proponent of the plan.

This statement is not generally filed for a number of months after the bankruptcy filing. It probably would not only be several months before this statement would be approved, but sometimes even years. Generally, then, you have a lot of time to file your Proof of Claim.

However, be alert and cautious because judges may issue an order shortly after a filing indicating that creditors must file Proofs of Claim on or before a specific date. Therefore, do not assume the general rule of filing applies as you must read each and every order and notice from the court.

This statement must set forth enough factual information to allow creditors to make an informed determination of whether they want to vote on the plan. It must, at a minimum, furnish enough information for creditors to compare what they are to receive under the proposed plan versus what they would receive if all assets were liquidated.

If a party other than the debtor is proposing a plan, that party must submit a disclosure statement. This may present real practical problems as the information necessary to be disclosed is usually only distinctively within the knowledge and control of the debtor.

As a practical matter, the bank may be better off when it can negotiate with the debtor and any other creditors and go along with a plan proposed by the debtor.

Plan of Reorganization

The final step in a reorganization proceeding is the submission of a plan. For the plan to become effective, it must be confirmed by the court. A plan of reorganization may take most any form so long as certain requirements of the Bankruptcy Reform Act are met.

Remember, creditors are ranked in the following order: secured creditors, priority creditors, unsecured creditors, and holders of ownership equity interests. Creditors of the same type may be placed into one class. Equal priority or unsecured creditors, for example, may be lumped together into one class. Each secured creditor is usually in a separate class as it is rare that two secured creditors have the same or equal rights sufficient to allow them to be treated in the same manner.

Creditors vote on a plan by class. The plan will be accepted by class if two thirds of the dollar amount and more than one half of the number of creditors in that class so vote. If a class of creditors rejects the plan, the proposal may still be confirmed over this objection if certain conditions are met, resulting in a "cram down." Broadly speaking, a plan can be confirmed over the objection of a secured creditor and the method of payment (for the amount of the secured claim) altered from that specified in the contract. But basically the secured creditor must be able to realize at least deferred payments for the full value of its collateral. It is usually in the best interest of creditors to negotiate the terms of a proposed plan that is acceptable to them, rather than be exposed to the expense and uncertainty of a sharply litigated confirmation hearing resulting in "cram-down" provisions. If the plan is confirmed, the rights of all creditors are fixed by the terms of the plan, and as long as the debtor meets the payments called for in the plan, creditors may not take any further action against the debtor or its property.

Other Chapter 11 Facts

There are often cases involving smaller borrowers where it may not be worthwhile to incur substantial legal or administrative costs.

You should file your Proof of Claim and appear before the judge to expeditiously settle the estate and have any available collateral abandoned to the bank. In such instances, the collateral may have been long gone or disappeared, so you may decide not to waste time or additional money. Also, consider cutting off efforts for reclaiming your collateral when you will only receive a few cents on the dollar, assuming the return would be less than the legal and other costs of acquiring and liquidating it. Alternatively, an abandonment may be an easy way out for the debtor; therefore, if your debt is secured, it may be worth your time and effort to have the debtor reaffirm your debt.

A Chapter 11 may benefit unsecured creditors because they could claim that the bank, as a secured creditor, is either too well secured or is really inadequately secured, which could impact the bank's position.

Larger creditors may serve on committees and can control actions. If you are invited to serve on a committee, even if you are a smaller creditor, it may be to your advantage to serve.

If the court authorizes use of your cash collateral, (receivables and inventory), request that the debtor maintain a cash collateral account with your bank in exchange for extending post-petition financing, which should continue your floating lien security interest in thereafter created collateral. Even if you do not extend post-petition financing, ask the court to order the debtor to open an account whereby all proceeds from inventory sales must be deposited. This way you can monitor progress of the business.

And, in the order, seek a provision requiring submission of a budget by the debtor at least on a monthly basis, a budget that details all anticipated disbursements, expenditures, and any other necessary expected costs and expenses. The order should authorize the bank's acceptance or rejection of any items indicated before the debtor is allowed to use cash collateral proceeds. Thus, the debtor would be prohibited from making any expenditures not specifically approved by the bank. The bank, under the court order, should remain responsible, so as not to control the debtor's specific spending or to discriminate by approving payment to one creditor at the expense of another, which could raise a control issue. The purpose of approval on the bank's part should be to see that the debtor does not indulge in any unnecessary or discretionary spending.

Exhibit G is a sample instruction sheet you would furnish your attorneys for them to set up a cash collateral account that may be approved by the bankruptcy court and maintained at your bank. It is followed by Exhibit H, regarding the actual cash collateral account to be approved by the bankruptcy court.

EXHIBIT G
Cash Collateral Instructions

To: (Name of Attorneys and Address)

1. Spell out the correct legal name of the debtor and its principal office or main place of domicile including the names of any other debtors who are obligated on debt instruments. In addition, furnish the lawyers with the Bankruptcy Case Number or Numbers if you have them.
2. Include the names and addresses of any contingent obligors to debt instruments, i.e., co-signers, endorsers, guarantors.
3. Provide the aggregate and individual note debt owed by the debtor as of the due date you submit the request detailed as follows:

A. Principal balance owing $ ______________
$ ______________
(use other side $ ______________
if necessary) $ ______________
$ ______________
Total $ ______________

B. Interest on each note above through ________ $ ________
(use other side if necessary)
C. Per diem from and after ________ is $ ______________
D. Advances used for, i.e., insurance, taxes, payroll, supplies, etc. $ ________.
E. Escrow balances, if any $ ________.
F. Escrow deficiency, if any $ ________.
G. Accrued Late Charges $ ________.
H. Attorneys' Fees incurred to date $ ________.
4. Payment History:
A. Date of the latest payment(s)
B. Date(s) that demand for payment was made

EXHIBIT G (*Concluded*)

C. Date(s) of debt acceleration, if different than demand dates.
5. An explanation and breakdown of the total payments required to bring each note current.
6. A breakdown of collateral value given, in the bank's estimation, to each item of collateral on which the bank holds a first or priority lien.
7. The names and addresses of all other lienholders of the debtor including a breakdown of those having a secondary or otherwise collateral interest in the debtor's assets, including the identification of those having a secondary lien position behind your bank's interest; or those having a conflict over a first lien interest with you; or those having a purchase money lien on a certain portion of assets on which you have a blanket lien; or those which may have signed a subordination or inter-creditor agreement placing them behind your lien position.
8. Detailed budget based on monthly expenditures, costs and other expenses as prudently estimated by the debtor broken down by item and category over the next 12 months.
9. Internal true cash flow forecast over the next 12 months prepared by the debtor specifically on each item the bank claims a first or priority lien on including rights to proceeds, income, rents, etc.
10. Your indication and willingness to allow or permit the debtor(s) to use some or all of the cash collateral assets, as defined by the court, in order to preserve any other assets on which you may have a lien, whether primary or secondary.
11. Names of loans officers who will be involved in the cash collateral negotiations and where they may be reached at the bank (department, phone).

Name of Bank ____________________
Officer Name and Title ____________________
(Signature)

EXHIBIT H
Cash Collateral Account

In the United States Bankruptcy Court for

THE ________ DISTRICT OF ____________ DIVISION
IN THE MATTER OF BANKRUPTCY NO.________
DEBTOR IN PROCEEDINGS UNDER CHAPTER 11

ORDER REGARDING USE OF CASH COLLATERAL

At ________, in said District, this ________ day of ________.
For consideration after due notice and hearing, the application of ________________ (debtor) came for the authority to use cash collateral in which the bank named herein has an interest and appearing before the court herein, and that the court finds the:

A. Bank has a valid pre-petition security interest and lien in and to the debtor's inventory, equipment, accounts receivable, contracts and general intangibles.

B. Debtor has on deposit with the bank cash and other deposit proceeds subject to claims of set-off and contractual security rights and that the bank's security interest and liens were perfected no earlier than ____________.

C. The use of cash collateral subject to the interest of the bank is necessary to the operation of the debtor's business and preservation of its assets including assets in which bank has security interests and liens.

D. The term "debtor" as used in this Order means (name of debtor) both in its capacity as a pre-petition entity and as Debtor-in-Possession, unless otherwise specifically designated.

It is accordingly ordered:

1. The debtor shall furnish to the bank within ten (10) days of the entry of this Order a full and complete list of all its accounts receivable, which list shall include the name and address of each account debtor, the outstanding amount of each said account as of , and a trial balance aging of each said account receivable;

2. The debtor will provide to the bank within twenty (20) days, a complete listing by type and item of its inventory, specifying the location(s) of said inventory, a breakdown of said inventory at each such location, and the dollar amount of inventory at each such location;

3. The debtor shall be entitled to use the cash collateral in the

EXHIBIT H (*Continued*)

ordinary course of its business in such amounts as is absolutely necessary to continue and uninterrupt its business operations. To effectuate this provision, the debtor shall on or before the 15th of each month submit to the bank a reasonably detailed budget for the succeeding month. The bank shall notify the debtor of the acceptance or rejection of such proposed budget by the 25th day of each month. If the budget is agreed to by the bank, the use of cash collateral shall continue pursuant to this Order and the proposed budget. If the bank does not approve any monthly budget, the debtor shall be prohibited from expenditures not specifically approved by the bank. Debtor shall furnish such financial information as the bank may reasonably request including but not limited to daily reports of inventory on hand.

4. The debtor shall deposit all funds generated in the ordinary course of business including cash collateral into a non-interest bearing Debtor-in-Possession account to be opened with ________________ and titled "(name of debtor) Debtor-in-Possession Cash Collateral Account" or as may be agreed to by bank and the debtor. All funds deposited in said account shall remain in said account subject only to the terms and conditions of this Order and/or further Order of the court.

5. In order to grant to the bank adequate security for the debtors use of cash collateral, the debtor hereby grants to the bank and bank is hereby granted a security interest and lien upon the assets of the debtor hereinafter described in paragraph 6, herein, to secure repayment of any and all obligations to the bank. Such security interest and liens are superior to all other liens and security interests in the collateral, save only creditors of the debtor holding prior existing and fully perfected and enforceable liens on such assets as of the time of entry of this order, or relating back to such time. The debtor is hereby authorized and directed to execute such other and further documentation of the above granted and authorized security interest and lien in the same form as the prepetition documents between the debtor and the bank and as may be required and deemed appropriate by the bank; provided that the failure of the debtor to execute any such documentation shall in no way affect the validity of the security interest and lien in favor of the bank granted pursuant to this paragraph. The bank is given leave to

EXHIBIT H (*Continued*)

take whatever action it deems appropriate to perfect any security interest or liens herein granted or authorized.

6. All indebtedness which may now or from time to time hereafter be owing by the debtor shall be secured by the following property of the debtor, subject only to valid and perfected liens and security interests existing on the date of the filing of the petition initiating these proceedings, and shall at all times be senior to the rights of the debtor or any successor Trustee in this or in any subsequent proceeding under the Code:

a. All present and future accounts, purchase orders, contract rights, documents, chattel paper instruments including the capital stock of (______________), general intangibles and the proceeds and products thereof, including but not limited to all accounts, purchase orders, contract rights, documents, chattel paper instruments and general intangibles and the proceeds and products thereof of the debtor to which the bank held a security interest prior to the date of the Petition;

b. All materials, supplies, inventory, work-in-process and finished goods now owned or hereafter acquired by the debtor including, without limitation, the proceeds and products of all the foregoing thereof owned by the debtor upon which the bank held a security interest at the time of the filing of the Petition.

c. All patents, patent rights, tax refunds, tax refund claims, and insurance policies now owned or hereafter acquired by the debtor, including without limitation, any and all proceeds and products of all the foregoing thereof owned by the debtor upon which the bank held a security interest at the time of the filing of the Petition.

d. All machinery, equipment, appliances, apparatus, tools, machine tools, supplies, accessories, parts, materials, furniture, goods and chattels of every kind and wherever located now owned or hereafter acquired by the debtor, including all of the proceeds and products thereof of the foregoing owned by the debtor upon which the bank held a security interest at the time of the filing of the Petition, and all substitutions, renewals, improvements and replacements of and additions to any and all of the foregoing, and products thereof; and

e. All other property and interests in property now owned or hereinafter acquired by the debtor.

7. The use of cash collateral by the debtor and the granting of

EXHIBIT H (*Continued*)

the security interest herein is necessary to preserve the estate of the debtor. All indebtedness which may from time to time hereafter be owing by the debtor to the bank shall have priority under the provisions of 364 (c) (1) of the Code over all administrative expenses incurred in the reorganization proceeding of the kind specified in 503 (b) or 507 (b) of the Code and shall at all times be senior to any subsequent proceeding under the Code, including any Chapter 7 trustee, and irrespective of the provisions of 726 (b) of the Code. No costs or expenses of administration which have been or may be incurred in these proceedings, any conversion of these proceedings pursuant to 1112 of the Code, or in any other proceeding related hereto, and no priority claims are or will be prior to or on a parity with the claim of the bank against the debtor arising out of the indebtedness of the debtor to the bank, or with the security interest and liens of the bank upon the collateral described herein; and no such costs nor expenses of administration shall be imposed against the bank, its claims, or its collateral.

8. The debtor shall not borrow any money on a secured basis unless and until the debtor shall have paid to the bank the full amount owed to the debtor on pre-petition accounts receivable and contract rights. The bank shall be given at least 20 days prior notice and an opportunity for a hearing before this Court in advance of any granting to any other party of any security interests or liens.

9. As adequate protection for the continued use by the debtor of the equipment in which the bank held a security interest at the time of the filing of the Petition, the security interests in the collateral described herein shall also be security for any decrease in the value of such collateral resulting from such use, from ordinary wear and tear, from uninsured destruction of any or all of such equipment collateral or from any other cause whatsoever, the entire risk of any such decrease in value expressly being assumed hereby by the debtor.

10. The right of the debtor under this Order to use cash collateral may be terminated by the bank without cause at any time; provided, however, that the obligations and rights of the bank with respect to all transactions which have occurred prior to such termination shall remain unimpaired and unaffected by such termination and shall survive such termination.

EXHIBIT H (*Continued*)

11. All cash of the debtor currently in the ________ account is proceeds of collateral of the bank existing prior to the date of the filing of the Petition and all such cash shall be delivered to the bank for application against pre-petition indebtedness owing by the debtor to the bank.
12. The debtor shall promptly reimburse the bank upon the request therefor by the bank, for all costs and expenses (including, without limitation, all filing and recording fees and reasonable attorneys' and paralegal fees and expenses) incurred by the bank in connection with;
• the preparation of this Order, the loan and security agreement and related instruments, and the other documents and agreements
• the preservation and protection of the bank's rights hereunder and thereunder
• the collection of all loans by the bank to the debtor.
The Bank shall not be required to file financing statements or other documents in any jurisdiction or take any other action in order to validate or perfect the security interests and liens granted to it hereunder and under the security agreement and related instruments, documents and agreements. If the bank shall, in its sole discretion, choose to file such financing statements or similar documents shall be to have been filed or recorded at the time and on the date of entry of this Order.
13. The signature of either ____________ or any other persons designated by the debtor, whether by letter to bank or appearing on any one or more of the aforesaid security agreements, instruments or documents, shall bind the other debtor.
14. If a plan of reorganization has not been confirmed by the ________ day of ____________, 19____, the bank shall have the right without further Order of the Court to exercise all of its rights to the collateral, whether such rights arise under contract, or under applicable state or federal law or under the provisions of this Order.
15. The debtor shall allow the bank access to its books and records during reasonable business hours, including the right to make copies of such records as may be reasonably required. The bank shall have the right at any reasonable time to inspect the collateral.
16. Any assets of the debtor constituting collateral of the bank not necessary for an effective reorganization shall be sold and

EXHIBIT H (*Concluded*)

any proceeds realized therefrom shall be applied to the claim or claims of the bank.

17. The terms of this Order regarding the use of cash collateral have been negotiated at arms-length and in good faith and are fair and reasonable under the existing circumstances.

18. The provisions of the Order shall be binding upon and inure to the benefit of the bank, the debtor and their respective successors and assigns (including any Trustee hereinafter appointed as a representative of the estate herein) and all other parties in interest.

19. This Order is hereby certified for immediate and emergency approval by the U.S. District Court for the ____________ District of ____________. Notwithstanding the foregoing, this Order is a final Bankruptcy Court Order subject to appeal.

Signed this ________ day of ____________, 19____

____________________ ____________________

Bankruptcy Judge

At some point you may feel that the company's future viability is questionable and that continuation of a Chapter 11 may only serve to diminish its assets and your collateral. In essence, this could shrink your bank's percentage liquidation recovery; the longer the business exists without a conversion to a Chapter 7, the more your assets shrink.

In a similar circumstance where the lender's principal, interest, and expenses are fully collateralized, being locked into a two to three year Chapter 11 may not be as advantageous as the relatively shorter Chapter 7 liquidation.

While Chapter 11's primary goal is to rehabilitate the borrower, it may be converted to a liquidation. If converted to a liquidation, the sooner you (as a secured lender) should petition the court for an abandonment of your collateral. Keep in mind that a Chapter 11 plan may be moved into or converted to a liquidation if the company cannot be rehabilitated. Thus, it would not be necessary to convert or move it into a Chapter 7. Therefore, in substantial cases when the solution is a sale or liquidation of the assets, you may continue in a Chapter 11 status without having to resort to a Chapter 7.

Partnership Debtors in Bankruptcy

You should be aware that partnerships are eligible as debtors under the Bankruptcy Reform Act. A partnership, with all the general partners joining in or approving the petition, may file a voluntary petition to reorganize the partnership under a Chapter 11 or to liquidate it under a Chapter 7.

An involuntary petition may be filed against the partnership by either the partnership's creditors or by a certain number of the partners themselves. Furthermore, if all the general partners are debtors in other bankruptcy cases, then an involuntary petition may be filed against the partnership by a general partner or by the bankruptcy trustee. As such, the general partners must prepare and file a statement of affairs or schedules in the partnership name in accordance with bankruptcy rules. And the court may order any general partner to file a personal statement revealing his or her personal assets and liabilities.

Once a Chapter 7 petition regarding the liquidation of the partnership is filed, it may not be converted to a Chapter 11 reorganization case without notice to all the partners, followed by a hearing, or unless consented to by all the partners.

While many of the same provisions under the Bankruptcy Reform Act apply to partnerships, as well as to corporations, there are certain provisions that apply to or affect partnerships specifically. As an example, in a Chapter 7 case, the trustee is allowed to recover any deficiency from the general partners. Also, under Section 723 of the Bankruptcy Reform Act, the trustee may be permitted to recover from each partner the amount of the deficiency in the partnership's property necessary to cover any allowed administrative expenses and claims filed against the partnership. The trustee is supposed to seek out nondebtor partners first in order to recover any necessary amounts from them to cover the partnership deficiency.

However, there may be grounds for defense in such cases when all general partners are not treated in an equitable manner. The court may enjoin any partners' disposition of property or assets in order to recover a deficiency from the individual's assets. Alternately, the court may require an indemnity agreement, or some other form of legal assurance, that guarantees an individual partner will pay the deficiency. Such court rights and powers appear to apply only to Chapter 7 liquidation cases, not to reorganization proceedings.

Distributions to partnership creditors under the Bankruptcy Reform Act are handled differently than distributions under the Federal Uniform Partnership Act, which is similar to a marshaling of assets doctrine.

In the latter case, partnership creditors must be satisfied first out of the assets of the partnership before the creditors of individual partners may seek repayment from partnership assets.

This works in the reverse as creditors of individual partners, which exhaust all effort to obtain payment from partners' assets, must be satisfied first before creditors of the partnership may seek payment from the assets of individual partners.

This is somewhat different under the Bankruptcy Reform Act as a trustee has a claim against all the individual general partners' assets to the extent of any deficiency in their assets to pay general partnership creditors, a claim which is equal in priority to that of personal creditors of individual partners. However, under the Bankruptcy Reform Act, creditors of an individual partner still cannot obtain any recovery out of the assets of the partnership until all partnership creditors are paid.

Fraudulent transfers by partnerships are voidable by the trustee under the Bankruptcy Reform Act. Thus, the trustee has the power to void certain transactions or transfers that occurred prior to the filing of the case thereby allowing it to reclaim those assets for the estate. Therefore, the trustee of a partnership may void any transfer of an interest in property or assets owned by the partnership or any obligation incurred by the partnership up to one year of the petition filing by the partnership, if the partnership was or became insolvent as a result of such transfer or incurred debt obligation. This becomes more apparent pursuant to Section 548 of the Bankruptcy Reform Act involving transfers to individual general partners by insolvent partnerships. In this case, the trustee may void any transfer made to a general partner or incurred to a general partner that was made or incurred on or within one year of the filing of the petition, provided the debtor was insolvent at the time of the transfer or obligation, or was rendered insolvent as a result of it. The trustee does not have to prove that the transfer was made for less than reasonably equivalent value; the insolvency of the partnership at the time of or as a result of the transfer is the critical key deciding factor.

If an individual partner files bankruptcy and the partnership is a debtor, then included in the estate of the individual partner is that partner's proportionate share of the partnership estate. Creditors of individual partners have no valid claims against the partnership estate until the creditors of the partnership and administrative expenses of the partnership have been paid. The automatic stay that goes into effect once the individual partner files a bankruptcy petition does not affect any actions against the partnership's property or assets. Courts have also held that the trustee of a partner may not assume the individual partner's right as a general partner in the partnership. Furthermore, courts have held that the bankruptcy of an individual general partner will not stand up as grounds to dissolve the partnership.

Under a Chapter 7 liquidation, discharge is limited to individual partners but is not available to the partnership. An individual who has filed bankruptcy may be discharged from a partnership debt, whether or not the partnership itself is a debtor.

Bear in mind that a partner can also be denied a discharge because of conduct in which he or she personally participated, relative to a bankruptcy case concerning the partnership, if such occurred within one year of the partner's own bankruptcy case.

Partners and partnerships may be discharged under Chapter 11 cases upon confirmations of a plan, although normally a general partner will not be discharged from the debts of the partnership in a Chapter 11 reorganization.

Guaranties and Fraudulent Conveyances

Another area we need to touch on is guaranties. Even though guarantors should fall outside of a Chapter 11, thus giving you the right to go against them, be cautious when taking guaranties from related entities.

Subsidiaries

If you take a guaranty from a subsidiary for a parent's debt and that subsidiary has a deficit net worth, such action could be deemed as fraudulent to the subsidiary's creditors because it was insolvent at the time of taking the guaranty and it did not receive any reasonable equivalent value or benefit for its guaranty. Of course, if the parent's net worth at the time of making the loan was equal or more than the subsidiary's obligation, it could be argued that the reimbursement right that the subsidiary would have against the parent would be sufficient to offset its obligation.

However, in all likelihood, the parent would probably be insolvent at the time the guaranty was called since the lender would not be calling on the guaranty in the first place if the parent could meet its obligation.

So then how would a court look at it? Basically, the test would be to see if there is an offsetting reimbursement right in value which in this case would be the contingent asset interest the subsidiary would have against the parent, while having an equal contingent liability for guaranting the parent's debt. Nevertheless, always look at the net worth not only of the party whose debts are being guarantied, but also the net worth of the party offering the guaranty to determine fraudulent conveyance risks.

Another instance where a fraudulent conveyance can occur is when a shell company buys the stock of an operating company under a typical leveraged buy-out arrangement. The buyer in turn assigns and pledges all of the subsidiary's assets to a lender who funds the purchase, thus the purchase also involves a typical bootstrap transaction because the lender is actually looking to the subsidiary to secure its loan.

Now, let us say that the loan to purchase the subsidiary exceeds its net worth at the time of purchase. Assume for a moment the parent has no other assets but the subsidiary's stock and thus has no operating income of its own and is fully reliant on upstream dividends or advances from the subsidiary to pay its debt to the lender. If the lender has to ultimately realize payment on its debt by repossessing or foreclosing on the subsidiary's assets because the latter does not have sufficient equity to liquidate the debt (thus forcing it into bankruptcy), there will be a good chance that this will render the lender's lien on the subsidiary's assets and the obligation void and subject to a fraudulent transfer.

Again, if the parent had some other substantive net worth besides the value of the subsidiary's stock at the time the loan was made, the subsidiary may initially have had some realistic right of reimbursement from the parent, which may have insulated the transaction from fraud.

Although the problem the writer has with the net worth test is how it will be decided by a court, if based on the time the parent or subsidiary, or both, are forced into bankruptcy, neither one evidenced the same net worth they had at the time of the original transaction. So you really do not know what the court would do in such cases. The lender would obviously have a better chance if the parent and subsidiary met the net worth test at the time the original transaction was granted.

Another important point to keep in mind before you get your bank involved in a similar transaction is to ask yourself whether all unsecured creditors are going to be better or worse off as a result of the transaction; forethought like this should help protect your bank from potential fraudulent conveyances. Keep in mind that the Bankruptcy Reform Act basically states that if a transfer is not made for a reasonably equivalent value within one year of bankruptcy, and the debtor was insolvent when it was made or was rendered insolvent by the transfer, then the transfer may be voided.

Remember, in a leveraged buy-out, the purchaser often uses the value of the acquiring corporation as security in financing the cost of the acquisition, especially when the acquirer is a shell company without any significant assets of its own. If the financing of the purchase can be accomplished simply by the granting of a lien to the bank on the acquired company's assets, it may be grounds for a fraudulent transfer especially if the purchased company is thereby rendered insolvent or undercapitalized in view of the buyer receiving the consideration for the financing and not the purchased company which assigned and pledged all its assets. Thus, a transfer solely for the benefit of a third party normally will not result or be for reasonable equivalent value. Even the defense raised by the buyer—that consideration should be evaluated because of the installation of new management into the purchased company—will not of itself, constitute reasonably equivalent value.

Uniform Fraudulent Transfer Act

The federal Uniform Fraudulent Transfer Act (UFTA) was approved by the National Conference of Commissioners on Uniform State Laws in 1984 as a replacement for the Uniform Fraudulent

Conveyance Act (UFCA). As time has passed, more states have adopted the UFTA, a movement similar to the adoption of the 1972 revision of Article 9 of the Uniform Commercial Code (UCC). The newer UFTA has significant impact on many areas of law, especially pertaining to those involving leveraged acquisitions, asset sales, and disputes with the IRS. The UFTA has been fashioned to a great extent after the Bankruptcy Reform Act, and contains significant changes from the UFCA, both in structure and in substance. Here are some important changes offered under the UFTA:

- Introduction of provisions making transfers to "insiders" voidable.
- Enhancement in creditors' remedies against transferees.
- Inclusion of a uniform statute of limitations.
- A newer, more objective definition of insolvency than the one in the Bankruptcy Reform Act.
- Elimination of the "good faith" requirement contained in the UFCA's definition of "fair consideration."
- Enumeration of certain areas considered fraudulent.
- Omission of a provision directed specifically at transfers or obligations of insolvent partner debtors.
- New defenses, in certain respects, for fraudulent transfer defendants.

The UFTA's definition of transfer is, for all practical purposes, identical to that of the Bankruptcy Reform Act. Also, under the bankruptcy code, the definition of insolvency requires a simple balance sheet test, which excludes from the fair value of the debtor's property any fraudulently transferred as well as exempt property.

The UFCA provides a somewhat more complex definition of insolvency than the Bankruptcy Reform Act definition which is as follows:

A person or entity is insolvent when the present fair saleable value of their assets is less than the amount that will be required to pay the probable liability on existing debts as they mature and become due. Present fair saleable value means the value that can be obtained if the assets are sold with reasonable promptness in an existing market. Under such a definition, a debtor may be insolvent for UFCA purposes even when the value of their assets exceeds the amount of their debts, if the assets are virtually all illiquid and the bulk of debts are mostly top heavy or short term (due within one year).

On the other hand, the UFTA's newer definition of insolvency is also complex, including the following points:

• A "balance sheet" definition similar to but not identical to the one contained in the Bankruptcy Reform Act.
• A debtor is considered insolvent if the sum of its debts is larger than the debtor's assets *at a fair valuation* (a term left undefined by the UFTA).
• A rebuttable presumption that a debtor who is generally not paying debts as they become due is insolvent.

The UFTA's proposed definition of insolvency makes it easier than under prior UFCA law for creditors to prove a fraudulent transfer when insolvency is a material element. The plaintiff creditor only needs to show, in most cases, that the debtor has generally stopped paying debts as they become due, placing the burden of proving solvency with the debtor. Proof by direct evidence of the insolvency of the debtor on the critical date of the transfer may be difficult; "insolvency must frequently be determined by proof of factors from which insolvency may be inferred." Courts have used the term *retrojection* to describe the process of working backwards from the date of the transfer to show factors from which the debtor's insolvency may be presumed. When using the accounting technique of retrojection to prove insolvency, however, the trustee must show the absence of any substantial or radical changes in the assets or liabilities of the debtor between the retrojection dates.

Leveraged buy-outs may become problematic as it pertains to the Uniform Fraudulent Transfer Act (UFTA) because assets do not include property to the extent of being encumbered by a valid lien under the UFTA. A leveraged acquisition that left a corporation with little or no unencumbered property would be even more readily subject to attack than under present UFTA law.

The best way to assure that a leveraged acquisition will not be voidable as a fraudulent transfer is to structure the transaction in a proper manner. For example, if you are the lender financing the acquisition, make sure the buyer purchases the assets held in the existing company's name, rather than its stock shares, as the bank may be better off by only taking a lien against the transferred assets that are being sold. If the company selling its assets receives an adequate price for those assets being sold to the buyer (which you are financing), the seller should not have made a fraudulent transfer. Alternatively, the buyer may obtain financing for the transaction by pledging the stock thereby acquired, if a stock purchase, but if the acquired company's assets are also assigned to the lender and the company remains as a subsidiary of the new owner, then consideration to the newly acquired subsidiary becomes a question.

As a precautionary measure, consider obtaining opinions from independent CPAs stating that at the time of the transaction, the acquired company was not insolvent nor was it rendered insolvent by the transaction, and that the transaction did not leave it undercapitalized, and further, that the transaction did not require it to incur debts beyond its ability to pay them at maturity.

More difficult to establish, but still potentially useful as part of a defense against a fraudulent transfer action, is some form or combination of forms of consideration provided the purchased company. These include provision for a right of subrogation to the bank's claims; a guaranty offered by the purchasing entity or by parties related to the buyer; opportunities made available to the company being bought such as access to new supplies or suppliers, markets, and better financing terms arranged to pay its debts. Therefore, fair consideration can exist when the transferor, that is, the company being bought which in essence is assuming (by way of upstream dividends) its new owner's purchase acquisition obligation(s) besides assigning and pledging its assets to the acquisition lender, receives some type of obvious, indirect if not direct, consideration or benefit. Other indirect economic benefits may exist for the newly acquired subsidiary such as a financially strong parent being a good source of financial assistance, and other support whether an enhanced market source or otherwise. However, a financially weak parent may impair a subsidiary's credit and even make it more prone and subject to liquidation, especially if it starts milking it financially or transfering valuable assets.

Another way to structure a leveraged acquisition may be available when there is an identity of interest between the parent and newly acquired subsidiary. The courts may treat them as a single entity, similar to the "alter ego" theory, so that the agreement becomes a simple two-sided transaction between the borrower and lender. Under this premise, bank funds loaned to the parent buyer will be deemed fair consideration for the assignment/ pledge by the subsidiary of its assets to the bank, provided that the relative amounts are not disproportionate although entities will be looked at as one by the courts, which can be to your advantage or disadvantage.

Disadvantages for the Bank of a Chapter 11

While there is certainly an adverse impact of a Chapter 11 on a business, there are also risks and disadvantages to creditors regarding the filing of a Chapter 11. Here are some.

- Loss of control over the credit due to the appointment of a trustee or because of the presence of a vigorous creditor committee.
- Risk of a claim against the bank of equitable subordination.
- Suit brought against the bank, based on one or more of the voiding powers.
- Long delay or deferral in receiving payment.
- Denial of an improvement in the bank's position during the case.

Chapter 7: Liquidation

The purpose of a Chapter 7 is to attempt to collect and liquidate all of the debtor's nonexempt assets and have the proceeds of sale distributed proportionately by class to all the debtor's creditors.

When a borrower files a straight liquidation Chapter 7 bankruptcy, there is usually a small amount of assets left in the estate, compared to the total debt owed creditors. At times, even a Chapter 11 will become a liquidation bankruptcy if the debtor cannot make it work within a reasonable period.

If you face a problem in a Chapter 7 case, you must decide whether it is worth filing an objection to the confirmation. Obviously, the larger your debt is and/or the more valuable the collateral, the greater the reason to follow up when you feel you are not being treated fairly. Your decision to file an objection or complaint to the confirmation plan should, therefore, be to have a change made in order to improve your position for relief from the automatic stay (allowing you to proceed with foreclosure), or just moving for a dismissal of the case.

Pertaining to an individual filing, you should closely scrutinize all income sources and expense amounts because if you show more available income than initially revealed by the debtor, you could have the case converted to a Chapter 13 reorganization instead of a straight liquidation.

In a Chapter 7, secured creditors are entitled to property on which they have a valid lien or to the proceeds of sale of such property. In case the debtor decides to exempt the property on which you have a lien, you have the right to have the debtor redeem the collateral by paying you a fair value for it or by giving up the collateral to you. The debtor may also be willing to reaffirm the debt with you; if this is the case have him or her execute a reaffirmation agreement. If the debtor later defaults under the reaffirmation agreement, proceed to repossess the collateral and sell it, as you would not be stayed under the bankruptcy filing.

Under a Chapter 7, certain unencumbered property of individuals is exempt from forced sale. A debtor can elect to take either federal or state exemptions. Some states, like Texas, have more liberal exemption statutes than the federal law allows. While federal law governs bankruptcy proceedings, states have the authority to prevent the forced sale of an individual's property. Individuals have the right to select which exemptions they want to take.

The prospect of undergoing a bankruptcy and discharging debts while at the same time retaining either the property protected by the state or federal exemptions may be attractive to debtors who do not own much more property than that which is protected by the exemptions. Once the Chapter 7 proceedings are completed, the debtor will receive a discharge and will be given a new financial start. It usually takes anywhere for 30 to 120 days after the first creditors' meeting for a debtor to be discharged in a Chapter 7. This date is usually given in the notice you receive from the bankruptcy court.

Chapter 12

Family farm business can now seek protection under Chapter 12. In order to qualify for relief, the farm debtor must meet the following conditions.

• A farmer and his spouse must operate a farm that does not have debts in excess of $1,500,000. At least 80 percent of the debt must have been created by the farm operation, excluding any home mortgage. In addition, more than 50 percent of the farmer's income must be derived from the farm.
• A farmer (or relatives) must personally operate the farm. If the operation is a closely held corporation or partnership, it may qualify if more than 50 percent of the equity is held by one family.

Some provisions of Chapter 12 have been adopted from Chapter 13, as seen in this list:

• The debtor will be given up to 90 days from the date of the bankruptcy petition to file a plan of reorganization, which may be modified any time prior to confirmation. This period may be extended by the court if "substantially justified." Any confirmation hearing of the plan in accordance with Chapter 12 of the Bankruptcy Reform Act, must be held within 45 days of the filing of the plan, with exceptions allowed for reasonable cause. If a plan is not filed within the 90-day period and no extension is granted by the court, the case may be dismissed, at which point the bank can proceed to foreclose or repossess its collateral, subject to state statute.

Creditors are not allowed to file a plan under Chapter 12. However, secured creditors are allowed to vote on the farm debtor's plan, which they must accept. Secured creditors retain their liens under the plan, including the values of their claims. Should the secured creditors opt not to approve the plan, they will only be assured of receiving an amount equal to the then current market value of the collateral, which may be paid over some designated time period. The debtor can surrender collateral to its secured creditors.

• The farmer may sell land or other assets, including those consisting of collateral, without the bank's consent before any plan is approved or confirmed, if such collateral is not essential for reorganization. This is considered an allowance of scaling down farming operations. Therefore, the bank's approval is not required if the court approves the sale, although the bank will continue to have a collateral interest in the proceeds if it originally had a proper lien on the assets that were sold. The intent of this authorization is to allow the farmer to scale down the farming operation to enable reorganization to succeed.

• The plan must at a minimum allow unsecured creditors to receive what they would have if the farmer's estate were liquidated in a Chapter 7, which would probably be very little anyway, if anything. Unsecured debts are covered under a plan limit of from three to five years. Payments to unsecured creditors must be in the form of "disposable income" which is limited to income that is not essential for maintenance or support of the farmer and his or her dependents, including the ongoing operation of the farm. Secured creditors, on the other hand, would have to receive the value of the collateral over the term of the plan or receive the actual collateral instead.

• Farm debtors, instead of providing adequate protection in the form of replacement liens and cash payments, may pay secured creditors a "reasonable rent" for use of farmland collateral in place of decline in value or in lieu of lost opportunity costs to creditors, (as allowed under the Bankruptcy Reform Act) such as losing use of funds that would have been received from a foreclosure sale. The rent payment is calculated on rental values, net income, and earning potential of the property within its community location. Farmers may also use payments to meet property taxes and to make repairs that benefit or maintain the value of the collateral.

"Indubitable equivalent" language in accordance with Chapter 12 of the Bankruptcy Reform Act has been eliminated, thus clarifying that the value of the property is clearly what needs protection; furthermore, this does not pertain to the creditor's collateral interest in the property.

Regarding other types of collateral, the creditor must be paid—in cash—the sum equal to the decrease in the collateral's value during the period the "automatic stay" was in force.

Banks should move quickly for dismissals when farmers do not comply with time limits, especially when creditors do not have the right to vote on a Chapter 12 plan. The farmer in possession may be removed if he or she commits fraud or is dishonest; incompetence and mismanagement are also grounds for removal. If a farmer is removed or ceases to be in possession for one reason or another, the trustee may take control of the farm, and then move the case to a dismissal, reorganization plan confirmation, or conversion to a Chapter 7. Farmers may also request conversions to Chapter 7 because they may conclude that after an attempt to reorganize, they are simply unable to succeed because of continued losses, or because of deteriorating, insufficient, or unavailable assets.

But the shield afforded by Chapter 12 won't offer farmers relief forever. It will terminate within seven years from the date it was adopted unless Congress makes an extension.

Chapter 13: Individual Debt Rearrangement

These plans, known as "wage-earner plans," are somewhat similar to Chapter 11 proceedings, but they apply to individuals and not to businesses. More specifically, an employed husband and wife, receiving regular income and having less than $100,000 in total unsecured debt and/or $350,000 in total secured debt, are eligible for Chapter 13.

Generally, the purpose of a Chapter 13 is to rehabilitate debtors rather than liquidate their assets.

A plan may be submitted only by the debtor(s). However, you may submit an objection to the debtor's plan to the trustee, who will set a deadline. At the time of the deadline, objections can be voiced at a confirmation hearing. Once any objections are heard and resolved, a final confirmation date for acceptance of the plan will be set.

An automatic stay against creditors and others is enforced,

beginning at the time of filing the petition, regarding any judicial or other similar proceedings that are undertaken. This includes a stay on actions or attempts to collect consumer debt from any individual contingent obligors, e.g., guarantors, or co-signers, who themselves may not have filed for relief under the Bankruptcy Reform Act, unless they became obligated in the ordinary course of their own business. The stay also imposes an automatic bar prohibiting foreclosure, repossession, or any other attempt to enforce a lien. This stay remains in force until the case is closed, dismissed, or converted to a Chapter 7 or 11.

Contempt of Court

Furthermore, you will no longer be allowed to make contact with the debtor, once a plan is filed and an automatic stay is in force. If you violate the law, it may render your bank, officers, and even attorneys in contempt of court and subject to a fine, including attorney's fees to be paid to the debtor's attorney. In this connection, immediately contact your loan operations/note department, requesting personnel to stop sending past-due notices to debtors, in view of this being construed as contempt of court because of the continued contact once the stay is in force.

Clearly, the bank needs to be aware of a Chapter 13 filing. That in itself poses a dilemma. How will you know whether your borrower has in fact filed a Chapter 13? How, indeed, will you know about such a filing when the courts are often congested. Also, the notice may not be sent to creditors for some time after such a filing. Thus, you unwittingly risk contempt of court in view of your continued contact with the borrower. What if you do not receive notice from the court, but are verbally told by the borrower of the filing, and you still in turn repossess collateral? The writer personally believes you could be held in contempt of court for such action. Therefore, even if you do not receive a notice from the court regarding the borrower's filing, but otherwise hear about it, we recommend that you contact the court to verify whether the borrower has filed.

If it is determined that the creditors will receive a larger repayment under the plan than under a straight Chapter 7 liquidation, the court will confirm the plan. Typically, these plans require all creditors to reduce their overall claims and to extend the repayment period. The intent is often to allow secured creditors to receive a payback equal to the present value of their collateral, plus some interest, while giving unsecured creditors the opportunity to receive anywhere from 1 to 100 percent return on the dollar.

Actually, these plans are often in a creditor's and a debtor's best interest. Since most individuals have few assets that can be liquidated for the creditors benefit (refer to the state and federal exemptions discussed in Chapter 7), the prospect of recovering somewhat less over a longer period of time from the debtor's ongoing income is preferable to receiving almost nothing under a liquidation.

The debtor also benefits because the onus of undergoing a Chapter 13 rearrangement where only parts of one's debt are compromised is not nearly as great as a Chapter 7 liquidation where nearly all of the debtor's debts are forgiven.

When debtors do not perform under the plan they submit, creditors are free to petition the court and request a Chapter 7 liquidation. Or, they can ask the trustee for a dismissal of the case or for relief from the automatic stay. Performance under the plan should not only call for payments in a timely manner, but also for insurance premiums, paid to protect the collateral. If the trustee fails to act in a timely manner or is uncooperative, the bank should take the initiative and request a dismissal from the court. If the bank wins the motion to dismiss the case, it should immediately repossess before the debtor refiles another Chapter 13,thus once again invoking the automatic stay. The creditor's rights are at least as protected under a Chapter 13 as they are under Chapter 11.

In most Chapter 13 cases, the payments received under the plan generally do not equal and are usually less than what was called for under the original note's terms, thus usually forcing the note into delinquency, although such notes probably have already been placed on non-accrual. Therefore, it is better to charge-off the balance of such loans (even though payments accrue on some regular basis), and to show the payments as recoveries.

In these instances, similar to handling charged-off loans, they should be rebooked on a dummy or open file computer system in order to show any new balances, interest rate accruals, payment schedules, and maturity as set by the court. This system should track and monitor the loans by evidencing payment history, balance, and future payments. If possible, add legal expenses and other costs incurred. Therefore, check out your bank's note system and its capability. If you are not on a system that provides this type of information, consider obtaining software that can do it. Such stand alone software programs could be placed on an existing personal computer. Otherwise, such data and record keeping could be maintained on a manual system.

A Chapter 13 debt readjustment can only be undertaken voluntarily; you can't threaten an individual with a Chapter 7 liquidation.

However, it may be possible to induce a debtor to "volunteer" for a Chapter 13 proceeding by agreeing to work with them on a favorable payout program or plan that they can bear, based on their present income and cash flow, but not in excess of the court-approved limit. Initially, you should receive a notice of the bankruptcy case containing case number; date and time of the first creditors' meeting; evidence of the bank's claim (whether secured or unsecured); and a short summary of the plan. In addition, the names and addresses of the trustee and debtor's attorney should be furnished. A Chapter 13 wage-earner proceeding involves a plan that must be filed within 15 days from the date of the bankruptcy petition, whereby individuals repay debt based on a percentage of their earnings. This percentage of earnings would then be paid to the court which in turn distributes them to creditors, generally on some pro-rata basis of these earnings.

Professional people such as dentists often use such plans to their advantage by allowing them an extended period of time to meet their obligations and eventually come out of this temporary bankruptcy or court-protected status. Such plans may also allow a self-employed professional to continue operating without creditors repossessing, executing, or levying on their equipment (collateral) or other properties.

Usually, debtors have to submit to the court up to 25 percent of their after-tax dollars for payment to secured creditors, with some balance beyond that to be paid to unsecured creditors. Plans have been observed whereby creditors have sought all available disposable income for repayment from the debtor. Wage earners under court supervision are normally allowed to take from three to five years to make full or partial restitution. The longer the period to repay debt, the greater chances of full repayment. Money may stem only from the debtor's income, or from a combination of income and liquidation of personal or real property assets.

Secured creditor's debts may be modified, excluding the debtor's principal residence. If debtors do not pay as agreed, they may be moved into a straight bankruptcy and their personal and other non-exempt real property assets (for example, dental equipment) liquidated.

Under a wage-earner plan, you only have until the first meeting of the creditors to file your Proof of Claim, stating evidence you are a secured creditor. Otherwise, you are deemed an unsecured creditor. Also consider the different options individuals have to file bankruptcy in either a federal or state court, which could have a bearing on what you may recover under a court order regarding a wage earner plan. (Note: Individual state bankruptcy exemptions will vary.) Here are some *federal* exemptions:

- Up to $7,500 equity ($15,000 if both husband and wife file) in a debtor's principal residence.
- Up to $1,200 equity in a motor vehicle; another $1,200 equity in a second vehicle will be allowed if both spouses file.
- All household and personal possessions with a resale value up to $200, excluding jewelry which is allowed an exemption up to $500, and miscellaneous personal property assets up to $400 plus any unused portion of the residential exemption.
- Up to $750 in professional books or tools of the debtor's trade.
- Any life insurance owned by the debtor.
- Certain benefits, e.g., Social Security, alimony, unemployment compensation, veteran's and disability benefits.

Informal composition is another bankruptcy term which involves informal proceedings that may involve varied and flexible plans under state court actions (per individual state bankruptcy acts) receiverships, and equity receiverships. States have their own bankruptcy laws which are not the same as the federal Bankruptcy Reform Act. Therefore debtors have the option of filing under either federal or state bankruptcy acts.

After you receive notice of a bankruptcy, check the petition schedule of liabilities. If your loan is not listed on the debt schedule, the debtor will not be able to seek bankruptcy protection from that amount. He or she may amend the petition at the first meeting of creditors; therefore, it is always a good habit to file your proof of claim within the designated period. If the trustee and creditors are satisfied with the repayment plan, the court must accept it. After this acceptance, the trustee will be responsible for payment collection and make proportional distribution to creditors.

After all payments are remitted, the debtor is entitled to a discharge. Although a hardship discharge may be granted (due to job disability for instance) before all payments are made, there are other times a case may be dismissed (for example, if a debtor dies or becomes destitute or mentally incompetent and has no assets or means of income). However, a discharge does not dismiss action against other contingent obligors liable for the debt, thus creditors may pursue these third parties for the unpaid portion of the debt. Once debtors pay out completely under the agreed plan, they will be discharged from bankruptcy.

5.08 BANKRUPTCY TYPES

Involuntary Bankruptcy

Under the Bankruptcy Reform Act, it takes only three creditors with claims aggregating at least $5,000 to force an involuntary petition on the debtor. If there are less than 12 creditors, it would require only one creditor to initiate an involuntary bankruptcy proceeding as long as this creditor's claim came to at least $5,000; therefore, watch trade debts closely. There are generally six recognized acts, any of which may justify an involuntary bankrupt proceeding on the part of creditors. The first three below would not usually require an allegation of insolvency.

1. Fraud (concealment of assets).
2. General assignment for creditors.
3. Admittance in writing of inability to pay debts.

These other three acts typically require proof of insolvency.

1. Preferences—collateral or debt that is voidable—in such instances more assets may become available. Preferences may be difficult to prove involving certain personal

property assets because of inadequate recordkeeping or monitoring by the bank. Possession may be a clear means to determine preference involving a collateral interest in certain assets such as instruments and chattel paper, because value should be more easily determined on any given preference date versus other tangible and intangible personal property assets that require filings in public records to complete perfection and which may have an unknown value as of the determined preference date.
2. Liens on property that are not dischargeable (e.g., judicial).
3. The debtor involuntarily or voluntarily allows the appointment of a receiver.

If the bank files an involuntary bankruptcy, it must allege that the debtor is either not paying debts as they become due, or that a custodian, e.g., receiver, trustee, or assignee, has taken over substantially all of the debtor's property within 120 days prior to the filing. Consider moving quickly to have a temporary trustee appointed after a filing if you are not confident that the borrower can properly manage the business or you think owner/managers are dishonest or have a lack of credibility with other creditors and suppliers. Without a temporary trustee, the borrower can continue business as usual.

At times, it may prove advantageous for the bank to file an involuntary petition against the borrower, especially when bank debt is unsecured versus other creditors whose collateral position will be deemed a preference. Indeed, bankers generally lock up all assets by taking them as collateral to keep other potential secured creditors out of the picture. Generally, it is not a case of the bank being purely in an unsecured position, but it is when your bank may have a chance to recover only $.10 on the $1.00 versus what the bank down the street or other creditors can recover. These other secured creditors may be in a preference position and have a chance to recover much more, namely, 80 or 90 cents on the dollar.

Therefore, even if the other bank does not have a preference problem, you could still restrain it from perhaps foreclosing by filing the bankruptcy petition. Thus, it behooves your bank to file an involuntary bankruptcy. Your bank has to be especially alert to other creditor collateral positions in order to respond and act in such a relatively short time.

At other times it may be easier to liquidate your collateral in a reasonably short period of time, especially involving a Chapter 7 where abandonment of property does not equate in value to the bank's debt.

One thing you should remember is not to violate the automatic stay. Thus, do not undertake any self-help action or seize collateral besides setting off any accounts, although you could temporarily freeze them once you find out about a bankruptcy filing.

Voidable Preferences in Bankruptcy

The bankruptcy code defines a voidable preference as any transfer by the debtor of its property to a creditor for the payment of antecedent debt extended by the bank while the debtor was actually insolvent within 90 days of the filing of bankruptcy.

This preference period extends back to one year from the date of bankruptcy if the debtor is deemed an insider. The term *insider* is subject to judicial interpretation, but basically it entails control of the debtor by the creditor. The court will have to determine the exact date of any collateral transfer involving any insider relationship.

This insider preference rule also means that loan advances could be set aside as null and void. The bank will only be exposed to the preference period if the trustee can prove that the bank would have received more for the collateral than it would have in a liquidation under Chapter 7.

No preference, other than the improvements test of prepetition collateral, applies to after acquired collateral pertaining to accounts receivable and inventory collateral, but does apply to other after acquired collateral (e.g., equipment).

As an example, if the bank has a blanket lien on equipment and does not take a purchase money lien on any equipment acquired by the debtor within 90 days of a bankruptcy petition, this could void the bank's interest in such after acquired property if challenged by a trustee. Regarding receivables and inventory, if there is an improvement in collateral from the 90-day period prior to the date of bankruptcy, this improvement differential may be subject to a voidable preference. The same thing holds true for depository accounts.

Therefore, the bank has to determine its exposure to preferences, such as measuring its improvements in receivable and inventory collateral or depository accounts during the 90-day period. The bank can determine only the trends because any improvements will be measured exactly from one date (take the date of bankruptcy filing, then go back 90 days prior to the filing). Apart from receivables and inventory, if there is an increase in market value (versus an increase in value because of additional purchases by the debtor) for other types of collateral, any such improvement should not count as a voidable preference.

Courts are deciding various issues these days. One major decision recently dealt with the fact that an undersecured creditor (collateral value less than loan balance) should not be compensated, such as being paid interest for the delay caused by a debtor's bankruptcy proceeding. The decision included a statement that creditors are only entitled to adequate protection for a decrease in collateral value whether by use, sale, or lease and not by a delay pertaining to a bankruptcy proceeding.

Courts in different jurisdictions have come to opposing conclusions about whether undersecured creditors are entitled to compensation because of being forced into a stay, that is, when the stay delays any repossession or foreclosure action. Of course, a creditor may move for relief of the automatic stay. In order to succeed, the creditor has to claim that its interest in the collateral was not adequately protected, or that the debtor does not have any equity in the property and that the property is unnecessary for an effective reorganization. The debtor in turn has to disprove the creditor's claim; otherwise the court must lift the stay or injunction.

Satisfying the Adequate Protection Test

A debtor can meet the adequate protection test in three distinct ways:

1. Make periodic payments to the creditor sufficient to reduce the creditor's interest in the collateral, e.g., equipment that is depreciating.

2. Provide replacement, substitute, or additional liens on unencumbered or other property.
3. Offer an equivalent; that is, when the court requires the debtor to offer an "indubitable equivalent" of the creditor's interest in the collateral. This concept is similar to some equivalency in collateral value granted the creditor while the debtor uses its collateral. This might involve a stay injunction whereby the creditor is not receiving any benefit in the way of additional collateral or a cash equivalent and/or payments for the use of its collateral.

The lesson that banks are learning is that the type and quality of collateral they are taking has a bearing on the outcome. Also, by being secured in excess, they have more assurance of receiving accrued interest or other compensation while being stayed. Consider building in rights in your loan and security agreements to require additional collateral or to take default action when collateral values decline. Otherwise, you may be caught in an undersecured position.

Reasons for Objecting to a Discharge in Bankruptcy

There are certain basic reasons why a judge will not dismiss borrowers from their obligations in bankruptcy. For these reasons, the judge will insist on trying the case. Some of them are grounds for criminal action, such as, misrepresentation and fraud, and they are included in this list:

- Submitting false financial statements (misrepresentation including destruction and mutilation of records) and making false oaths.
- Making false claims or claiming money by false pretenses.
- Mutilating collateral; also failure to preserve collateral, and asset concealment.
- Committing fraud (e.g., not paying wages, delinquent alimony and child support, and maintenance damages to property); if a borrower commits an act of fraud, you may work out a repayment arrangement with them without court protection or intervention.

It is often easier to work with borrowers outside bankruptcy; therefore, do not unduly force them into bankruptcy. Negotiations may be in order. You may decide not to press criminal charges against a borrower. Also, you may be willing to allow the borrower to file a bankruptcy petition if they agree to reaffirm their obligation (sign an agreement to repay your debt which would be excluded from other debts) to you at which time the borrower will basically be prevented for six years under federal law to seek protection of the bankruptcy court; check state law in this respect if bankruptcy is filed that way. Certainly state filings, depending on the state, have different conditions and exception rules versus federal law.

Pre-Bankruptcy Planning by Creditors

Secured creditors are obviously always in a preferable position over unsecured creditors. Hopefully, a secured creditor will be able to obtain the value of its security out of the bankrupt's estate.

In some situations, a trustee can void a secured creditor's lien after a petition is filed. For example, a security interest obtained within 90 days of the filing of a petition can be voided if it is shown that the creditor was previously owed money by the debtor and was obtaining the security interest simply to obtain a favored position over other unsecured creditors.

However, such action cannot be taken until a petition is filed. This means that prior to the filing of a petition in bankruptcy, a creditor is free to execute his or her security interest in any collateral if a debtor does not perform. For example, a car or boat can be repossessed and sold. You can also set off the debt against a depository cash account.

Protecting Your Interests Once a Petition is Filed

If you are a fully secured creditor (margin of collateral is determined to exceed the debt), then you need not file a Proof of Claim with the court. This is based on the fact that creditors' claims and stockholder interests are to be listed on schedules to the court by the debtor or the trustee. You must only await the judge's decision as to whether the debtor will be given a discharge in bankruptcy before you take action against either property you have a security interest in or any depository accounts.

However, the writer suggests as a matter of practice you go

ahead and file a claim with the court, especially if perhaps your claim was listed as disputed, unliquidated or contingent, which would then require you to file a claim anyway although it could be objected by the debtor or trustee and even other creditors or third parties of interest. The standard Proof of Claim form is fairly easy to complete and can be done by someone in the bank as an attorney is not necessary. Some banks use in-house paralegals or personnel assigned to the charge-off/recovery section or department to complete and file such claims.

If you are only a partially secured creditor, then definitely do not overlook filing a proof of claim for that portion of your debt that is unsecured. If you are a totally unsecured creditor, then it strongly behooves you to file a claim for the amount of the debt. A plan for rearrangement will be confirmed by the court and imposed upon the creditors. A creditor who believes its rights will be adversely affected may and should file a complaint with the court or trustee and should request a modification of the plan.

5.09 ADEQUATE PROTECTION: ADDITIONAL QUESTIONS

The *American Mariner* case concerned the question of whether an undersecured creditor, whose collateral was worth less than the amount owed against it, was in fact entitled to adequate protection payments for the loss of the use of the money tied up in the collateral during the time the case was pending. This case concerned a question of adequate protection payments ordered as a condition of the continuation of the automatic stay as to a piece of undeveloped real estate. Although the land was not declining in value, either through use, wear and tear, or through the simple passage of time, the creditor argued that it was entitled to protection payments for the loss of the opportunity to foreclose on its collateral, sell it, and reinvest the proceeds elsewhere. The Court of Appeals in the American Mariner opinion found this a valid argument and upheld an award of adequate protection payments for loss of the time value of money tied up in the collateral, even though there was no depreciation in the value of the collateral during the pendency of the bankruptcy. This same reasoning followed in other Circuit Court of Appeals cases.

However, in the *Timbers of Inwood Forest Associates, Ltd.*, case, the court held that an undersecured creditor is not entitled to adequate protection payments to compensate it for the delay of the Chapter 11 reorganization during the pendency of the automatic stay, or for the loss of the opportunity to reinvest the money tied up in its collateral. The judge reasoned that adequate protection reimbursement for loss of the time value of money tied up in collateral is tantamount to interest, and the bankruptcy code allows interest for secured claims only pertaining to oversecured creditors whose collateral is worth more than the amount of their debt.

Therefore, on the one hand, it appears that the appeals courts have taken the position that protection payments will, henceforth, generally be available to compensate an undersecured creditor for depreciation in the value of its collateral during the pendency of the bankruptcy. Furthermore, undersecured creditors did come away with the right to be protected from a decline in collateral value and the right to be compensated due to deterioration, waste, or erosion (e.g., rust and spoilage).

The U.S. Supreme Court ruling, by contrast, left the undersecured creditor with only the option to move for a quick confirmation of a plan or for a dismissal of the case, thus attempting to minimize the period that it would not be realizing interest and opportunity value of money reinvestment.

This court also held that the undersecured creditor does not have a right to full reimbursement of attorneys' fees, even though a note and/or security agreement provides for it. Beyond that, the court did move to speed up Chapter 7 proceedings and indicated that debtors must show a viable reorganization is possible within a reasonable time and to show that the collateral in question is essential for a successful reorganization.

5.10 POST-PETITION FINANCING

If your bank is a creditor, whether one or one of many, that has a collateral interest in the debtor who has filed a Chapter 11, you will more often than not be requested to provide ongoing reorganization post-petition financing.

Obviously, more money will increase your debt exposure when added to your prepetition debt and the original loan(s). In this connection, you should analyze the chances of recovery of the existing debt (plus new money), based on the chances of the borrower achieving a successful reorganization, whereby it may, with your new financial assistance, emerge from bankruptcy.

Bear in mind that this will depend on such factors as the continued improved management of the company and the potential of it succeeding, including the approval, attitude, and cooperation of any creditors committee.

There may well be negotiations with committee members, namely, moratoriums and subordinations of their debt and collateral positions, in view of your commitment to advance additional post-petition funds.

Before advancing new money, make sure that the additional funds will strengthen the bank's position when collecting its existing debt. You do not want to find yourself advancing good money after bad.

If the committee and your bank are in agreement on advancing additional funds, make sure you receive the following consideration:

- Adequate collateral protection on additional loans.
- Adequate interest rates charged on these funds.
- Proper amortization and repayment of funds.
- A priority on payment (in the form of administration expense allowed to the bank) should be approved under a court order.

CHAPTER 6

CHARGE-OFF, JUDGMENT, AND RECOVERY

6.01 GENERAL

First of all, you must define when to charge off the loan according to your own bank's policies. Most banks adhere closely to the regulatory rules. As a matter of practice, it should be bank policy to charge off loans when they are deemed uncollectible.

The appropriateness of charging loans against the reserve for loan losses should be seriously considered on all commercial loans 90 days or more past due (and on installment loans that are 120 days or four payments past due).

A charge-off should be made whenever a loan is inadequately protected by either the current sound worth and paying capacity of the obligors or by the collateral assigned or pledged; that is, when these weaknesses make collection or liquidation in full highly improbable, based on current facts, conditions, and values. This does not mean that salvage value is absent, but rather that it is not desirable to defer writing off this virtually worthless asset. Even so, partial recovery may be realized in the future.

There is no real formula that covers all the possible circumstances and all loan loss situations. Therefore, charge-off decisions need to be made according to a review of many factors that include but are not limited to the following:

• Borrower's financial condition (and trends in the financial condition). Review working capital, debt payment due currently, accruals, and net worth (in the form of liquidity). Check on financial capacity by looking at earnings potential and true internal cash flow.

• Secondary support from guarantors or other contingent obligors, and from available collateral.
• Attitude—will or will not the borrower be cooperative?
• Sharp deviations from the original proposed use of funds.
• Questionable source of funds from which to repay debt.
• Total debt obligations, both short and long term; those in a senior or subordinated position; debt instruments; debentures; capital notes, including the impact from letter or loan agreements, security agreements indentures, and other agreements in force.
• General and local economic conditions that might have a bearing on the collectibility of loans. This includes deep business recessions and even local area depressions; recent plant closures; substantial industry cutbacks; and long, extended strikes in one-industry towns.
• Anticipated factors that were to deter charge-off, but in fact never did materialize, e.g., sale of a borrower's business, merger or acquisition, capital injection, substantial sale or liquidation of certain assets, additional financing or refinancing of debt by others

Obvrously, charge-offs should occur when losses are apparent, rather than at some stated period. However, timetables and other criteria are used as benchmarks in addressing these issues and in undertaking a more timely, disciplined, and realistic view. A charge-off, or at least a charge-down, should also be considered in cases where the remaining balance of a loan is less than the fair value of the collateral and where it would be too costly in time and money to practically pursue collection.

Initially, a charge-off request form, giving a write-off summary, should be completed by the servicing loan officer and then reviewed by managers at higher levels for final approval or disapproval.

If a charge-off is rejected, the request form and the file should be returned to the servicing loan officer, along with recommendations for additional collection efforts. If the request is approved, it should be initialled by the manager and others, if required. Accounting, or some other designated department, should first determine the exact figures that will be charged against the reserve for loan loss accounts. The request form should give the account number of the reserve for loan loss; the form should identify the department or cost center to which the loss will be charged.

Accounting, with the assistance of the loan and collateral department or the loan operations/note department, should then make up the proper charge-off entries. Some banks leave this entire process up to the charge-off/recovery department. The charge-off request form should include a brief history of the credit and the reason for charge-off as well as information on any other live bank debt.

After the request is approved, the files (bank's credit file, officer working file, if on hand, and collateral files) should be delivered to the charge-off/recovery or reclamation/asset recovery department. The asset recovery manager should initial the charge-off debit. This step acts as a purchase and a transfer of the debt.

The recovery staff should review the forms and files for completeness before signing off on the recovery form and accepting full responsibility of the files and charge-off. They should also verify the total amount to be charged off against reserves.

Index

A list of approved charge-offs, as well as recoveries received through the end of each month for the prior month, should be submitted in report form as part of the overall director's report. This material should be provided all directors at monthly board meeting, as well as to the directors' credit review and any other designated audit or review committees for their perusal. Ratification may be necessary.

Once entries have been made by the accounting or loan operation/note area, the original notes and any negotiable collateral documents should remain in the note area under dual control, rather than being delivered to the recovery staff. This allows separate control of them.

The loan operations/note or accounting areas should post all recoveries, which should be maintained in a separate computer file system. Either of those departments should also balance the recoveries to the charge-off ledger. Thus, one of these departments should prepare all entries to the charge-off trial balance and reserve for loan loss account, including a subsidiary charge-off or general ledger. Prime codes on each charge-off should be changed in order that the charge-off ledger reflects to whom the file has been assigned, e.g., collection or repossession agency, in-house collection without judgment, bankruptcy, pending or recorded judgment, inactive or skip.

Control Register

If the accounting department or another designated department does not have a charge-off control system, it is suggested that one be implemented. It should use a control register, whereby details can be entered into the register that is maintained. Here is a sample:

1. Index.
   a. Name.
   b. Loan number.
   c. Charge-off date.
2. Control register.
   a. Active subsidiary ledger.
   b. Workable subsidiary ledger.
3. Monthly report of total year-to-date activity.
   a. Per note department.
   b. Summary.
      (1) Balance at beginning of month.
      (2) Plus: charge-offs for month.
      (3) Less: collections for month.
      (4) Less: uncollectibles transferred to archives.
      (5) Balance at end of month.

Monthly Report of Total Year-to-Date Activity

The control register should be posted daily, and monthly year-to-date re-posts should balance to a memo control (for account entries) to the general ledger.

6.02 RECLAMATION (CHARGE-OFF/RECOVERY) DEPARTMENT

A department or section within the bank should be designated to handle all charged-off loans.[1] If you are in a branch system, a

---

[1] Such departments are known by various titles, ranging from "reclamation" to "charge-off/recovery." Or a bank may simply call it the "charge-off department." Depending upon the number and size of charge-offs, and the size of its staff, it may be accorded department status or section status.

regional headquarters may be given the responsibility to recover at least the larger, more complex charge-offs. Therefore, it will often receive all charged-off loans from branches.

This is similar to having a central department handle workouts (or "problem loans" which implies live debt). As in the workout area, personnel assigned to the recovery department should be considered quasi-specialists. They need a good working knowledge of the bankruptcy code and the governing rules. Also, they should know the ins and outs of the local bankruptcy legal system, including its rules.

The bank should always obtain the *Bankruptcy Rules of Procedure* and official forms, as sanctioned by the U.S. Supreme Court. These rules affect such procedures as notices and time of hearings that must be given to all parties of interest.

It will also be beneficial for you to know as much as possible about the local judges who oversee cases in your jurisdiction. This may be of assistance to you in knowing how to proceed with a particular case, especially if you find out how the judge has ruled on similar cases in the past.

You also have to learn to deal with bankruptcy clerks because these are the people who manage the day-to-day files and access thereto. You may find them very restrictive concerning the use of files, such as when and how you can see them. Get to know these clerks and their staff and learn their rules and procedures.

Trustees: They Frequently "Talk" Only by Letter

Seek background on the trustees handling your cases. Appointed by the court, they are usually attorneys who have a private practice. They have their own way of handling proceedings; some do not even answer questions on the phone. They often insist on only answering inquiries by letter. Knowing how to deal with the trustee can save you considerable time and money. If you have rapport, you can clear up simple matters of misunderstanding or miscommunication, even clerical errors and omissions.

One way to get to know trustees better is to attend creditors' meetings where you can observe how they operate and conduct business and where you *can* ask them questions.

It may even be to your advantage to get to know the debtor's attorney, as this could make negotiations easier; however, be cautious. The debtor's attorney often acts as an adversary. If you are not an attorney, you may need your own attorney to advise you on more sensitive and delicate legal matters. Negotiating on your own may be imprudent.

You should also get to know creditor committee attorneys who represent the class (particular group of creditors) that you belong to; or they may represent unsecured creditors. In either case, these attorneys can be a special source of assistance and information on bankruptcy matters in view of their experience and day-to-day dealings in the courts, especially as it relates to new or unusual circumstances. This may apply to some particular issue they have or have seen others litigate. You may find sharing ideas and getting to know them very meaningful.

One particular area relative to the Bankruptcy Reform Act that reclamation personnel should understand concerns "voidable preferences," that is, preferences both within the 90-days rules and within the one-year period (when the bank is deemed an insider), or when there is a fraudulent transfer of borrower assets.

In addition, charge-off/recovery personnel need to be knowledgeable in local and state statutes as they govern judgments, foreclosures, garnishments, and how to levy and execute on assets. They should have a fair understanding of financial statements and loan documentation, and have knowledge of the Uniform Commercial Code (UCC), as it applies to liquidating collateral in a "commercially reasonable" manner.

Income and Expense Savings Opportunities

A good loan recovery department may not only let the bank recoup much of its loss, but it can certainly significantly reduce ongoing expense.

Take the cost of bankruptcy cases as an example. Initially, before and after a borrower enters bankruptcy, the bank has probably spent a substantial amount in time and money. This includes the time and effort of loan officers, management, and other specialized personnel within the bank, besides the time spent by outside attorneys.

More specifically, it takes time to review loan documentation and files, deciding strategy before meetings with debtors, then discussing and deciding on issues at meetings, and acting upon them afterwards, including follow-up. Even before a loan is charged off, a substantial amount of time and money may have been devoted to the case. With a Chapter 11 corporate reorganization, this can especially become an expensive exercise.

Therefore, a good internal control system, together with increased bank participation (namely, an active recovery unit) may contain some of these costs, especially outside legal fees. Moreover, a good system of monitoring accounts may improve repayments and perhaps help obtain collateral that may be liquidated against the debt. Remember, every recovery dollar goes straight to the bottom line, and in turn can be reinvested.

Departmental Management, Staffing, and Expense

Optimally, the reclamation department or section could come under the umbrella of an in-house attorney. A large bank may have a number of in-house attorneys, but many banks cannot support this level of personnel.

Another problem that banks have with an in-house attorney is that it is often hard to find one who fits the mold of a banker. Typically, the more aggressive, better attorneys want to get out on their own, setting up a practice or joining a firm where they enhance the utilization of their skills. However, let us qualify this statement as some attorneys have sought out their certification or licenses because they really wanted to or eventually decided to become a banker. As such, they knew they could put such credentials to their advantage on the job.

With or without an attorney in charge, the Reclamation Department is often under the senior credit or lending officer. It may even be the same one who oversees workout loans or loan/credit administration.

It may be to your advantage to have recovery personnel come under the reporting responsibility of the workout area because workouts normally deal exclusively with the problem loan portfolio and often are closer to these same cases prior to the charge-off. Also, workouts probably operate in many of the same ways as the charge-off/recovery department including similar experiences as far as monitoring cases and dealing with attorneys.

In summary, the workout area is already familiar with many of the cases, so workout supervision may be a natural sequence of events in the handling process.

On the other hand, if you have the commercial loan side manage charge-off cases, it may work less diligently due to its new business development emphasis. Moreover, this commercial side lacks expertise with problem loans, especially those that have been charged off. Of course, in a smaller bank there may not be any other choice.

Some bankers believe that charge-offs should come under the responsibility of the credit/loan administration, but if it acts strictly in a support capacity (including the management of the note and collateral or loan operations/note department), credit/loan administration may not be the one to oversee the charge-off function. Why? Personnel, especially the manager of the credit/loan administration, may not have experience in collecting charge-offs.

Even if he or she has experience and is given such responsibility, it is best to have the loan operations/note area retain charge-off notes, receive payments, and reconcile entries for reporting purposes, thus continuing to allow for independence from the actual charge-off/recovery functions in order to meet security and internal audit and dual controls.

If the bank does not have an in-house attorney in charge, it should have either an experienced loan collector or an ex-lender who is tenacious and experienced enough with problem loans to manage them. The same type of person should also be hired for recovery positions within this department, too. If the bank can not line a good in-house collection attorney for charge-off/recovery work, then it should consider hiring a paralegal to undertake many of the mundane, clerical legal matters. Perhaps the paralegal can even curb outside legal fees. However you decide to staff this department and manage its responsibility within the bank, you should tailor it to your needs and particular situation in order to maximize recoveries and minimize costs.

Banks have come to realize that outside attorneys' fees have become exorbitant. When your outside counsel handles a case from the filing a petition and/or Proof of Claim to finalizing a discharge, you will quickly find that out.

Once the debt has been charged off and the borrower has not filed bankruptcy, you should pursue further collection action.

If you give a case to outside attorneys or it is determined that outside legal assistance is needed, photocopies of the loan and collateral documents should be made, along with copies of other pertinent information from files. They should then be checked out and transferred to the law firm. In case the attorneys are attempting to obtain a judgment and the court requires the original debt instrument, a photocopy of the original should be kept in the file, while the originals are forwarded to the attorneys or court. Attorneys should sign for any original documents removed from the bank and a follow-up procedure should be implemented to assure the return of such originals.

6.03 CHARGE-OFF/RECOVERY POLICIES AND PROCEDURES

Initially, the bank should write a good charge-off/recovery policy and procedures manual. This should begin with the process of charging-off the debt.

Procedures Prior to Charge-Off

Once the borrower fails to respond to your standard demand letter then charging off the loan is the next step. However, before charge-off steps are taken, the servicing loan officer should discuss the loan with his or her manager, and/or with the appropriate loan committee, in order to determine if demand should be taken. If the decision to make demand is made, copies of the demand letter should also be sent to any co-makers, co-signers, endorsers, guarantors, and other third-party contingent obligors or assignors of collateral to the debt. The demand letter should state if payment is not made within 10 days, for example, you will need to take the necessary legal action to collect this debt in full. Besides issuing copies of such letters to any other contingent obligors or assignors of collateral, a copy of the demand letter must go into the credit file.

It should be the bank's policy that loans are to be charged off when deemed uncollectible. The appropriateness of charging off loans against the reserve for loan losses should be considered on all commercial loans 90 days or more past due. For closed-end consumer installment loans, charge-off should be considered at 120 days or more past due. For open-ended signature credit and installment loans with no remaining payments (having a balance as a result of late, past due or extension and renewal charges, or unpaid single interest (USI) insurance the bank had to pay), which is 180 days or more past due. These loans should be charged off and interest charged to the appropriate expense account.

Whenever a loan is determined to be inadequately protected by either the current financial condition or paying capacity of the borrower and by any collateral pledged or assigned, and these weaknesses make collection or liquidation in full highly questionable or improbable, based on currently existing facts, and conditions and values, a charge-off should be made. This does not necessarily mean that there is no recovery or salvage value in the collateral, but rather that it is not practical or desirable to defer writing off the loan balance, even though a partial recovery may be realized in the future.

In this manual, the writer recommends that there be three types of charges made to the loan loss reserve account:

1. Charge-off of loan principal.
2. Write-downs of loan assets to their market value of collateral acquired through foreclosure, up to 90 days after the date the collateral was acquired. Any subsequent write-downs later than 90 days after foreclosure should be charged against income.
3. Deposit account overdrafts, excluding those created by bank service charges and other internally generated charges.

Generally, no other types of charges to the reserve should be made. Loan-related charges, such as reversal of accrued interest, attorneys' fees, expenses related to the maintenance of foreclosure properties (or properties abandoned to you by bankruptcy courts), loan collection expenses, fee income reversals, and overdrafts caused by internally generated service charges should be charged to the appropriate expense account.

Any expenditure incurred to improve or enhance the value of foreclosed property/collateral should be expensed unless its recorded book value (including the expenditure amount) is less than the fair market value of the property, based on a current appraisal. In these instances, such expenditures may be capitalized.

Any gain or loss realized from the sale of foreclosed property/ collateral within 90 days after foreclosure should be recorded as a recovery or charge-off, respectively, to the loan loss reserve. Any gain or loss which occurs later should be recorded as income or expense, respectively. Any deviation from this policy should be approved by management.

Charge-Off Procedures

After it is determined that a loan should be charged off, the charge-off request form should be completed by the servicing loan officer and signed by his or her supervisor and perhaps by a higher level of authority. The request could then be submitted to a designated department for verification before being finally signed off by management. An example of the request form is seen in Exhibit I on page 214.

After all signatures are obtained, the form should be sent to the note and collateral department or loan operations/note department and to the accounting department for processing and preparing the general ledger debit and credit entries. All entries should then be prepared and executed and should include any appropriate counter-signatures on tickets.

Next, the note department should remove the loan—and any accrued, but unpaid, interest—from the appropriate subsidiary note systems and ledgers (commercial or installment). The note department or the accounting department should post the charge-off to the subsidiary charge-off records utilizing the information contained on the charge-off memo entries and request form.

When an installment loan is charged off before maturity, a debit for a rebate of unearned interest or discount should be made if the loan was originally made on an add-on or discount-note basis.

In respect only to commercial loans, any unpaid interest that has accrued should be debited against the interest income account and respective cost center to which it was made at the time the loan was placed on non-accrual. The principal balance of any loans should then be debited to the reserve for loan losses account. Therefore, charge-off loans should be debited for the total amount of principal charged off, plus any interest reversed and any interest lost (not accrued) through the date of charge-off. Any legal fees or other collection expenses should be included. Those items should

EXHIBIT I
Charge-Off Request Form

Borrower(s) ____________ Social Sec. No. ____________
Street Address ______________________________
City ______________________ State ______ Zip ______
Endorsers, Co-makers, Guarantors
Address
Amount and Date of Indirect Obligations:
Charge-Off No. Date Orig. Note Date Orig. Amount
Type of Loan or Acct. No. Date of Loan (overdraft)
Face Amount Gross Balance Maturity Date Interest Paid To
Unearn. Disc. or Acc. Int. Net Charge-Off Balance Orig. Off.

A. Current Loan Status
    1. Number of Days Past Due or Date of Overdraft:
    2. Other Bank Debt and Department:
        a. Commercial and Installment:
        b. Open Credit:
        c. American Express, Gold Card:
        d. Credit Line Checking:
        e. MasterCard, Visa:
    3. Deposits:
        a. DDA:
        b. TDA:
B. Original Loan Information
    1. Collateral Description:
    2. Original Approving Officer(s):
    3. Original Purpose:
    4. Original Payment Program
C. Assessment as to Cause of Loss: (Be specific, e.g., lost job)
D. Action Taken to Collect (Include disposition of collateral)
E. Suggested Course of Action to Effect Recovery (if assigned to an attorney(s), state name(s) and phone number(s).

Prepared by Acct. Off ____________ Date ____________
Approved by Department Mgr. ____________
Approved by Division Mgr. ____________
Approved by President/CEO ____________

be broken out separately on a memo account debit entry. These entries should then be posted to the charge-off loan ledger. The posting date should be the date the entry went into the general ledger. Total debits should be offset with the credit to the correct account in order to balance these entries.

When the recovery department receives the processed charge-off form, it should arrange to have the note department also add any interest accrued but unpaid to the date of note maturity, or the last payment before the note went past due, or (as indicated above) to the date of charge-off.

Past-due interest may also be included from the time the note went past due. The note department, therefore, may calculate the balance of the charge-off from that date forward at the maximum past-due interest allowed in accordance with the note contract. Any accrual option beyond the principal amount owed should be approved by the recovery department and any other necessary higher authority.

Reversed or lost interest, legal fees, and other collection expenses should not be charged to the loan loss reserve, but rather to the appropriate expense account. Interest accrued, but not paid from prior years, should be instead charged to the loan loss reserve. Legal recourse should be used by the bank against the debtor in order to gain repayment of the debt, including unpaid but accrued interest, legal fees, and any other collection expenses as allowed in accordance with the terms of the note.

Upon completion of the charge-off, the case should be transferred to the reclamation or charge-off/recovery department for recovery action.

On a regular basis, the charge-off/recovery department should verify that all entries have been properly made as they pertain to continued accrued interest and that other legal and collection charges have been made, including the application of recovery proceeds to the charge-off balance. The note department should have a computer program to set up the charge-off balance, accrue interest continuously, and record any recoveries on a separate system from the live debt on the bank's books. The note department should balance all postings during the month to the general ledger at the month's end.

In some banks, charge-off balances may be handled separately by the accounting department or even the charge-off recovery department itself. However, for audit purposes use dual control; it is suggested that the latter department not be held responsible for the accrual or recovery entries, while also being responsible for undertaking the actual recovery collection work.

Each charged-off loan could be manually summarized on a liability ledger form or card and a new ledger card could be prepared for each new charge-off based on information obtained from the charge-off request form and charge-off entries. A manual system such as this may be applicable if you do not have a computer system that will print this information out sufficiently enough for you. A sample of the charge-off liability ledger instructions is shown in Exhibit J.

EXHIBIT J
Charge-Off Liability Ledger Instructions

1. Name and address of customer.
2. Type of note, e.g., commercial, installment, credit card.
3. G/L index number, if applicable.
4. Description of transaction, e.g., charge-off loan balance, legal fee expense, partial recovery.
5. Initials of the loan officer.
6. Date of the note.
7. Note number.
8. Interest rate.
9. Amount of note.
10. Service charges, legal fees, or other charges.
11. Interest reversed or lost.
12. Amount of any payment, recovery, or proceeds from collateral received.
13. Date posted.
14. Current balance: Columns 9 + 10 + 11 − 12 (that is, amount of note; plus service charges, legal fees, or other charges; plus interest reversed or lost; less amount of any payment, recovery, or proceeds from collateral received).
15. Sheet number (if more than one is required, sheets should be numbered consecutively beginning with "1").
16. Subtotals at bottom of page, when sheet is full; these subtotals should be carried forward to the next sheet.

A copy of the charge-off ledger can be filed alphabetically in the charge-off/recovery department file. Charge-off activity may also be recorded manually to the liability ledger, if you want to run a dual system with your computer records or until you implement a satisfactory EDP system for charge offs/recoveries. The computerized system should generate a detailed charge-off balance by customer. Of course, if you do not have a computerized system to reconcile the posting of all entries, you will have to maintain the manual liability ledger or a similar system.

Therefore, all activity affecting a charged-off loan's outstanding balance would be recorded on the liability ledger. Such activity might include: initial and subsequent charge-offs, partial or full recoveries, legal and collection fees, interest accruals, or other adjustments. Information may be obtained from entries made by the note or accounting departments each month. A full description of each transaction should be reflected on entries which then may be clearly recorded and updated monthly to the liability ledger.

The charge-off department should complete a central information form (CIF) in order to have this information inputted into the bank's central account and loan record information system. If the bank does not have a computerized CIF system, then a manual one should be maintained by making up cards properly marked to indicate that the particular account has been charged off. This will allow all loan officers to first check the CIF system for past charge-offs regarding that particular borrower before granting it future loans. If you do not have a CIF or manual system, loan officers may have to review charge-off files or some other previous loan history records or other print-out reports to check for any past charge-offs before making new loans to that borrower.

Handling and Filing Charge-Offs

Voluntary Credit Reports

At the time documentation is compiled for a charge-off, pertaining to an individual (or an individual was liable), a voluntary credit report should be prepared, reflecting the bank's loss. This report should be sent, possibly by computer, to local credit bureau(s). A copy should be retained in the charge-off file. Exhibit K on page 218 is a sample report.

The consumer banking department, or its counterpart, can file

EXHIBIT K
Voluntary Report

Credit Bureau ID #
R: (Date Reported) C: (Your Code No.)
Your Company Name Authorized Signature
Debtor's Name Suffix Spouse's Name
Social Security No. (His and Hers)
Current Address (No., St., City, State, Zip)
Former Address (No., St., City, State, Zip)
Current Employer
Former Employer
Your Customer Acct. No.
Address and/or Employment Wanted:

A: (Action Code) W: (Whose Acct.) D: (Date Opened)—(Mo./Yr.)
L: (Date of Last Pay—Mo./Yr.)
H: (Highest Credit or Last Contract Amount)
Present Status:
O: (Balance Owing) P: (Amount Past Due)
B: (# Payments Past Due) N: (# Months History Reviewed)
Historical Status: Times Past Due
E. 30–59 Days Only F. 60–89 Days Only G. 90 Days & Over
TY: (Type of Account and Terms, e.g., I.O.R. & S.)
S. - Select Proper 3 -Letter Remarks Code

Authorization is hereby given to discuss this account with the subject if he or she contacts the Credit Bureau to review this record. Mail to Credit Bureau of: Ames, 10 Peach St., Kansas, 44352

the reports immediately prior to completion of a charge-off for personal, consumer retail, and indirect loan accounts.

Documentation Transfer Procedures

Before a charge-off file is made up, certain documentation needs to be transferred. Here are some guidelines:

Transfer of Original Promissory Notes and Negotiable Documents by Note Department to Collateral Vault. After charging off the loan and entering the balance on the system, the note department should pull the following documents from its files:

Original Notes and Collateral. The note department should make one copy of the note and any other negotiable collateral, including titles, for transfer to the charge-off/recovery department. Non-negotiable documents may be transferred to the charge-off/recovery department in original form. The original note, title, and other negotiable documents should be placed in a note jacket or in a legal file if they are too cumbersome.

Note jackets or legal files can be filed alphabetically in the collateral vault. Negotiable collateral could be refiled in the collateral vault in accordance with note and collateral or the loan and note operations department procedures. Such documents should be separated from active loan documents.

The Remaining Collateral Documents. Any remaining non-negotiable collateral which can also be delivered to the charge-off/recovery department should be first reviewed, and then approved and authorized for transfer.

Access to original charged-off notes could be made under the dual control procedures established by the note and collateral or loan operations/note department.

A chronological, vault activity log could be maintained for all transfers of notes to or from the vault. The log should be initialed by two vault custodians and kept in the vault. A sample copy of a chronological vault activity log is shown in Exhibit L on page 220.

Transfer Copy of Notes, Collateral Documents, and Credit Files to the Charge-Off/Recovery Department. Prior to the delivery of any collateral documentation to the charge-off/recovery section from loan operations note department, a transfer sheet should be completed with an original and one copy.

The transfer sheet should contain a description of all documents delivered. The manager of the charge-off/recovery department should then review the documents and sign the transfer sheet for each document received. A copy could then be placed in the charge-off file. For a sample of a transfer sheet, see Exhibit M on page 221.

EXHIBIT L VAULT ACTIVITY LOG

Charge-Off Notes

Date	Cust. Name	Note No.	Check (In/Out)	*Reason	Init.	Init.
/ /						
/ /						
/ /						
/ /						
/ /						
/ /						
/ /						
/ /						
/ /						
/ /						
/ /						
/ /						
/ /						
/ /						
/ /						
/ /						
/ /						

* Example: In—New Note Out—Account paid out or closed. Note: This log is to be maintained in the collateral vault for a minimum of two years or until the account is paid out or closed.

The loan operations/note department could then deliver the above mentioned documentation items to the charge-off/recovery section, along with a copy of the transfer sheet, while retaining the original in the note jacket or legal file.

The charge-off/recovery section could obtain the credit file from the credit department using similar transfer procedures. Optimally, such charge-off/recovery files are retained in a separate section of the credit department.

Completing and Organizing Charge-Off Files. Upon the receipt of a copy of the debit, note, collateral documents, and credit files, these items could be merged into one charge-off file by

EXHIBIT M
Transfer Sheet

From: Loan Operations

To: Asset Recovery Department

Re: Smith's Shoe Store—Charged Off 9/31/90

1. Copy of promissory note (Describe)
Note # 300000—Smith's Shoe Store—$10,000.00—dated 12/1/87, with maturity date of 3/31/89. Secured by shoe inventory.
2. Copies of Negotiable Collateral Documents (List)
3. Non-negotiable file

Duplicate debit—reserve for loan losses in the amount of $10,000.00

charge-off/recovery personnel or credit department file clerks who in turn could deliver it to the charge-off/recovery department. Only that portion of the file applicable to the charge-off (if there is other live debt owed by the debtor) should be transferred because of the retention of other actual loan documents.

Consider developing your own forms and checklists for following the case or reviewing material. To quickly keep abreast of the case, it's best to maintain checklists and forms on the top of files.

Certain charge-off files should not be moved to the recovery department, but should be retained by the central workout or commercial loan group in view of partial charge-downs and other live debt tied to the borrowing relationship. However, once the workout or commercial loan group stops processing that particular case and the accounts have been fully charged off, the reclamation department should receive full responsibility for collecting any recovery on the charge-off debt. Unless the charged-off debt is moved to another specialized unit within the bank that handles other assets in the bank's possession or foreclosed real property, the reclamation department should handle it. Another specialized unit should only assume responsibility if the asset is transferred out of the loan portfolio to another asset category at the current market value.

Maintenance of Charge-off Files. These files should be maintained alphabetically in the charge-off/recovery department until the account is paid out or closed.

If these files have to be kept in the credit department, a special color label or tab should be used, distinguishing charge-offs from all other credit files. If the customer has other debt or relationships with the bank and separate credit files are retained, a memo record to that effect should be attached to the front of those files. Therefore, if there is ever any inquiry or new activity on this customer, it would put bank officers on notice that this borrower has both live and charged-off debt. Here is a recommended two-sided format for a legal charge-off file, organized in two columns.

Right Side—Chronological Order, Top to Bottom

Recovery activity diary (see Exhibit N).

Repayment/workout agreement, including terms, rights, remedies, and events of default.

Copy of ledger and accrual work sheet.

Legal bills, invoices.

Legal action request form.

Copy of petitions.

Judgments and abstracts.

Interrogatories and bills of discovery.

EXHIBIT N
Recovery Activity Diary

For ____________________
(Debtor's Name)

Date of Action______________ Action/Results______________

Notices of bankruptcy.

Copies of negotiable collateral documents received from the note department.

Original non-negotiable collateral documents received from the note department.

Left Side—Chronological Order, Top to Bottom:

Note jacket/copy of notes.

Duplicate charge-off/memo debit account entries.

Charge-off request form and transfer sheet.

Voluntary credit report.

Charge-off repo checklist and other repo documents.

Demand letters and certified mail receipts.

Memos and correspondence (debtors, attorneys, collection agencies).

Loan applications fact and term sheets.

Financial statements.

Credit bureau reports.

Inquiries.

Miscellaneous.

The primary purpose of the charge-off file is to serve as a reference source for the various documents that will be needed to collect a charged-off loan, to document the recovery collection efforts that have occurred, and to indicate the current status of the case. The charge-off/recovery department is responsible for maintaining these files in an orderly, up-to-date condition. A file should be prepared for each loan, in accordance with customer name. The diary should serve the purpose of documenting each step taken to collect any recovery on the charged-off loan, whether on a daily or weekly basis. Planned and pending action should also be included.

Statute of Limitations. When a debt is set up on the charge-off trial balance, dates should be noted in the statute of limitations' suspense or tickler system, reminding the staff six months in advance of the limit (the timetable varies by state). This assures that the debtor's liability is not inadvertently lost, due to the expiration of the statute of limitations. The tickler system could also be used to remind staff of any judgments that are nearing expiration (this time table also varies by state).

Monitoring Case Activity. Each month, the recovery department should review the entries posted to the charge-off trial balance. Loan operations or accounting may even separately post or manually update the charge-off activity to the liability account ledgers if there is not an EDP system in place.

Foreclosure and Repossession. Foreclosing on real property or repossessing other collateral should be undertaken prior to or at the time of charge-off. All expenses involved in repossessing and disposing of collateral should be charged to a collection expense account by using general ledger entries submitted to the loan operations/note department for posting. Copies of the general ledger entries should be sent to the charge-off/recovery department. Foreclosure or repossession may be the best alternatives for recovery.

As for repossession of personal property, fast movement is the key, as this should allow for greater salvage value. In a number of states (check your own state law), the law permits the bank to repossess motor vehicles, recreational vehicles, mobile homes, and boats without judicial process, provided repossession is done without breach of the peace. If the bank itself does not repossess, maintain a list of reputable recovery agencies to carry out a repossession within the letter of the law of your state.

After the bank obtains possession of the collateral, a letter (certified with a copy to file) should be sent to the debtor notifying them of the repossession. Failure to send this letter may result in the loss of the right to pursue the debtor or any guarantors for any deficiency after the sale of collateral. The debtor could then be given at least 10 days, which is reasonable, before the collateral would be sold. The debtor would additionally be responsible for any related costs, e.g., repossession and legal fees and storage.

When the 10-day period elapses, the bank could sell the collateral either publicly or privately for the highest possible price. The debtor, any co-signer, co-maker, endorser, guarantor, or third-party collateral assignor should be sent a final letter advising them of the disposition and any remaining deficiency. Money from the sale would be applied to the net balance. Proceeds in excess of the balance and fees should be returned to the borrower. These balances, after receipt of proceeds, would be handled by the charge-off/recovery section in accordance with charge-off procedures after the loan officer completes the charge-off request form and obtains approval.

Due to this means of repossession, the bank may become more vulnerable to litigation. To minimize exposure, officers should document each step they take relative to repossessions and should consult with their managers and in-house legal staff or higher levels of authority if they have a problem. All the above steps, therefore, should be handled in a "commercially reasonable" manner as defined by Article 9 of the Uniform Commercial Code (UCC).

Banks must consider the tax impacts of any mortgage foreclosure that will be treated as a sale or exchange of the mortgaged property by the former owner. The results will be either a gain or loss, whether the former owner had any personal liability on the mortgage debt or not. Actually, the sales price should generally equal the discharged mortgage debt, including any accrued and unpaid interest. The fair market property value should not have any bearing when determining the amount of the gain. Because the transaction is treated as a sale for tax purposes, the normal depreciation recapture provisions apply if there is a gain. The impact on deferred income tax recapture should result from the standard straight line depreciation method versus an accelerated depreciation method the borrower may have been using.

Use of Attorneys. Filing suit, obtaining judgments, and executing and levying on assets for recovery will involve the use of an outside attorney if you do not have an in-house one.

The supervisor of the charge-off/recovery section, or even with higher management approval, should first determine if it is feasible to pursue legal action. That manager may decide that recovery can be arranged by the charge-off/recovery section or through a collection agency without filing suit. If this cannot be arranged, staff then has to consider the size of the debt, the level of cooperation by the debtor, and the borrower's financial condition as well as available assets. In short, does the case merit legal fees? All this analysis is important because the cost of obtaining and collecting a judgment can be expensive.

Furthermore, the recovery process can be lengthened or become more costly if the debtor or its attorney uses defensive tactics to prevent judgment or collection.

When legal assistance is used, photocopies of the documents and of other pertinent information in the file are necessary. These copies should be forwarded to the law firm for post suit and/or collection efforts. The following guidelines concern the use of outside attorneys whether before or after charge-off:

- The recovery department should only use certain outside attorneys, cleared through the proper level of authority. Many attorneys have different areas of expertise.
- Prior to charge-off, a loan officer seeking the assistance of an outside attorney should first obtain approval of his/her manager before an outside attorney is engaged.
- Legal costs should ultimately be borne by the debtor, whenever possible.
- Attorneys should not be allowed to "trade deals" or make business decisions that can be properly handled by the bank's staff members, based on their knowledge of the facts pertaining to the cases.
- Bank personnel should not be placed at an unfair disadvantage when in conference with the borrower. Therefore, if the borrower is accompanied by an attorney, bank staff should consider having an attorney present, too.
- Bank officers, generally, should not negotiate with the borrower's attorney in the absence of the debtor or without the assistance of their own bank counsel.

Procedures to Obtain Judgments. The attorney assigned to the case should proceed to file suit in order to obtain a judgment by way of the following steps:

- Plaintiff's original petition is filed with court.
- Service of citation is made on the debtor, (now known as the defendant). If the defendant cannot be located, it may be legal to serve by substitution or via a newspaper notice.
- If the citation is not served due to an incorrect address and if the correct address cannot be obtained from the bank's files, pull credit bureau reports to locate the debtor. This may include skip tracing. Use other sources to locate defendants, such as cross reference or

criss-cross directories. If these other sources or the credit bureau is unable to locate the debtor, the bank should ask the credit bureau to list the bank in bureau files as desiring the current address of the debtor. If a substantial amount of money is involved and you cannot locate a debtor, then it may be appropriate to use a private investigative or collection agency, or whatever other source necessary. Once the debtor is served and is responsive, the attorney should move for a summary or agreed judgment. If the debtor is unresponsive, the attorney should move for a default judgment.

- Should judgment be obtained and the court require the original debt instrument, a photocopy should be made and retained in the note department's vault or a central vault where other instruments, and negotiable and transferable collateral may be stored. Originals should then be forwarded to the court. The attorney should sign a receipt for any original instrument he or she receives.
- Once the judgment is obtained, it should then be abstracted. The original abstract should be returned to the bank after recording. Record your judgment in the county or land records where the debtor may own property. Your judgment is normally recorded behind any other existing liens or prior recorded judgments that is, they are normally based on the first-to-file rule. You generally have to see if there is any equity in the property before deciding to buy out any other prior recorded lienholders' position.

Of course, in states that have homestead laws, you are not allowed to execute on your judgment, if property is a primary residence. However, years later after your judgment has been recorded, a charged-off debtor might try to sell a residence, only to discover that the title company frequently finds the judgment in the deed or land records. If the buyer was unable to obtain clear title because your judgment had not been released, it may nullify the sale, thus the sale will not be closed. When first issued and abstracted, the judgment probably included interest to that date and legal charges; plus it accrued interest on this new total at another interest rate, as sanctioned by the court. Sometimes the debtor or their attorney may try to settle a judgment for a smaller amount, without informing you of the reason for their call. So be alert to this, particularly in case they are selling a residence that has more equity than what they are offering to settle the judgment.

Set up a tickler file on computer or manually of all judgments obtained so they can be renewed properly before they expire. Check your state statute of limitations on judgments, for tickler purposes when judgments have to be renewed. Once a judgment is obtained and abstracted, the charge-off/recovery department should prepare new entries to correct the balance in accordance with the judgment amount, which may include legal and court costs, along with the new rate of post-judgment interest to be accrued.

Other post-judgment action and steps to collect the judgment by your attorneys may include the following:

The attorney can initiate a Bill of Discovery, send some interrogatories, or take depositions in order to locate assets belonging to the debtor. If assets are located, the attorney can garnish accounts, or levy on personal assets, or execute on real estate.

Relative to legal action by your attorneys to collect on judgments, two avenues often used by counsel are the attachment of real and personal property assets and the garnishment of bank accounts in the debtor's name. Attachment involves an execution to foreclose against real estate or a levy to repossess personal property assets. Should your attorney attach property? The size of the debt, and whether the borrower owns exempt real estate with sufficient equity or personal property assets (where your judgment is first or second in line) should have a bearing on a decision. Also, be sure you can seize such property without breaching the peace.

Your attorney may proceed under a Bill of Discovery when it is suspected the debtor has hidden assets, not previously disclosed. This bill will take a debtor into court; under oath, he or she will have to testify on personal financial records and tax returns which hopefully can detect additional assets that were previously not disclosed or which were accumulated since the date the debtor submitted the original "Statement of Affairs." The Statement of Affairs should consist of a statement comprising financial details including assets and liabilities of the debtor and any contingent assets and liabilities. If the debtor lies under oath, he or she is punishable in accordance with criminal statutes. Such action may be a strong inducement for debtors to make better arrangements with the bank to pay off their debt, especially if additional assets are discovered.

Check the statute of limitations in your state to see how long judgments extend before they expire, unless properly renewed. In this connection, any unsatisfied judgments should be renewed within a reasonable time prior to their expiration. Manual or computerized suspense or tickler files should be set up and maintained so that sufficient time will be available to prepare for renewal. This will ensure that the debtor's liability is not inadvertently lost due to the expiration of the statute of limitations. Judgments may be moved into an inactive status once it is determined that it is no longer advantageous to pursue recovery collection. Still, the judgment will remain of record.

Collection Entries and Other Expenses. To provide dual internal control in view of potential vulnerability to defalcation, the loan operations/note area should receive all payments on charged-off loans. All recoveries should be received at the loan operations window, and receipts should be issued for any in-person check or cash payments. Loan operations should prepare the entries to be posted to the reserve for loss account and to the general ledger. Credits from recoveries should be made to designated accounts relative to the reserve for loan losses and charge-off records. Loan operations should submit copies of memo account entries and process all payments, including the recording of recoveries, on a computerized or manual ledger system. The latter processing could be handled, if necessary, by accounting, particularly if a manual system is used.

All legal, judicial, and collection expenses involved in judgments, garnishments, repossession, and disposal of collateral should be debited to the loan loss (charge-off) ledgers, and then recorded and debited to the computer trial balance (loan loss control) in order to adjust balances. Upon receipt of abstracts and judgments, new charge-off balances should be made to the ledgers and trial balance in order to adjust the records to the new amount owing.

Charge-off recoveries collected through an outside agency, for which a commission has been paid, should include the above entries, besides the amount withheld by the collection agency, as a charge or debit to fees. A credit in turn should be made against the reserve for loan losses account. Before you deem it appropriate to return any remaining excess funds to a debtor based on collections in excess of a balance, someone needs to first recalculate accrued, but unpaid, interest and any other incurred costs or charges, such as collection, repossession, appraisal, inspection, maintenance, or legal, in order to determine the exact excess amount. If it is then determined that a credit balance is owed to the borrower, the excess funds should then be returned to the borrower. Proper debit and credit entries should then be made to a reserve for loan loss account. The charge-off/recovery manager should approve these entries which should be verified, also approved, and made and processed by the loan operations/note department, which in turn should forward a cashier's check for any excess credit balance to the borrower.

Purging Procedures. When a loan is paid in full or the file is to be closed, the following steps should be taken:

1. Paid notes.
   a. The original note should be stamped "Paid" and returned to the borrower.
   b. The credit bureau should be notified, if appropriate.
   c. The judgment, if any, must be released.
   d. The charge-off file should be marked "closed—paid in full," and sent to permanent storage.
   e. All internal accounting records should be updated to reflect the paid status.
   f. Loan operations should only release notes upon written memo and approval by the charge-off/recovery manager and other specified senior officers.
2. A file should be considered for closing and purging for the following reasons:
   a. If the judgment has expired and was not renewed or extended.
   b. If collection is futile because the debtor is a skip (i.e., you are unable to locate the debtor), and you have exhausted all efforts to locate him or her, or you have not been able to find property, on which to execute or levy.
   c. The borrower is virtually judgment proof (has no or few, or very little in the way of value regarding non-exempt assets).
   d. The debtor has been adjudicated in bankruptcy.
   e. The debt is beyond the statute of limitations for recovery and you have not been able to obtain a judgment.

f. In the opinion of the bank, chances of recovery are not worth pursuing the case.

When a loan has been fully worked and the decision has been made to close the file, or when the loan has been fully paid and recovered, the file should be removed from the regular charge-off files and retained temporarily in a segregated charge-off file section for future transfer to permanent retention/storage records. Paid or closed files should not be purged or moved by the recovery department without the approval of some higher level manager.

Removing Notes from Charged-Off Ledger and Other Records. Loan operations or accounting should prepare general ledger entries to remove charge-offs from the ledger and trial balance loan loss control reports. Appropriate debit and credit entries should be made to charge-off and reserve for loan loss accounts. Entries should be counter-signed or initialed by the charge-off/recovery manager and then processed by loan operations. Loan operations note department should maintain a copy of the subsidiary ledger for all purged loans.

6.04 FOLLOW-UP TO BANKRUPTCY PROCEEDINGS

Careful follow-up is always necessary, even if the borrower has filed bankruptcy. The bank needs efficient internal controls to handle all charged-off loans. Remember, any recoveries will affect the bottom line of the bank.

Bank staff should be constantly alert to the receipt of notices and other bankruptcy case matters. Frequently, the first notice of bankruptcy, especially on individuals, will come from the debtor's attorney. It is important that the right staff member receives such notices as soon as possible in order to allow recovery staff members as much time as possible to review, prepare, and plan their recovery strategy. In this connection, all other departments within the bank should be notified to immediately deliver any bankruptcy notices they may perchance receive to the charge-off/recovery department or other designated department.

Once the first notice of bankruptcy is received, the recovery staff should immediately check for any accounts or deposits in the borrower's name or on which it may sign, particularly since the bank may have a right of recourse or security interest in such accounts because the signature or account agreement includes security agreements. If any such accounts or deposits are found, put a hold on them immediately and do not allow any further checks to be drawn on them unless it is a check that must be honored. Do not set-off against the accounts if the debtor has filed bankruptcy (in view of being stayed), but just freeze them until the court resolves the case. Also, you have to stop accruing interest as of the bankruptcy filing date if the debt is not already on non-accrual since the bank's claim cannot exceed what the debtor owes on its debt, once the petition is filed.

In addition, the charge-off/recovery department should in turn notify all other bank departments requesting that they have no further contact with the borrower as all future contact will be made by the charge-off/recovery staff. As a safety precaution, some reference on the case should be made on all internal bank records and computerized system screens so that all bank personnel can adhere to your request.

If the borrower has not filed bankruptcy and you have obtained a judgment against the debtor, you can attempt to garnish bank accounts at other institutions. Various ways to locate other accounts include running credit bureau reports which may reflect them. You can also call other banks directly if you are aware an account in the borrower's name may be located there. You can even do a study on any of the borrower's time or demand accounts that he or she has maintained at your bank in order to pursue a historical search of deposits, which would probably involve re-searching microfilm records. Such deposit information may assist in locating other banks where money may still be maintained.

6.05 FAIR DEBT COLLECTION PRACTICES ACT

This law is designed to eliminate deceptive and abusive debt collection practices and to make sure that reputable debt collectors are not given an unfair advantage. A debt collector is defined as any third party who regularly collects or attempts to collect, directly or indirectly consumer debts asserted to be owed to other parties. The Fair Debt Collection Practices Act became law in September 1977, effective March 1978.

Business or agricultural loans are not subject to this act. Therefore, we want to reiterate that this law does not pertain to business transactions, but only to individual consumer or retail debt (such as for personal, family, or household purposes). Also, for this law to apply, the bank must be using an independent third party for collection. Furthermore, a bank would be subject to the act's requirements if it uses a name other than its own in its collection efforts.

The impetus for this concern over compliance is to warn and caution many of you who use third-party collection agencies. Often these agencies are used to track down skipped accounts, involving individual consumer debtors. But their aggresive behavior is not tolerated by the act. The act prohibits these practices:

- Abuse and harassment, e.g., threatening violence or using profane language.
- False and misleading representation, e.g., threatening to communicate false credit information, or giving a false impression that collection documents represent some sort of legal or judicial process.
- Unfair practices, e.g., misusing postdated checks, or engaging in communications by postcard.
- Contact with the debtor's employer, except to obtain information on how to locate the employee.
- Communication with the debtor at his or her place of employment if there is reason to believe that the employer prohibits such communication.
- Contact with a debtor at any unusual place or time, e.g., before 8 A.M. or after 9 P.M., unless agreed to by the debtor.
- Instigating court debt-collection action in a jurisdiction other than those permitted by the act.

If the bank as represented by the collector violates the act, it is subject to civil liability. Private civil action must be brought by the debtor against the bank within one year from the date of the violation. In an individual action, the debt collector is liable for actual damage plus punitive damages of up to $1,000. In a class action, the debt collector is liable for actual damages, plus punitive damages up to $1,000 for each named plaintiff and the lesser of 1 percent of net worth or $500,000 for all other class members.

CHAPTER 7

GUARDING AGAINST LENDER LIABILITY

7.01 GENERAL

With the proliferation of lender liability suits, the bank needs to act in a judicious manner when handling problem debtors. Banks have been vulnerable to many actions that have drawn them into lender liability suits, e.g., control issues, bad faith, negligence, and fraudulent actions. Appropriate training of lending or workout officers in this regard is necessary.

Of particular concern is the information that finds its way into bank credit files and other bank records. Officers should be aware that anything they write could someday represent prima facie evidence that may eventually be presented in a court after being discovered via a subpoena of bank records, thus what is written should be couched in tactful terms.

For instance, do not make discriminatory or derogatory remarks about borrowers, nor express opinions about their character. In particular, do not do this in a memo or other documentation that may find its way into a credit or some other file including desk files. Nor should vindictive attitudes be evident in correspondence; always think of the possible implications of what you say or write. Also, be sensitive to unintentional remarks that may later haunt you. For example, if you express the opinion that a borrower may actually be insolvent, even though the borrower's current financial statements do not reveal such a condition, this could be held against you if the borrower later enters bankruptcy and/or if a question of fraudulent conveyance surfaces. Therefore, be cautious about documenting the file at any time you believe the debtor is insolvent.

Do not file sensitive legal opinions or memos in files since this is privileged information (when not written on bank letterhead) and legally may be held in confidence. Such opinions are at times written in blatant violation when graphically describing how the creditor may take advantage of other parties of interest or the debtor itself.

All of this also applies to verbal comments made in the presence of debtors; agreements should be in force prohibiting verbal discussions between the bank and its debtors from becoming binding. Attorneys at times offer action that may set up or harm the position of other creditors, which could result in grounds of an "equitable subordination" against the bank. The bank should always scrutinize credit correspondence and memos, and other significant documents before making demands for payment or calling loans because of an event of default. Files should always reflect the bank's good-faith attitude.

Remember, anything that you do not want to hear read in a court of law or before a jury should not be in your files. Do not think that just because you have a private desk file you can overcome any exposure or hide information, or be more candid in stating your opinions.

7.02 CAUTIONARY MEASURES

You may find the following cautionary statements helpful:

• Make sure loan monitoring procedures are consistent with written loan policies at the bank.

• Be consistent in completing loan agreement compliance checks, and provide evidence to the borrower of all violations and events of default; declare such when calling a loan. Your rights and remedies may be modified or even lost if you become lax by not requiring compliance to loan agreements. If the borrower is not in compliance, always send out notices of agreement violations followed up by waivers or amendments. By not following up in this manner, you could be exposing yourself by waiving your rights. Also, do not just call the loan when a default exists without offering evidence of what represents a default as this could result in a cause of action by the debtor against you. Therefore, always provide adequate notice to borrowers before you ever exercise your rights and remedies under the loan or security agreements.

• Do not get caught in a trap of "overreaching." Thus, have your borrower acknowledge written agreements pertaining to any extensions, additional collateral, or other implemented requirements; review of such documents by its legal counsel should strengthen your position.

• Do not change written agreements or contract terms without properly notifying your borrower as a court could nullify such action on the grounds of acts of commission or omission; therefore, be consistent in word and deed regarding any spoken or written word.

Judges have recently held banks liable to their borrowers for refusing to make further loan advances; the courts held that refusal was bad-faith action on the bank's part. Therefore, if you decide to terminate a borrowing relationship, first contact your attorney if you have any reservations about immediately proceeding.

Next, assuming that a clear violation has occurred under the loan agreement, which has now become an event of default, inform the borrower that you want the debt moved or paid within a given period of time. Preferably, this request should be made in a personal meeting. Make sure there is no misunderstanding on the borrower's part.

Follow up the meeting with a certified letter, return receipt requested, indicating that you are demanding payment under an event(s) of default and demanding that the debt be paid within so many days. It's better to give the borrower a 30-day grace period to repay the debt, rather than the customary 10-day period, especially if a company borrower has a sizable credit facility or sizable loan balance. Thus, attempt to give the borrower a sufficient amount of time to move the debt even if the note is due on demand. It is important to offer a sufficient amount of time because when you make demand, you should stand by your decision.

When there is an unfriendly termination of the relationship, the following strategies should also reduce the risk of lender liability suits:

• Always fully document any event of default in your files and in letter form to the debtor. This may give the bank some amount of protected assurance under a good-faith termination of the credit, unless you have made a habit of arbitrarily waiving defaults in the past. Make it a practice to always document waivers by giving debtors letters in this respect rather than being complacent, or only informing the debtor verbally that you are aware of the default.
• Do not modify, supplement, restructure or create a novation of debt without legal assistance, especially so as not to expose the bank to further waivers of debt or events of default under loan agreements.
• Never accelerate the debt without first giving a written notice of demand, unless such action will prejudice your position. If you have been acting in a complacent manner regarding waivers, then first send a letter (certified return receipt requested), before you forward the actual demand letter, indicating that you will not be waiving any more violations or events of default and that they must be cleared in the time allowed under the agreement. Furthermore, you should indicate in the notice that strict performance under the loan agreement will be required and enforced.
• Be cautious in relying too much on certain minor or so-called boilerplate covenant violations (that result in defaults), or those that could perhaps be easily cured. Calling a loan on these grounds could be deemed bad faith. Therefore, make sure that you are acting in good faith and believe that the prospect of payment or performance is impaired and that there are definite or clear-cut reasons to call the loan, e.g., obvious lack of performance or numerous occurrences of events of default under the note and loan agreement.
• Do not induce borrowers to renege on other obligations or infringe on another creditor's collateral rights in order to gain an advantage in some way, e.g., taking collateral knowing it would violate another creditor's loan, security, or other collateral agreements.
• Be very cautious in the use of discretionary-advance clauses in agreements, e.g., bank's right to stop making advances or of cutting back on borrowing base formulas arbitrarily.
• Be very sensitive when calling loans where the borrower has a great deal of vendor or borrowed debt because if you cut the debtor off, this may mean it will be too difficult for it to move or obtain

other credit and capital; the latter applies more to publicly owned companies.

• Be very cautious when calling a loan under an insecurity clause provision in your note or agreements or using an acceleration clause to call a loan under an event of default. Compared to your previous dealings with the borrower it may appear that you are now taking unwarranted action; therefore, make sure there is valid and fair justification for calling the loan and that it is being done in good faith. Your previous manner of dealing with the customer may be tested in court. For instance, you may be challenged on waiving your rights because in the past you accepted late payments routinely; and you allowed violations to agreements and events of default to continue without proper notice or authorizing any waiver or amendments to agreements. Insecurity clauses should only be used when you strongly believe that the prospect of future payment has been impaired or is in jeopardy; you may even have to prove to a court quantitatively how much future repayment of the debt has been impaired.

• Be careful that loan commitments do not vary greatly from acceptable loan policies and procedures especially when initially establishing loan relationships. This may become a different issue when initiating standstill or moratorium agreements.

Standstill or Moratorium Agreements

If you feel that the relationship is or is going to be adversarial, consider implementing a standstill or moratorium agreement whereby the bank will agree not to call the loan because of a default, or take legal action. The bank may even offer continued advances in order to prevent legal action.

As consideration for the bank extending such an agreement, the borrower should be willing to sign an agreement not to sue the bank. Or the borrower could even furnish a statement releasing the bank of any liability based on the negotiated favorable action offered by the bank and accepted by the debtor.

Such an agreement can certainly diminish, alleviate, or reduce the possibility of any legal repercussions of a later filed suit by the borrower because of its earlier acceptance not to take action against the bank under the circumstances, at least for a specified period of time. It should at least limit a defense later raised by the borrower. Be cautious when the borrower's attorney insists that by signing this agreement, the borrower is not waiving its rights to bring suit after the expiration of the standstill or moratorium period.

The key to such agreements is that the arguments have been settled and neither party thinks it has a leg up on the other or is making a power play based on its feeling that it is in a better negotiating position. Here are some tips:

- Work for proper communication and disclosure in agreements.
- Act with good cause based on reasonable expectations from all parties.
- Avoid fact issues involving detrimental reliance.
- Avoid errors and surprises.
- Develop plans and strategies to avoid and resolve controversial issues.
- Verify all the facts about the adversarial relationship—especially when the borrower threatens suit—before you extend any standstill or moratorium agreement.

Make sure the borrower is serious and that there is sufficient justification on its part to take any further action. Cautionary measures like those listed above may protect the bank against committing the following types of wrongdoing:

- Obvious violations as an insider.
- Genuine lack of good faith in calling a loan because of the past action of accepting late payments or allowing loan agreement defaults without formal notice, thus waiving the bank's right to demand payment.
- Verbal or written discriminatory remarks by bank officers or staff against the company and/or its personnel.

Again, review all the facts, advantages, and reasons why you should enter into a standstill or moratorium agreement with the borrower before you do so. Furthermore, do not move too hastily in this regard because the borrower could take the offensive by believing they have the advantage and immediately file suit.

Moving towards a standstill or moratorium agreement should be a last resort for the bank because this is all that it can do under the circumstances, or because it is really at risk or in jeopardy of losing a lawsuit because of its past actions.

Potential Bank Violations

Reasonable Care Standards. One trap a bank can find itself in is a violation of the "reasonable care" standards as governed under the Code regarding the possession of company stock in the name of the borrowing entity. This is not to say that the bank cannot hold company stock as collateral, but if it has a loan agreement which has a covenant prohibiting a change in management without its approval and at the same time holds the controlling shares, the bank could be in a strong position to control or have great influence on any management changes.

Therefore, if the bank uses its controlling shareholder influence, along with its loan agreement covenants, to install management who subsequently weaken, diminish, mismanage, or ultimately ruin the business or deplete the value of its assets, the bank could find itself in court being charged with a breach of its "reasonable care" of the stock besides being charged with an insider violation.

Obviously, as one can visualize, if the bank holds the borrowing company's stock, without even voting it (which of itself would be a clear violation of insider rules), all it has to do is to have an influence, especially when coupled with loan agreement covenants controlling management changes.

A good rule of thumb is not to use covenants or violations thereof to coerce the borrower into doing or taking other actions that you want done. Thus, you will have to be very cautious because the lender's attorney will place your bank under close scrutiny and will go to extremes and great lengths to prove lender liability on any such issues.

The bank should never use excessive control over the borrower or unreasonable interference in its business. For the bank does not want to be placed in a position of being faced with accusations of duress, or economic coercion as a result of pressuring the borrower to do certain acts clearly for the lender's benefit, e.g., forcing it to sell off or liquidate assets still being used in the business to pay debt. In addition, it has to be careful of being accused of violations of the following legal principles:

The Deceptive Trade Practices (DTP) Act. Even though you may not have done anything directly wrong, you may have bought from a dealer a contract or chattel paper pertaining to a vehicle purchase by a consumer (who may have misrepresented the sale). In this case, you are involved as assignee under the contract regarding consumer allegations.

Therefore, whenever possible, consider obtaining an indemnification agreement from those third parties from whom the bank buys paper in order to protect it against debtor suits for violation of the DTP Act by such third parties. This way the bank may be somewhat protected against the wrongful acts of others.

Fraudulent (Knowing) or Negligent Misrepresentation. Related violations include wrongful control, duress, economic coercion, bad faith, breach of contract, promissory estoppel, conspiracy, security law violations, and violations of the Racketeer Influenced and Corrupt Organization Act (RICO), the Sherman Act, the Bank Holding Company Act, and the Anti-Tying Act.

RICO claims and allegations may arise against banks and other creditors based on accusations of involvement in a pattern of racketeering relative to fraud. RICO allegations are occurring more frequently as they relate to securities fraud in account and loan relationships with limited partnerships and closely held private corporations and some public companies. This has resulted in banks being accused of aiding and abetting involving unregistered securities fraud through subsequent conversion of unlawfully obtained securities to cash and debt repayment, and also direct and blatant acts of mail fraud to promote the sale of those securities and handling such transactions. Securities fraud can result from misrepresentations of material facts. It can also result from failure by corporations and partnerships to disclose material facts which should have been disclosed in order that an offering not be misleading. RICO violations relating to securities fraud and deceptive practices have been alleged in more lender liability cases recently because of the many offerings and sales of unregistered or improperly registered limited partnership and company interests to unsophisticated investors. Plaintiffs who win RICO suits can collect treble damages and attorney's fees; such awards are not generally available under state anti-fraud laws. The writer predicts a large number of RICO suits in the near future against financial institutions for alleged wrongdoing and fraud. Remember, RICO has broad and far-reaching powers, and the legal system and law enforcement agencies are starting to use it more in combating white-collar crime.

Violations of State Consumer Codes, Insurance Laws, and Deceptive Practices Statutes. The bank needs to be alert to potential violations of this type. These include breach of warranties, and unconscionability, including defamation of character such as slander and libel as it relates to credit reporting and related areas.

Also, if a bank misrepresents its borrower's financial condition to other creditors, and does not make accurate or full disclosure in order to intentionally disguise the true financial picture of the borrower, it could be held liable to a plaintiff. Therefore, if the bank agrees to respond and answer another creditors' questions, it has a duty to properly and fully disclose any material information that is requested of it regarding the borrower's true financial condition. Failure to accurately respond may subject the bank to liability under federal securities acts, too.

On the other side, plaintiffs have charged banks with breaching their trust relationship by not properly informing them—or not disclosing derogatory information—regarding companies for which they requested the bank to undertake credit investigations relative to extending credit. Worse, banks have improperly convinced borrowers to assume ownership of companies to which the bank also had outstanding loans—companies whose chances of success were worse than they were made to appear. Plaintiffs charged a breach of trust and fiduciary relationship.

Other Potential Violations. If you enter into any contracts with the borrower, be cautious of such areas as the "parol evidence" rule, oral agreements, and waivers and estoppels.

Banks are also being impacted by tort cases pertaining to causes of injury to debtors which may be concluded as intentional or absent of any justification, e.g., wrongful call of a demand note, therefore, being held as prima facie evidence under a tort theory or tortious interference with contract rights. This tortious interference may also carry over to control of decisions of managing the borrower's affairs to the lender's benefit and borrower's detriment.

Damages and Penalties

Some of the different types of damages and penalties the bank may sustain—which may not all be legal—that are important for you to consider in a lender liability suit include the following:

- Actual consequential (awarded for actual losses) and exemplary (punitive damages awarded to punish and deter) and legal expenses (includes attorney's fees). A violation of the Deceptive Trade Practices Act and RICO would also result in treble damages.
- Injury to borrower's reputation; mental anguish.
- Statutory penalties (discretionary, automatic and multiple).
- Forfeiture of debt and interest or any anticipated deficiency.
- Court reimbursement orders.
- Economic losses and bad community publicity.
- An "equitable subordination" of claims to other creditors. This could result from the bank taking unfair advantage or using inequitable conduct resulting in the injury to other creditors of a bankrupt entity.
- Decline in bank personnel's time and energy including morale.
- The bank being deemed an insider e.g., voidable preference on debts and collateral, and being found to have control over the debtor's ability to pay creditors, including not paying IRS withholding or other federal and state taxes as they become due. It may also find itself jointly liable for federal withholding taxes and any penalties therefrom.

In this connection, courts have developed functional tests in determining responsible actions by bank personnel and others by examining their control over the borrower's entire payment process and ability as it pertains to what bills the borrower pays.

This could become more precarious for the bank if it monitors and controls account debtor payments coming directly to the bank under a notification arrangement or through a blind lockbox (disguised notification arrangement regarding direct remittances of accounts receivable proceeds or contract payments from other obligors of the borrower) and such are first deposited to a cash collateral (restricted) account under the bank's exclusive control. Therefore, regarding the direct collection of account debtor remittances, make sure your debt is paid down accordingly in order to keep the borrower within its borrowing base, but do not restrict any excess or remaining funds received, or advances that are credited to the borrower's operating account nor control payments made to others from unrestricted accounts.

You could also forfeit your right to dishonor checks by controlling the proceeds derived from receiving checks "in kind" or through a lockbox that is applied to debt or credited to a cash collateral account. Basically, it will come down to the bank's actions being found to be a "voluntary, conscious, and intentional" act to prefer itself and perhaps certain creditors over others, the government, or other third parties of interest.

Preventing Potential Lawsuits

The bank should adhere to the following rules when dealing with customers in order to prevent potential lender liability suits:

- Never mislead the borrower or any of its other creditors, whether intentional or by way of being negligent; always be factual and straight-forward as it relates to business transactions. Always follow through on what you say you will do.
- Do not attempt to falsely persuade a third party to purchase your troubled borrower, or improperly inform a third party or misrepresent facts about the debtor including material omissions
- Always undertake business dealings in an atmosphere of a fair course of conduct.
- Lenders should never manifest abusive actions whether by the way they conduct themselves or speak to borrowers.
- Lenders should not change their course of action or conduct without prior written notice to borrowers. For example, they should no longer accept late payments or honor overdrafts as a continued general matter of business practice, as this course of action of itself could modify the bank's rights under any preexisting agreements. This also applies to prior negligence—to not doing anything while the borrower was in default whether under a

provision of the note or pertaining to a violation of a covenant in a letter or loan agreement.

• Bankers should always provide the debtor and contingent obligors, assignors, and pledgors of collateral to the borrower's debt, prior reasonable written notice of debt acceleration or collateral foreclosure. It may be wise, if possible, to provide one short-term loan renewal before calling the loan in order to give the debtor some time to arrange payment of the debt, unless this will further jeopardize your position.

• At the time you call the loan and accept a partial payment from the debtor, you should always send the debtor and other contingent obligors a demand letter, giving them reasonable notice, if you again decide to call the loan.

• Lenders should not deal harshly or use severe tactics with borrowers just because they may rely on agreements in force which the debtor has violated or may have defaulted under.

• Lenders should alway refrain from becoming involved in a control situation over the borrower's business affairs, e.g., determining what bills and creditors should or should not be paid, influencing management decisions or changes because of holding control of the business through company stock pledged to the bank or by way of governing covenants in letter/loan agreements.

• Lenders should not make commitments or other agreements with borrowers verbally. All dealings should be on an arms-length basis. Follow-up letters should be sent to the debtor indicating the lending officer's understanding of any agreements and describing the discussion. A copy of the letter or separate memo should be put in the credit file.

In the recent *Krause vs. Bank of America* lender liability case, the appeals court properly overturned a prior award granted the borrower in accordance with a jury verdict. The appeals court based its decision on the fact that the bank had not entered into a formal contract or commitment with the borrower; thus the bank was not legally obliged to fund future advances. A formal commitment involves a legal contract between a bank and a borrower. If the bank does not want to be legally obligated to the borrower, it should enter into an informal agreement written in a qualified manner so as never to formally obligate it to fund future advances, which also applies to verbal credit agreements. If the bank does enter into a formal commitment with a borrower, any commitment letter or letter/loan agreement should also have an added clause that the borrower waives its right to a trial by jury. This may protect the bank against any sympathetic attitudes that jurors often have for debtors and their ignorance about such legal matters.

- Lenders should not overstep their bounds when giving financial advice to borrowers so there will be no question that the banker is not acting in more than a fiduciary capacity. This is not to say that the banker should not be able to frankly discuss the borrower's financial condition with it and point out noticeable trends and concerns whether positive or negative.
- Lenders should not get entrapped by threatening to call a loan when that is not really their intent, as they may only have wanted to get the borrower's attention by using such a tactic, and actually they may not have made a final decision to call the loan. Therefore, do not act in a cavalier manner, or use bluff tactics to gain the borrower's attention or cooperation, as a court could construe such action on the bank's part as being fraudulent, irrespective of the rights and remedies provided in loan and security agreements.
- Lenders or other credit department personnel should never give out erroneous or false information relative to incoming credit inquiries on borrowing customers as the bank may find itself being sued for misrepresentation based on injury or harm suffered by such other creditors that relied on your information in making credit decisions. This may even include negligent misrepresentation on the bank's part based on unknowingly or unintentionally giving out false or misleading information on your borrower.
- Lenders should never represent themselves to be knowledgeable or sophisticated in a particular lending or documentation area to customers, when in fact they are not. This could backfire on the loan officer when a borrower is harmed or injured because of relying on this type of lender misrepresentation (similar to a malpractice suit). It may have valid grounds for winning a suit.

Regarding guaranties, make sure they are written explicitly relative to why they are requested in order to protect you later from being accused of overreaching. Also, consider inserting jury waiver provisions in a conspicuous location within your other loan and collateral documents. Check your local statutes to determine if such waiver clauses are enforceable. Make sure the debtor understands such provisions by acknowledgement thereof. Consider including a forum selection clause in your loan documents, too, in order to specify the state or forum in which a trial will be held regarding lender liability, should it occur, and that it is enforceable. Also, include a clause in documents, whereby the debtor agrees that they are "commercially sophisticated" and that the bank has not used duress or undue influence over them to execute any agreements.

CHAPTER 8

REPOSSESSIONS AND PRIVATE SALES OF TANGIBLE PERSONAL PROPERTY

8.01 GENERAL

This chapter sets forth the guidelines and procedures a creditor can follow in order to repossess a motor vehicle or other personal-goods collateral after loan default. This chapter is devoted to these topics because vehicles and certain other personal goods are commonplace types of collateral that the bank frequently deals with when personal and consumer loans fail. Before embarking on repossession, always confirm that a default has indeed occurred as defined in the terms and conditions of your security agreement.

8.02 DEFAULT IN SECURITY AGREEMENTS

Your security agreement should contain "events of default" clauses that protect your collateral interest. Some of the more typical clauses are as follows:

- An "event of default" shall exist upon the borrower's failure to make a loan payment when due.
- Default shall occur upon the borrower's failure to perform any of the terms herein or requirements of any other documents executed in this connection.
- Default may be triggered if in the bank's good-faith opinion, the borrower's prospects of performing under its obligation have been seriously jeopardized.

• Default may be initiated if the collateral, in the bank's judgment, becomes impaired or unreasonably decreases in value.

These last two default clauses are often referred to as "insecurity clauses." Section 1–208 of the Uniform Commercial Code (UCC) authorizes such clauses, provided the creditor in good faith is of the opinion that the prospect of payment or performance is highly questionable or impaired for one reason or another. However, the burden of proof to perform is on the creditor. The Code also defines "good faith" as "honesty in fact." However, the courts have found the entire area of insecurity clauses difficult to deal with; they seem uncertain about what constitutes good faith. Therefore, even though you may have such clauses in your security agreements, use them judiciously, only when you have reasonable assurance of expected impairment or nonperformance on the borrower's part.

In most instances, however, the bank should have no problem in determining that the borrower has in fact defaulted on his or her obligation as the debtor will be delinquent in its payments. Before declaring the note in default under the security agreement or accelerating the maturity of the note for any reason other than a past-due payment, though, cautiously determine whether an "event of default" has actually occurred under one of the other default clauses exhibited in your security agreement.

Once you have determined to call the loan because of a payment default or because of an event of default, you should give the debtor and any contingent obligors (guarantors, endorsers, or co-signers) formal notice of payment demand and a reasonable period to correct or cure the default. Notice to any contingent obligors may not be necessary, but it is suggested that you notify them anyway, just as extra caution in case they later raise a defense if you sue them for a deficiency judgment. Furthermore, by giving such a notice you will not waive any right against third parties in order to protect your collection efforts. A normal, reasonable period to cure a default is 10 days. Anything less may be considered unreasonable by a court of law. Your demand letter should indicate that acceleration of the maturity of the entire balance of the note, including any unpaid and accrued interest in full, will be due if the default has not been corrected or cured within the stated period.

If an add-on interest note, any unearned interest that was originally added to the face of the contract has to be deducted or credited from the unpaid balance of the note, based on the payoff of the debt before maturity. Failure to make the appropriate deduction could result in a usurious interest rate charge. Check your own state interest-rate limits pertaining to usury violations.

8.03 REPOSSESSIONS AND COLLATERAL SALES

In accordance with Article 9.503 of the UCC and upon the event of default and acceleration of the debt obligation, you should be allowed to repossess your collateral without judicial process unless otherwise governed by state statute. Of course, in most states this is allowed as long as there is not a breach of the peace. In this connection, cautiously choose your repossession agents as their actions could have serious and harmful consequences, if not properly undertaken, as it relates to potential liability to the bank.

As an example, when a vehicle is repossessed from a closed or locked garage, it could be considered breaking and entering; even taking a vehicle out of an unlocked or open garage could result in possible liability. Beyond such an instance, the usual claims of damage possibly done to a vehicle during repossession (including claims of theft, or loss of personal property items missing from the vehicle after repossession) may be alleged by the debtor. These are reasons enough to hire a reputable and financially responsible agent.

At the time of repossession, have the agent make a list of all personal property items in the vehicle; these items should be immediately delivered to the bank. Also, have the agent photograph the vehicle in order to determine what the vehicle looked like and to determine what possible damage may have existed at the time of repossession. This is especially important when recovering damaged vehicles. It is imperative that you maintain good records.

Reasonable Care, Custody, and Preservation of Collateral

Store the vehicle in a reasonably safe place, and do not utilize it unless necessary, such as showing it to potential buyers. Also, preserve the value of the vehicle, e.g., minor repairs, and paint touch-ups.

After repossession, borrowers should always be advised where they can pick up any personal items that may have been left in the vehicle; let them know of a designated location and the time during normal working hours that they can pick up their personal items. Normally, this contact should be done by phone, followed up by a letter indicating that you plan to sell the vehicle.

Under Section 9.506 of the Code, the borrower has the right to redeem the collateral at any time prior to a public or private sale for a discharge of the debtor's obligation. This discharge should not only include the balance owing (principal and interest), but also include payment of the creditor's reasonable expenses of repossessing, storing, maintaining, and preparing the collateral for sale. These costs should be authorized in accordance with the bank's security agreement and not be prohibited by law. Add any reasonable legal expenses and attorney's fees to the obligation, too.

Disposing of Collateral or Taking It for Debt Satisfaction

According to Chapter 9.504 of the UCC, the vehicle may be sold at public auction or by private sale within 90 days after you have taken the car when it is considered consumer goods and the debtor has paid 60 percent of the loan amount and has not signed a statement modifying or renouncing his or her rights to a purchase of the vehicle after default.

When less than 60 percent has been paid, the creditor, after default, may propose to retain the collateral in satisfaction of the obligation according to 9.505(b) of the UCC, provided proper notice of such a proposal is sent to the debtor. Should the creditor or secured party receive an objection in writing from the debtor or any other person entitled to receive notification within 21 days after such notice is officially sent, the secured party must dispose of the collateral by private or public sale under Section 9.504 of the Code. Of course, if the creditor does not receive such a notice, it may retain the collateral in satisfaction of the indebtedness. In such instances, the bank will be waiving any rights to a deficiency against the debtor or any other contingent obligors. However, at the same time the bank will be relieved of the burden of proving that the sale of the collateral was "commercially reasonable" as required under Section 9.504 of the Code, a proof which is necessary when seeking a deficiency judgment against the borrower or other third parties. As a creditor you may also be subject to individual state laws regarding repossession and sales of vehicles.

It is safe to say that a private sale will bring the highest price for the car. Therefore, remember when selling the collateral that you have to comply with "commercial reasonableness" which includes giving the debtor and other interested parties proper notice of the time when any private sale of the vehicle is to occur. Assuming the collateral is consumer goods, no other notice is necessary except in those instances of a Federal tax lien whereby proper notification must be given to the IRS.

For various reasons, debtors at times are willing to voluntarily surrender the collateral. Each instance may be somewhat different and should be treated accordingly to realize the best recovery for the bank and the least problem for the debtor. The sale price of the vehicle may be more easily determined if the debtor has filed bankruptcy because many courts have concurred with the value in some official car guide book. Such books usually provide both wholesale and retail trade-in prices.

If you have any rapport at all with a bankrupt's attorney, call him or her if the debtor's schedules or plan does not reflect a reasonable price. Together, you can easily correct the matter. Otherwise, as an alternative, you will have to file a motion for a hearing on the vehicle's value, referred to as a "valuation hearing," which would entail an inspection, appraisal, and possibly testimony from expert witnesses. Then there is the cost of holding the hearing. As you can see, this alternative can be time consuming, expensive, and prolong the case; therefore, the amount of debt and value of the vehicle should have a bearing on going this far. You may find more cooperation than anticipated with debtor attorneys because it will cost them time and money to go through a second process, too.

If a commercial vehicle is at stake, such as a truck or limousine used by the bankrupt in a sole proprietorship, it may be worth taking the second alternative if the debtor (or attorney) is not cooperative in correcting the schedule or plan value of the vehicle. You can even object to the bankruptcy plan on the grounds that the borrower is acting in bad faith if he or she (or attorney) is not cooperative in amending the plan, especially if the collateral value of the vehicle is greatly understated. Whatever alternative you take, once you undertake the task, follow up. If you win, you will often get a fair value on the vehicle, plus any insurance premiums you paid and even some reasonable amount for the attorney's fees you incurred.

Often, when collateral consists of a vehicle, the debtor will exempt it. If the case is or shortly moves into a Chapter 7 liquidation and the debtor is discharged, they will have to redeem the collateral at its current value in one lump sum payment, or surrender it to the bank, or be willing to reaffirm the debt with the bank.

You need to analyze the above options, especially as they relate to the payment history on the debt. To begin with, determine when the loan was made, the time span after the petition was filed, and the number of delinquent payments, assuming the loan was on a monthly amortization program. If the bankruptcy filing was made shortly after the loan was granted, this may be a valid reason to object, thus possibly obtaining an exception to discharge for the debt. If you allow the debtor to reaffirm the debt, the borrower should understand that all payments in arrears will have to be immediately brought current.

If the collateral represents inventory, notification also has to be sent to other subordinate parties that may have an interest in it within a reasonable time before the sale. A time period of five business days is reasonable. This minimum time factor is based on the Code requirement for giving debtors sufficient time (even though an actual period is not specified), to undertake the steps to protect their interests by taking part in the sale or disposition of the collateral.

When goods are perishable, the notification requirements may be excused in case the collateral is exposed to a rapid decline in value or is of a type that is sold on a recognized market. Of course, it is questionable whether there is any recognized market for used vehicles versus, say, perishable goods. The notice of any sale which is subject to Article 9 of the Code should be given, not only to the debtor but to any guarantor or other accommodation maker such as a co-signer or endorser. Otherwise, you may waive certain rights you have against such parties for a deficiency.

When conducting a private sale, always include the method, manner, time, place, and terms of the upcoming sale in order for it to meet the "commercially reasonable" Code criteria. Selling the vehicle too cheaply is usually the primary reason debtors and other obligors raise a defense. Sometimes resale prices become difficult to deal with, especially when measuring between supposed retail and wholesale values. Measuring and recognizing sales of collateral to or through dealers is probably the best indicator, besides often being the easiest source and best possible means of realizing a return on resales. This is often true because the bank is not really set up to sell vehicles, or for that matter, nor does it usually have the facilities to sell any other type collateral. Therefore, selling vehicles to dealers, if fairly conducted, should meet the "commercial reasonableness" test. If you opt for a private sale, take three bids in order for the sale to meet "commercial reasonableness" criteria. Also, take photos of the vehicles, especially when they are substantially damaged, and perhaps even obtain an appraisal in certain cases.

If you sell a vehicle by way of a private sale to a surety or third-party obligor for less than the unpaid balance, you will waive your rights of deficiency against the debtor unless some other form of agreement is reached.

Deficiency Collections

After you have undertaken a private sale of a vehicle, advise the debtor of the terms of the sale and return any proceeds in excess of the amount of the indebtedness, (retain costs consisting of interest, attorney's fees as allowed by law and the terms of your note, and costs to ready the vehicle for sale and store it).

You should send a letter to the borrower and any accommodation parties breaking down the costs of the deficiency after receiving the resale proceeds. The letter should list the remaining amount owed. It should also be in the form of a demand letter, thus showing your intent to collect the deficiency. By sending such a letter, you may prevent the borrower or third party obligors from claiming satisfaction of debt strictly based on the sale of the collateral and any assumption on their part that the obligation was satisfied from the proceeds of the sale.

Failure to Comply with the UCC

The bank is subject to certain statutory liability penalties if it does not comply with the rules of the Code. The debtor does not have the right to set aside the sale of the vehicle, but he or she does have the right to receive any lost proceeds from the sale as a result of failure caused by the secured party to comply with the provisions of the Code. In respect to consumer transactions, the bank may also be subject to an additional service charge penalty and even additional penalty interest based on the amount of the debt. These potential penalties may be costly when such charges are computed on an add-on interest basis over a term of years. Furthermore, besides incurring such penalties, the bank will assuredly be denied a deficiency judgment against the borrower and any third party obligor and could even be subject to civil liability or criminal liability under the Consumer Credit Protection Act.[1]

Federal Tax Liens and Bankruptcy

In case a federal tax lien has been filed, you must give notice of any sale (conducted without court authorization) in writing by either registered or certified mail to the IRS not less than 25 days prior to the date of sale. If you do not provide this notice within that time and do not adhere to the regulation requirements of such a notice, the IRS lien may remain in force, thus any title conveyed to a buyer in good faith could still be subject to a federal tax lien.

In the event that the debtor files a bankruptcy petition, you will be faced with a stay on any action to repossess the collateral. You should first file a Proof of Claim of your previously perfected lien. If the vehicle is worth less than the balance of the debt, the trustee may approve an order of abandonment, thus lifting your stay and permitting repossession. If the trustee is not cooperative, a formal request for "adequate protection" should be filed with the court, or possibly a complaint seeking abandonment.

---

[1] There may be Code exceptions from state to state including specific governing rules pertaining to respective state Certificate of Title Acts that affect repossession and sales of vehicles and other personal property assets.

CHAPTER 9

BANKRUPTCY AND THE CONTRACTOR

9.01 GENERAL

Bankruptcy certainly is a difficult matter to face, whether you're a debtor or creditor; however, it may be particularly precarious when you are a contractor. As you know, when a bank lends working capital to contractors it frequently takes a blanket lien on all accounts (contracts), contract rights, and general intangibles, now owned and hereafter acquired including all proceeds therefrom. As part of this collateral, the bank also has an interest in contract retainages, which are not paid until the work on a particular job is completed and accepted.

The unique thing about the contractor as opposed to other businesses is that if the contractor is bonded, the bonding company automatically has first claim on contract proceeds under the "equitable doctrine of subrogation rights," according to federal bonding company law rights which preempt and are not subject to the bank's priority filing under the Uniform Commercial Code. Therefore, besides not being subject to the Code, the surety's subrogation rights also act as a secret priority lien because the surety is not required to give public notice in the form of filing. The bonding company usually bonds all labor and material cost for completing the job.

9.02 BANKRUPTCY FILING

Suppose the contractor is in the midst of a job. Now, if you are lending against the borrower's bonded contracts and it files bankruptcy, the surety's rights should prevail. Then, say, the bonding company has to step in and take over in order to complete the job. It will have a right to all proceeds due, and to off-set any amounts owing the bankrupt estate as a cost to complete the project. Therefore, it is generally understood that the surety has a right to use all unpaid contract proceeds owed as an off-set against any costs to complete the job or against any losses it sustains in paying off filed claims for unpaid work by subcontractors and material suppliers.

As a banker, besides the inherent risk in lending against executory (performance) contracts which are subject to completion and performance, you face even greater prospects of loss in case the contracts you lend against are bonded and the borrower defaults on properly completing those jobs. This is another reason why bankers should insist on securing the loan with additional other types of collateral.

9.03 CONTRACTORS OF GOODS AND SERVICES

Even borrowers who make, distribute, and sell products can become involved in contracts. For example, they may have to make or deliver products to certain specifications. Or they may have to perform some sort of process in connection with the sale and delivery of those goods.

Sometimes, such borrowers act as a subcontractor who has to deliver the material to a job and who in turn must perform or complete a process under a contract. At times, the general contractor is bonded. Furthermore, your subcontractor would certainly have its mechanic and materialman's (M&M) lien rights, which should indirectly mean further protection for payment under the bond. However, the question is how good are the subcontractor's contracts which are assigned to you if it defaults on its work for the general or prime contractor? Or if it is unable to perform under those contracts or files bankruptcy?

Any way you look at it, whether your borrower enters into a contract to fulfill a service or to perform a job, you are at risk if you have to rely solely on the performance of the contract assigned for repayment of your loan.

CHAPTER 10

LIQUIDATIONS GOVERNED BY THE UCC

10.01 GENERAL

The principal theme behind the rules for liquidation in the Uniform Commercial Code (UCC) is that it should be handled in a "commercially reasonable" manner. As a banker, if you do not follow these rules you will be subject to a loss of any deficiency judgment against the debtor or any contingent obligors. Furthermore, you could be vulnerable to suit by other creditors or even third-party collateral owners in the event you were negligent in liquidating the collateral for its reasonable value or worth.

When liquidating collateral, keep in mind the following matters:

• Be cautious; do not get in the precarious position of confronting the debtor and engaging in physical or harmful bodily injury to repossess the collateral. Also, do not breech the peace or force your way into the borrower's premises in any way. When the borrower does not surrender the collateral voluntarily, proceed to seek judicial action through a court of law to enforce your rights.
• Preserve the collateral to the best of your ability (this may exclude perishable goods in those instances where it may be out of your control to preserve them). The Code requires what it refers to as reasonable care in your custody, i.e., protecting the assets from alteration, theft, and vandalism.
• Undertake prudent action when preparing the collateral for sale. The UCC allows the bank to prepare the goods for sale or to sell them in their present state. It is strongly suggested that you

preserve the goods and undertake a minimal amount of preventive maintenance, making whatever repairs that are necessary—perhaps painting, cleaning, and restoring to make the goods sell at a fair value. You may find it advantageous to have language in your security agreements requiring that the borrower assemble the goods on its premises for sale and to render the goods unusable any further by the debtor, thus allowing you to dispose of them on the borrower's property. Of course, you need a cooperative borrower to allow you onto its premises where the collateral is located.

• Always furnish proper notice when collateral involves marketable securities or perishable commodities, or goods that may be sold on a recognized market. In this way, the bank will comply with notice requirements to those who have ownership interests in the collateral, or who are obligated in order that they may protect their interests. Proper notice is at least five business days, and longer when possible. Regarding federal tax liens, you must give the IRS at least 25 days advance notice of any sale of personal property asset collateral. If this compliance is not met, the lien will continue and hence the cost thereof to the bank.

Giving Notice of Sale

Some of the general requirements of notice are: place and time of any public sale of collateral; in the case of a private sale, when it will occur and how contact can be made with the bank selling the goods.

The time of the sale after repossession can be important as it determines if a sale has been made within a reasonable period after repossession. For instance, if the collateral is sold within 90 days of repossession, this should be a satisfactory period. Any time beyond that period—especially if the sale is not accomplished within six months—could be deemed unreasonable.

In such instances, you should document why it took so long to accomplish the sale if you perceive it was necessary and reasonable under the circumstances. As an example, an unusually long period to repair certain technical or specialized goods may occur; or an unexpected delay could have been encountered because of a back order for a very technical or specialized part needed to fix equipment.

Whatever your reason, document it if for legitimate reasons so the transaction will not be deemed "commercially unreasonable." If you have delayed the sale purposely, or had an unjustifiable delay, or if you just procrastinated too long, a court may rule that you waited too long to liquidate the collateral, thus ruling that you have accepted the collateral in satisfaction for a discharge of the debt.

Notices of sales should be given to the debtor and any secured creditor who requests them in writing. If there are competing creditors, who believe that they have valid rights to the goods, you may be notified by them if their payment claims with the borrower have not been satisfied. If these other so-called secured creditors do not request a notice of sale from you in writing, they will not have any right to share in the sales proceeds. However, these same creditors can still sue you for failure to conduct the sale of the collateral in a commercially reasonable manner. Keep in mind that you may have to notify any contingent obligors, to whom you have recourse, of the sale. You can obtain limited recourse as a result of a repurchase agreement with a manufacturer, or it can be obtained through the purchase of chattel paper from a dealer of goods, even if you do not have direct recourse from the dealer.

Good record-keeping of notices and proper mailing is also essential. This means sale notices should include the names and addresses of the correct parties and the dates when sent. While notices can be sent by regular mail, they should also be sent by certified or registered mail, return receipt requested. In this way, you are assured that the notice is received; and if not accepted by the recipient, then notice by regular mail may get the job done. If the certified or registered notice is returned, you should make an effort to locate the party being notified at his or her current address. This is an extra precaution.

Advertising the sale properly is another important aspect of complying with the "commercial reasonableness" test. Advertise in appropriate trade journals and in local newspapers or sales media to draw suitable interest. You, as the secured party, must make a concerted effort to publicize and solicit interest in the goods for sale. You should even independently contact potential buyers, too, to draw as much interest as possible in any forthcoming sale. Defenses have been raised by obligors, collateral owners, and other creditors having a possible interest in the collateral. They have contested sales based on the grounds that not enough advertising or publicity was undertaken by the bank.

Conducting the Sale

• The manner in which sales take place is very important, too, as it pertains to a "commercial reasonableness" sale. This applies to the time and place of sales, meaning it should be conducted during a reasonable time of the business day and at a convenient and readily accessible location, if applicable, based on the particular goods being sold and the potential interested parties. Of course, this is not always possible, due to the goods involved and their present location. Some goods may be more easily moved while it may be harder to move other larger items. When it is necessary to sell goods at public locations pertaining to public auctions, it may be more advantageous to move smaller items or parts of those goods that can be easily transported. Obviously, if the collateral consists of vehicles, they can be more easily relocated, while other goods can be more difficult to move due to size and immobility. Private sales could entail more difficulty if not on the bank's or owner's premises. When the collateral is in a remote area, the bank has to decide how, when, and where to move it. The bank needs to evaluate if it is worth providing guard service or other costly security services temporarily until the goods can be transported to a more convenient and accessible location for sales purposes.

• The manner and method of sales is important, too, besides realizing the best price in return. The bank might consider acting as the fiduciary agent for the debtor or collateral owner regarding the collateral. Check with your legal counsel to determine if this is a viable alternative that may be to your advantage legally or otherwise. At times, it may prove advantageous to provide owner financing, if you have taken the collateral in satisfaction of debt. This may be the best possible alternative to selling the goods and obtaining the optimum return.

Determining the Sales Price

All this leads up to the price the collateral should be sold for. Therefore, all the factors above—time, place, manner, method and terms—are germane to the proper sales price.

Just because you have made a best-efforts attempt to sell the collateral at the best price based on these considerations, it does not necessarily guarantee that you have met all the "commercial reasonableness" standards of the UCC. Any time the sales price is low, compared to the fair or general market value of equivalent goods, make sure the sales price is well documented and that sufficient reasons are given to justify it. The sales price and the circumstances leading up to it may have to be explained in a court of law. A low selling price can result, for example, from the badly deteriorated or decomposed state of the goods when repossessed. A low price can stem from badly damaged goods which do not warrant fixing. You might consider first having the court sanction the disposition and ultimate sale, when you are of the opinion that a low selling price is most likely. This sanction may also have to be approved by a creditor's committee or trustee in bankruptcy. By taking these precautions, you will be assured and guaranteed of a "commercially reasonable" sale of the collateral.

CHAPTER 11

REAL ESTATE FORECLOSURE

11.01 GENERAL

At the time the bank decides to foreclose on real property, it must be conscious of preventing and controlling excessive cost and deterioration of the physical properties. If in the bank's best interests, it may attempt to gain control of other assets owned by the borrower.

If your bank decides to accept the borrower's real property securing the loan in full satisfaction of the debt, the property should be written down and recorded at its fair value. This value should be supported by a current appraisal. The difference between the recorded amount of the debt including accrued interest, and any lower fair value of the real property taken in, should be charged to the allowance for loan losses. Any future write-downs of the real property should be charged against operations. When your bank decides to bid on the foreclosed property, the bid-in price should be the lower of the fair value of the property or the cost the bank has recorded for the property.

11.02 FOLLOW-UP PROCEDURES AFTER BANKRUPTCY

The following guidelines may assist you in the appropriate procedures of foreclosure:

- Obtain a good attorney early on who will quickly act in your behalf.

• Verify all insurance coverage if improvements have been made to the property, and make sure there is sufficient coverage.
• Inspect the premises and estimate any necessary maintenance, possible renovation, or improvements to the property that need to be undertaken that would make it more appealing and marketable. This may also require having a reliable real estate broker walk the property in order to provide a preliminary assessment of marketability.
• Arrange for a developer or contractor to come in to help determine recommendations for renovation or improvements, followed by a bid to establish a cost for such work.
• Attempt to arrange for a "friendly foreclosure," whereby the owner will hopefully turn over the keys to you.
• Have a title company complete an abstract or update the policy which should include a search for tax liens, filings of suits, and conveyance and judgment recordings.
• If the property consists of raw land, seek out a surveyor to undertake an updated survey.
• Find a good management company to oversee the property, especially if it is income producing.

Appraisals

Obtain an independent current appraisal from a qualified appraiser of the fair market value of each parcel of real property now owned by the bank. This should be done initially, with certain exceptions, once the bank takes the property over, and annually thereafter. Alternatively, a qualified appraiser can certify in letter form that the fair value has not declined. The appraiser should include an estimate of the cash price that could potentially be received in view of exposure to the open market for a reasonable period, considering the property type and local market conditions.

If it is unlikely that a sale can be consummated within one year of the acquisition, the appraiser should discount all existing cash flow received from the property by virtue of tenant payments, or from ownership, development, operation, and sale of the property in order to determine its fair value. This discount should reflect the appraiser's judgment of what a prudent, knowledgeable purchaser, under no obligation to purchase the property, would be willing to pay for it, based on current sales. Fair value is the cash price, net of all closing and sales costs, that might reasonably be expected to be received from a sale. This cash price should also be based on exposure to the open market for a reasonable time in view of the property type and local market conditions. Basically, a fair sale means that both the buyer and seller have acted prudently, knowledgeably, and are under no pressure to buy or sell.

In accordance with national banking regulations, for each parcel of other real estate owned (OREO) that has declined in value, the bank must establish a valuation reserve in an amount at least equal to the excess of book value over fair value of the parcel or record the decline in value by a direct write-down of the asset. When a later appraisal indicates that fair value of the parcel has increased, the reserve for that parcel may be reduced, but not below zero.

Real Estate Sales

A covered transaction will be considered in place when one of the following conditions exists:

- If a sale of real estate is undertaken by the bank when less than 10 percent of the total sales price is received in cash or where the bank carries back all or a portion of the sale as owner financed on terms more favorable than generally granted by the bank for similar transactions not involving property acquired under foreclosure.
- When the bank finances the sale of the property it owns and does not transfer the normal risks of ownership or the rewards thereof.

In turn, a covered transaction will cease and no longer exist once 10 percent of the sales price has been paid in cash, and when that portion of the sales price guaranteed to the bank by a private mortgage insurance (or an equivalent third-party guarantee) equals or exceeds 10 percent of the property's sale price.

CHAPTER 12

TROUBLED REAL ESTATE DEBT RESTRUCTURES

12.01 GENERAL

Many borrowers, caught in financial difficulties, have been unable to make loan payments in the past few years. Particularly hard hit are manufacturing and more recently, agriculture, oil, and real estate. It has often been necessary for borrowers in these fields to arrange for the restructure of debt.

Restructuring by financial institutions has entailed extending repayments, reducing interest rates and principal amounts, and even extending new funds. These changes have been arranged by way of new or modified terms. In certain instances, borrowers have even transferred assets to banks in partial satisfaction or for full settlement of their debt.

Foreclosure

Subsequent foreclosures have occurred, too, in many cases when there was no possibility of restructuring the debt to the satisfaction of both parties. In such circumstances, the bank has become the owner of the property and then has attempted to sell it for a reasonable recovery of its debt. If the bank takes its real property collateral back under foreclosure or by way of a deed in lieu of foreclosure (friendly foreclosure) to satisfy the debt, the property should be transferred to other real estate assets on the bank's books and should be recorded at the current fair value, per appraisal. If the appraisal (based on the fair value of the property) comes in less than the foreclosed amount or existing loan balance (including the recorded amount of all accrued and unpaid interest on the bank's books), the shortfall should be charged to the reserve for loan losses. Then, any future write-downs should be charged against operations as non-interest expense. Turn to Chapter 11 for an in-depth treatment of foreclosure.

FASB Accounting Treatment

Bank regulations call for following generally accepted accounting principles (GAAP) in regard to loans that have been formally restructured.

In particular, the *Financial Accounting Standards Board Statement No. 15 (FASB 15)* governs the accounting treatment by debtors and creditors relative to troubled debt restructuring. This *Statement* basically defines troubled debt restructure as a loan whereby the bank has granted a concession to the borrower because of its financial difficulties that the bank would not otherwise consider.

Many restructurings involve modifying terms to reduce or defer payments in the near future to attempt to improve the borrower's financial condition and eventually allow it to pay the financial institution in full.

Another form of restructuring involves the bank's acceptance of cash, other assets, or an equity interest in the borrower's company in satisfaction of debt, even though the value received is less than the amount of debt as the bank may believe that this step will maximize the recovery of its investment. Furthermore, any transfer of assets whether receivables, real estate, or other assets to fully or partially satisfy a debt (including transfer through foreclosure or repossession) could be considered a debt restructure.

Restructuring may also entail, depending how it occurs, use of Accounting Principles Board (APB) No. 21, as it applies to discounting present values and interest on receivable and payables, in addition to the use of the *Financial Accounting Standards Board Statement No. 66,* Accounting for Sales of Real Estate.

These accounting standards allow the bank to carry a loan on its books at the value of the restructured credit without recognizing any losses when a loan is properly restructured, whereby there is a good probability and reasonable estimation in the bank's opinion that the borrower will repay the loan under its modified terms.

Keep in mind that the recorded amount of the loan on the bank's books determines the accounting method used for the restructured debt. *FASB 15* provisions call for recording the principal amount of the loan, plus accrued interest, less any previously charged-off amounts to the loan. Once a loan is restructured, the bank may not reverse any previously charged-off amounts to increase the recorded loan amount. Additionally, interest may not be accrued to the date of restructuring if the loan has also been previously placed on non-accrual.

The restructured terms will also have to be enough that the total future cash payments, including principal and interest, will at least equal the present loan amount on the bank's books. If the future combined payments consisting of principal and interest do not equal (or are anticipated to be less than) the loan amount, the recognized loss will be limited to the expected cash flow deficiency.

Beyond this, in view of the regulators' attitude towards forbearance, banks will not be required to automatically and immediately charge-off loans or portions thereof that have been restructured and that comply with *FASB 15*. Financial institutions also do not have to report conforming renegotiated loans with non-performing loans.

Furthermore, the regulatory agencies appear to have modified the reporting and disclosure requirements for restructured loans that are performing in accordance with the terms. Another point to keep in mind is that many loans, considered perhaps as restructured loans, will not meet the above criteria of a troubled debt because they may not be an actual problem loan where the bank has offered any concessions. Instead, they are only renewals or novations of debt; that is, an extension because of an emergency need of working capital, or renewed payments tied to a change in cash flow ability, or decrease in rate because of a general decline in overall market rates.

For example, a troubled debt restructuring is not involved if:

- The fair value of assets accepted by the bank in full satisfaction of a debt at least equals the bank's recorded investment in the loan, including accrued interest.

• The creditor reduces the effective interest rate, primarily to reflect a reduction in rates in general or a decrease in the risk, so as to maintain a relationship with a borrower who can readily obtain funds from other sources at current market interest rates.
• The borrower issues—in exchange for its debt—new market debt having an effective interest rate based on its market price that is at or near the current rates for borrowings with similar maturity dates and interest rates issued by nontroubled borrowers.

Before you deal with troubled debt restructure, you should be able to recognize the signs involving these potential problems. The following may assist you in identifying them, relative to project indicators or market conditions:

1. Rent concessions being offered or sales discounts being given resulting in a cash flow decline below the level originally expected based on lease commitments.
2. Sales discounts offered below what was originally forecasted and projected, relative to the original appraisal.
3. Construction delays, including cost overruns, that may require renegotiation of loan terms.
4. A slow down in leasing or lack of sustained sales activity.
5. An increase in cancellations, which may result in delinquencies or default.

12.02 ACCOUNTING FOR TROUBLED DEBT RESTRUCTURE

Basically, restructuring of debt occurs when the bank grants a concession to a debtor having financial problems and difficulties meeting payment on its debt that the bank would not consider under normal conditions. The bank in such instances must plan its strategy and properly negotiate its position with the borrower who has been identified as having a troubled real estate loan on the bank's books.

FASB 15

Accounting for troubled debt restructure is based on the particular type of restructuring to be undertaken. The following describes the accounting that should be taken into consideration by the bank under *FASB 15*

• A financial institution that receives assets from the borrower or another third party should account for them at their fair value at the time of restructuring. The excess of the recorded loan, including accrued interest, over the fair value of assets received should be recorded as a loss. After this restructuring, the bank shall account for this asset as if it had been acquired for cash.

Fair value is the amount that the borrower could reasonably expect to receive for the asset in a current sale between a willing buyer and seller, that is, other than in a forced or liquidation sale. The fair value of an asset is measured by the market value if an active market exists. If none exist, but one exists for a similar asset, that value can be helpful in estimating the fair value; a forecast of expected cash flows can aid in estimating the fair value, provided they are discounted at a rate commensurate with the risk involved.

• A financial institution that modifies the terms should not account for a loss and change the recorded loan amount on the bank's books at the time of the restructuring unless that amount exceeds the total future cash receipts specified by the new terms. Interest income should be computed with a constant effective yield over the remaining term of the loan. The new effective interest rate should be the discount rate based on the present value of future cash receipts under the new term of this restructured loan. If, however, the total future cash receipts, specified by the new terms of this loan before restructuring (including accrued interest) do not equal the recorded loan amount, the financial institution should reduce the recorded investment in the loan to an amount equal to the total future cash receipts specified by the new terms of the loan. In this circumstance, no interest income shall be recognized on the loan for the remaining term of the restructured debt.

• A bank receives debt satisfaction from a combination of receipt of assets and a modification of terms. In this case, the bank shall account for the assets received at their fair values and reduce the recorded investment in the loan. No loss on restructuring will be recognized unless the remaining recorded loan (including accrued interest) exceeds the total future cash receipts specified by the terms of the new loan which remain after the restructuring. Future interest income will be accounted for as previously discussed under modification of terms. Some of the primary types of restructuring are discussed below.

Modification Terms of a Debt

Under such transactions, GAAP allows a loan to remain on the bank's books without requiring it to recognize a loss if the loan is properly restructured in such a way that it is both probable and estimatable that the borrower will be capable of repaying the debt under the new and modified terms, and that the future cash payments (which include principal and interest combined) at least equal the loan amount on the bank's books. The modification terms may take many different forms, including one or more or even a combination of some of the following:

1. Absolute or contingent reduction of the interest rate over the remaining original term of the loan.
2. An absolute or contingent straight reduction of any accrued interest on the loan.
3. Absolute or contingent reduction in the face or principal amount or maturity amount of the debt as stated in the note or any other agreement thereto.
4. Extension of the maturity date or payment dates at a stated interest rate lower than the going current market rates for new debt with similar risks.

Accounting for modification terms includes the following calculation. When the new or modified terms of the troubled debt restructuring call for a reduction of either interest or principal or both, the amount carried on the bank's books, both principal and interest, should be compared to the expected, total contractual cash payments. These cash payments should be calculated to cover both principal and interest. A loss should only be recognized if the total of the combined future payments is less than the recorded amount of the loan. Otherwise, no loss needs to be realized. See Exhibits O, P, and Q on pages 272–73 regarding impacts of a reduction in interest rates and recorded loan balance before restructure.

EXHIBIT O—Reduction in Interest Rate

Assume a borrower in financial difficulty is indebted to the bank for $250,000. The following example demonstrates the effect on the loan, based on a reduction in the current interest rate from 12 to 6 percent with both principal and interest due within one year.

New contractual payment amount	$250,000
Plus: New contractual interest payment at 6 percent	15,000
Less: Current recorded loan balance	(250,000)
Interest income difference of excess of new contractual payment amount over current recorded loan balance	$ 15,000

No loss is recorded since the total new restructured contractual payments exceed the current recorded loan balance. Interest income of $15,000 should be recorded at the stated 6 percent over the one-year loan term.

EXHIBIT P—Principal Reduced with Loss Recognized

Presume we take the same borrower, as in Exhibit O, who owes the bank $250,000. Alternatively, the bank is willing to reduce the current recorded loan balance to $200,000. Assume the interest rate is reduced from 12 to 10 percent. Also, the total principal and interest will be due within one year. In this restructure, the bank will record a $30,000 loss.

Current recorded loan balance	$250,000
Less: New principal amount	(200,000)
Less: New interest payment at 10 percent	(20,000)
Loss: Excess of current recorded loan balance over future cash payments	$ 30,000

The restructured loan amount will be recorded on the bank's books at $220,000, versus the new contractual loan amount of $200,000. The $220,000 total is also the recorded amount of the loan prior to the restructure reduced by the loss. No interest income will be recognized during the term of the restructured loan as all payments will be applied against the current recorded amount of the loan.

EXHIBIT Q—Principal Reduced with No Loss Recorded

Presume we again take the same borrower who owes the bank $250,000. Alternatively, the bank is willing to reduce the current loan balance to $200,000. Assume the interest rate will be reduced from 12 to 10 percent and interest will be paid annually while the principal will be due and payable in full in three years. Furthermore, there will be no loss recorded on this restructure because the future total principal and interest payments should be in excess of the recorded amount of the current loan. Additionally, the bank will record $10,000 in interest income at a 1.43 percent rate over three years.

New contractual principal amount	$200,000
Plus: New contractual interest payments at 10%	60,000
Less: Current recorded loan balance	(250,000)
Excess of new contractual payment amounts over current recorded loan balance, considered interest income	$ 10,000

Because there is no loss recorded on this restructure, the loan will remain on the bank's books at the current recorded loan balance totaling $250,000 versus the new contractual loan amount of $260,000.

The new effective annual interest rate is computed on the current recorded loan balance, based on annual scheduled cash payments of $20,000 for each of the first two years with the balance of $220,000 due in the third year. An effective annual interest rate on the restructured debt will yield a constant 1.43 percent return over the remaining term of the loan. This return calculation is based on reducing the current recorded loan balance of $250,000 by the annual scheduled cash payments, less the total amount of interest income of $10,000 to be recorded from these cash payments over the three-year period.

Thus, *FASB 15* requires that the recorded amount of the loan on the bank's books be measured against the total future contractual cash payments stipulated by the modified repayment terms including both principal and interest and ordinarily excluding any contingent payments. Losses on restructuring should normally be recognized by a charge to the loan loss reserve, and only if the total of future principal and interest payments is less than the recorded loan amount; or else, no loss on the restructuring will be identified relative to the restructured debt. The only remaining accounting requirement will be to determine the new effective interest rate on the restructured debt for purposes of income recognition.

Frequently, the new effective interest rate will equal the stated interest rate included in any new restructured loan, although adjustments may be necessary, e.g., loan principal being reduced, if the new contractual interest rates are on a gradual basis (increasing each year), and if due and unpaid interest is not added to principal or included in the contractual interest rate, or if the repayment terms have some other unusual provisions or requirements.

Thus, the effective and the stated rate will generally not be equal when the loan principal is reduced, or when the new contractual interest rates are on a graduated basis, e.g., a five-year loan with 7 percent the first two years, then a one-point increase over the next three years. Another time when these rates may not be equal is when accrued (but unpaid) interest is not added to the principal or else is included in the contractual interest amount, or when there is some other unusual repayment terms. If an effective interest rate computation is required, it should be based on future new or modified contractual payment terms excluding all payments which are contingently payable or receivable, irrespective of principal or interest designation.

This effective interest rate should be a discounted rate that equates to the present value of the future cash payments with the recorded amount of the loan on the bank's books under the new or modified contract terms. Also, this new rate should yield a constant rate of interest income over the remaining life of the loan. It should be anticipated that the rate will generally be less than the original one and may be as low as zero, without any requirement of recognizing a loss on the restructured debt.

Combination: Restructure plus Taking Assets

At times, you may have to combine a restructure of debt under modified and new terms, along with the taking in of real property collateral, resulting in a partial satisfaction of the debt.

In these cases, the accounting procedure is normally a two-step process. Initially, the loan balance on the books is generally reduced to the fair value of the property taken in, based on a current appraisal of the property. Next, you have to compare the future anticipated cash payments under the new restructured contractual agreement to the remaining available amount of the loan recorded on the bank's books and the new interest rate therein, which is computed under the modified terms and provisions entailing the new effective interest rate. Exhibit R gives an example of reducing the outstanding principal and accepting property as a partial satisfaction of debt.

EXHIBIT R—Principal Reduced and Property Accepted

Presume we again take the same borrower who owes the bank $250,000. In this case, the bank is willing to take back its real estate collateral, which has a current fair market value of $30,000 in partial satisfaction of its debt. In addition, the bank is agreeable to restructure the borrower's debt under new or modified terms. Under the modified loan agreement terms, the borrower will repay $200,000 of principal within one year, and in turn will be forgiven $20,000. Interest will be reduced from 12 to 7 percent and will be paid at the end of the one year. Under this scenario, the bank records a loss of $10,000 at the time of restructure, which should be charged to the reserve for loan losses.

Current recorded loan balance	$250,000
Less: fair market value of property taken back as partial satisfaction of debt	(30,000)
Adjusted recorded loan balance	220,000
New contractual principal amount	200,000
Plus: New contractual interest payment at 7 percent	14,000
Total cash payments under restructure	214,000
Loss: Excess of adjusted recorded loan balance over future cash payments	6,000

The restructured debt will be carried on the bank's books at $214,000, versus the new contractual principal amount of

EXHIBIT R—(*Concluded*)

$200,000. The restructured amount is the adjusted recorded loan balance after subtracting the fair market value of the real property taken in as partial satisfaction of debt and further reduced by the loss recorded on restructuring.

No interest income will be recorded over the remaining loan term as all payments will be applied against the recorded amount of the restructured loan. If the interest rate on the restructured debt was set at 10 percent, the bank would break even and recover the full amount of the adjusted recorded loan balance without sustaining any loss.

If the interest rate is increased to 12 percent, the bank would realize $4,000 more than the adjusted recorded loan balance.

This interest income amount would be recorded over the remaining term of the restructured loan. In this latter case, since no loss is sustained on restructuring, the modified debt will continue to be carried on the bank's books at the adjusted balance of $220,000, instead of the new contractual principal amount of $200,000. The new effective annual interest rate is computed on the adjusted recorded loan balance, thus income recognized will be at a rate of 1.82 percent for the one-year term of the restructured loan.

New contractual principal amount	$200,000
Plus: New contractual interest payment at 12%	24,000
Less: Adjusted recorded loan balance	(220,000)
Interest income over remaining term of loan	4,000

Friendly Foreclosure

At other times you may have to take the property in for full satisfaction of the debt, which is often accomplished by taking a deed in lieu of foreclosure. The bank may be willing to undertake such a friendly foreclosure when it believes that the fair value of the property is sufficient to cover the loan balance and it will not be advantageous to foreclose because of the time and expense. In sum, the bank can accomplish better results by not foreclosing.

If permitted by state law, the bank could bid-in the property at the courthouse, which could satisfy the obligation, instead of letting it go to the highest bidder under a judicial foreclosure and then having to sue the borrower—or any contingent obligors—for any deficiency.

Furthermore, a troubled debt restructure can even include transferring the real property ownership to the bank for full satisfaction of the debt. If the bank then sells the property outright, and if the sales price exceeds the book value of the property, the bank will record a gain to its operating statement. The bank will reflect a loss to its operations if the property is sold for less than its book value carried on the bank's books. Thus the bank takes a gamble when it becomes the owner of the property by either bidding it in or by transfer from the debtor in satisfaction of debt.

Novation of Debt

Restructuring often involves new and substitute borrowers, based on owner (bank) financed arrangements after the bank has foreclosed on the property, or in other instances, when a new borrower, who is unrelated to the existing debtor, assumes the existing obligation.

Under these situations, the new borrower receives a novation of debt, while the old troubled loan to the former unrelated borrower is considered fully satisfied. See Exhibit S on page 278 regarding the substitute borrower.

Even though the term *novation* is generally used in combining debt under existing obligations owed by a borrower, we feel a novation applies in this case. Novation is defined as "the substitution of a new obligation for one already existing." Thus, a novation creates a new transaction which seems to apply in this case, based on the assumption by a new borrower of the old debt (owed by the former debtor) which is fully satisfied.

The new loan will generally be carried at its fair value. Frequently, the interest rates on such new loans are granted below current market rates for similar transactions. Therefore, when this is the case, APB No. 21 stipulates that the loan be discounted on a present value basis at a current market rate in order to have it bear a market yield and to determine its fair value.

Financing the Sale of Property

At other times, the bank may finance the sale of property taken in as a result of foreclosure, now carried on the bank's books as Other

EXHIBIT S—Substitute Borrower

In another example, the bank finds an unrelated third party to assume the balance of a $250,000 loan owed by an existing borrower, and take over ownership of the real estate securing the loan in return for a reduction in the interest rate to 6 percent. Under the modified assumption, both principal and interest will be due in one year. The current market rate for such transactions is 12 percent. The loan will have to be discounted to its present or fair value under applicant APB 21 rules. The fair market value of this loan discounted to yield a market rate of 12 percent equals $236,607. The loss on the restructuring that the bank must charge against its reserve for loan losses based on approving the assumption of the existing loan at a lower interest will be $13,393.

Current recorded loan balance	$250,000
Less: Discounted value of assumed loan at 12 percent	(236,607)
Loss on restructuring	$ 13,393
As income over the life of the loan as follows:	
Current face value of loan	$250,000
Less: Discounted value of assumed loan at 12 percent	(236,607)
Loan Discount	$ 13,393

Real Estate Owned (OREO). Normally, as in the substitute borrower case, the bank will have to finance most of the sale at a concessionary or below-market rate versus similar transactions, which means APB 21 again applies as the balance of the new loan will have to be discounted to its present or fair value.

Basically, the impact of the discount is to reduce the gain or increase the loss as a result of the transaction. Interest income should be recognized at a constant yield over the life of the loan. An increase in interest income or accretion of discount should be realized on a constant yield over the term of the refinanced sale. If this new value is below the current recorded loan amount on the bank's books, owed by the former borrower—which is often the case—this difference will have to be charged to the reserve for loan losses. Any interest income realized on the new loan, including discount accretion, should be at a constant rate over the term of the loan. When you calculate the effective discount rate on the new debt, as an example, and the annual interest exceeds the actual annual payments on the debt, then the net difference will be the accretion amount of the unearned discount earned each year.

When there is little or no down payment on the bank-financed sale of real estate, then *FASB 66* applies to accounting for the new debt. A minimum down payment must be made, along with other conditions, if the bank is going to immediately realize the full amount of any profit on the owner-financed property sale, or else such profit will have to be deferred. The sales price will effectively be reduced based on the bank's offering a below market interest rate on the financing of the sale, thus this discount impact on sales value will, in essence, minimize any down payment.

A gain is realized based on the new receivable, which is the remaining principal amount after the interest is discounted, to a market rate that is greater than the book value of the real property. Profit on the sale will be recorded on an accrual method (record the receivable [loan] and recognize the gain immediately at the time of the sale) if certain criteria are met. Such as when, upon completion of sale, the purchaser continues to evidence a commitment to pay for the property in full; when there is no subordination by the bank of the buyer's obligation; and when the bank has properly transferred ownership of the property to the buyer on a continuing arms-length basis.

The sale will not have to meet the criteria for straight accrual accounting in order to record an accrual profit. Instead, the bank may record the sale on an installment basis such as collecting a minimum amount on the loan in the first year and deferring the profit on the sale. Other accounting methods that may apply if the gain is deferred include the cost-recovery method, deposit method, and reduced-profit method.

The sale may also produce a loss if the new loan (receivable) is less than the book value of the real property; that is, the principal and interest income of the new loan is greater than the current book value of the property. This could involve a covered transaction (see the end of Chapter 11). Therefore, when a loan involves a covered transaction and remains that way, it must continue to be carried on the bank's books as other real estate owned (OREO). When the sale does not entail a covered transaction, the bank may record its loan (receivable) and record a loss at the time of the sale. For more on OREO, see Exhibit T.

EXHIBIT T—Other Real Estate Owned, Sold, and Financed

Take another case when the bank has foreclosed on real property which is carried on its books as Other Real Estate Owned (OREO) at a fair market value of $205,000. The bank in turn sells the property for $210,000 and extends owner financing of $200,000 to the buyer who puts down $10,000. The bank also extends a concessionary interest rate of 6 percent to the buyer on its financing. Payment on the new debt consists of repaying the principal fully in five years, while paying interest annually. The comparative interest rates in the market for such transactions is 14 percent.

APB 21 requires that the loan be discounted to its present value, which if discounted to yield a market rate of 14 percent, totals $145,071. Thus, the adjusted sales price of the real estate is $155,071, based on adding the down payment and the discounted present value of the loan. The following example shows the loss to the bank on the sale of the real estate.

Recorded amount of the land	$205,000
Less: Down Payment	(10,000)
Less: Discounted Present Value	(145,071)
Loss on real property sale	$ 49,929

In view of the real estate being sold at a loss, the full amount of the loss will be booked on the day of the sale as a non-interest expense. If the sale would have resulted in a gain, *FASB 66* would require it to be deferred because the down payment was less than 25 percent.

The discount of $54,929 will be accreted into income over the term of the loan. While the face value of the loan will remain constant, the accretion of the unearned discount accruing into income each year will be the net difference of the discounted interest income over the scheduled annual payments, while the remaining balance of the unearned discount each year will be the difference between the net loan balance and face value.

12.03 ADVANCING NEW MONEY

At other times, the bank lends a troubled borrower new money below market interest rates. This can assist the borrower in some way to return to profitable operations or possibly enhance its future earnings or cash flow. Hopefully, then, the debtor can pay off existing bank debt. However, the bank is wise not to throw good money after bad.

The new loan may not entail restructuring of debt, thus no special accounting rules apply. However, if the loan is arranged by the bank as a part of restructuring existing debt, the new money will be included as an integral share of the recorded amount of the existing debt on the bank's books as it relates to the accounting of the borrower's total debt for restructuring. This combination of debt may then be considered a modification of terms including perhaps a new effective interest rate restructure.

Keep in mind that troubled debt restructure does not always work out, thus the future collection of payments may not be realized. Therefore, besides any recorded loss relative to processing the restructured loan, the bank needs to be ready to charge-off or charge-down additional amounts based on the existing or new borrower's inability to meet the restructured debt schedule or because of obvious questionable credit quality of the new borrower.

Pertaining to the restructure of the existing debt, the bank should first recognize a loss before the restructure is consummated in view of inadequate credit quality of the borrower. If there is any question on the existing or new borrower's credit ability or capacity to meet a reasonable repayment schedule, do not make the loan just to keep the transaction moving or in order to delay future charge-downs or write-offs—which would be really a disguise. Thus, use judicious underwriting credit standards when restructuring debt. In order to assist you in determining the borrower's credit ability or capacity to meet its debt obligations, the bank should undertake a thorough credit analysis which should also be used in determining if any additional amount should be set aside or allocated from the reserve to cover any possible loan losses.

The allocation should be based on the final credit rating given the credit. Most banks today include examiner credit ratings in their standard loan review grading system which should assist you. The significant areas in any credit analysis of this type should include the borrower's ability to service the debt based on the new terms after giving consideration to true cash flow and projected cash flow, besides any other important credit conditions relative to the borrower.

The following simple examples will provide you with some further guidance on handling the accounting procedures for troubled debt restructure of other real estate owned, based on the many possible ways to restructure and change the terms of the debt. You should work closely with the specialists in your bank on restructuring debt for accounting purposes. Such specialists include the accounting staff, credit/loan administrators knowledgeable in these areas, and loan operations/note and collateral department personnel.

Some examples are offered below for clarification of the required accounting under *FASB 15* as well as the restructured loan classification relative to modifications. The restructured loans used in Exhibit U would be classified as reduced rate or non-accrual loans.

Original Terms before Modification. A creditor holds a loan calling for $100 in interest at the end of each year for five years and the receipt of $1,000 principal at the end of five years. The stated interest rate is 10 percent annually. The loan is booked at a face amount of $1,000.

Modification No. 1 (Timing of Interest Only). Terms modified to defer collection of interest until loan matures at the end of five years is substituted for five annual collections of $100 in interest.

Modification No. 2 (Amount of Interest Only). Terms modified to leave unchanged the timing of interest and the timing of principal payments to be made, but the annual interest payments are reduced from $100 to $60.

Modification No. 3 (Amount of Principal Modified Only). Terms modified to leave unchanged the amount and timing of

EXHIBIT U
Additional Loan Modifications

	Before Modification	Modifications #1	#2	#3	#4	#5
1. Amount by which initial cash receipts specified by terms exceed recorded investment in the loan:						
Interest	$ 500	$ 500	$ 300	$ 500	$ 500	$ -
Principal	1,000	1,000	1,000	800	800	800
Total Cash Receipts	$1,500	$1,500	$1,300	$1,300	$1,300	$ 800
Recorded Investment	$1,000	$1,000	$1,000	$1,000	$1,000	$1,000
Excess/Receipt over Investment	$ 500	$ 500	$ 300	$ 300	$ 300	$(200)
2. Effective interest rate on recorded investment	10.0%	8.5%	6.0%	6.5%	5.4%	–% *
3. Restructured Classification		Rate Red.†	Rate Red.	Rate Red.	Rate Red.	

* Non-accrual, $200 charge-off to reserve.
† If this rate of interest is considered a market rate, the loan could continue to be classified as a performing asset.

interest, but the principal required to be paid at the end of 5 years is reduced from $1,000 to $800.

Modification No. 4 (Combination of Change in Timing of Interest and Amount of Principal). Terms modified to defer collection of interest until loan matures; principal reduced to $800.

Modification No. 5 (Forgive Interest and Reduce Principal). Terms modified to forgive payment of interest and reduce the principal amount due from $1,000 to $800.

INDEX

A–B

C

D–E

F

G–H

I–J

L

M–N

O–P

R

S–T

U–W